Praise for *Data Engineering Design Patterns*

The book you now have in your hands is the seminal work for the future of data engineering design patterns. This should be required reading for any data professional, and is as important to the future of the profession as the Gang of Four's design patterns were for software design.

—*Scott Haines, coauthor,* Delta Lake: The Definitive Guide

Data engineering often feels like solving the same problems over and over—Bartosz Konieczny changes that with this book. Covering everything from idempotency to error handing and data observability, this is the definitive guide to building resilient data pipelines with reusable, proven design patterns.

—*Adi Polak, director at Confluent*

Bartosz has made a great contribution to drive data engineering forward! Data engineering is the technical backbone on which the leading tech companies build their dominance, and this knowledge needs to spread beyond the technical elite. *Data Engineering Design Patterns* is a great step in that direction. It captures years of experience crafting solutions to common data engineering challenges. It gives names and concise descriptions to recurring architectural patterns that are folklore among data engineering veterans from the Hadoop age, and can now spread to a wider audience.

—*Lars Albertsson, data engineering entrepreneur*

Stoked to see that some of the data engineering principles I've advocated for in the past— like immutability, deterministic transformations, and idempotency—are not only taking root but getting expanded upon and developed to a whole new level in this book. A great resource for data engineers looking to build reliable, scalable pipelines.

—*Maxime Beauchemin, original creator of*
Apache Airflow and Superset

Data Engineering Design Patterns
Recipes for Solving the Most Common Data Engineering Problems

Bartosz Konieczny

Data Engineering Design Patterns

by Bartosz Konieczny

Published by O'Reilly Media, Inc., 1005 Gravenstein Highway North, Sebastopol, CA 95472.

O'Reilly books may be purchased for educational, business, or sales promotional use. Online editions are also available for most titles (*http://oreilly.com*). For more information, contact our corporate/institutional sales department: 800-998-9938 or *corporate@oreilly.com*.

Acquisitions Editor: Aaron Black
Development Editor: Michele Cronin
Production Editor: Jonathon Owen
Copyeditor: Doug McNair
Proofreader: Piper Content Partners

Indexer: BIM Creatives, LLC
Interior Designer: David Futato
Cover Designer: Karen Montgomery
Illustrator: Kate Dullea

April 2025:   First Edition

Revision History for the First Edition
2025-04-14:   First Release

See *http://oreilly.com/catalog/errata.csp?isbn=9781098165819* for release details.

978-1-098-16581-9

[LSI]

Table of Contents

Preface

As a data engineer coming from the software engineering world, design patterns have always accompanied me on my journey. Adapter design pattern (*https://oreil.ly/ J8yQe*) helped me write a backend with pluggable I/O abstractions, Template Method design pattern (*https://oreil.ly/ZA1yz*) let me write an easily adaptable business logic, and thanks to the Builder design pattern (*https://oreil.ly/yK8A5*), I could set up an easily maintainable unit tests layer. Having these great experiences in mind, I have been looking for similar standardized solutions since my first day in the data engineering space.

Over time, in each new project, I found something that was similar to previous projects. By connecting these dots I first completed a list of data engineering patterns for cloud services.[1] Meantime, I have been continuing to enrich my data engineering design patterns list, despite working on different business domains and with different technologies.

That's how, by summer 2023, I ended up with a quite solid list of data engineering design patterns that I included in the proposal for this book—which, since you are holding the book in your hands, was accepted. I hope the book will add a missing standardization piece each data engineer can rely on to identify a problem, its solution, and warning points, and I also hope it will help data engineers work with the data engineering tools of tomorrow.

---

[1] I was very into the topic of cloud and data engineering between 2020 and 2022. Following this interest, I self-published the book back in 2022. The first chapter is available for free on my site (*https://oreil.ly/fYn8M*).

Conventions Used in This Book

The following typographical conventions are used in this book:

Italic
> Indicates new terms, URLs, email addresses, filenames, and file extensions.

`Constant width`
> Used for program listings, as well as within paragraphs to refer to program elements such as variable or function names, databases, data types, environment variables, statements, and keywords.

 This element signifies a general note.

 This element indicates a warning or caution.

The Structure of This Book

This book follows the workflow of a classical data engineering project that starts with data ingestion and ends with day-to-day monitoring. The steps of the project correspond to the main chapters, so you can easily identify the stage to which each pattern in a chapter applies.

Additionally, each chapter has a two-level structure, with the levels being design pattern categories and the design patterns themselves. Why this two-level organization? First, a given data engineering problem can have at least two possible solutions, and it wouldn't be possible to logically group them without having this first level of design pattern categories. Second, data engineering design patterns have their own names that sometimes sound mysterious, and design pattern categories provide extra application context that helps you know where to apply a particular pattern without requiring you to delve into details.

Finally, for each pattern, you'll find the following subsections:

Problem
> This subsection provides a real-world example of when you can use the pattern.

Solution

    This subsection describes the pattern in more technical detail. Usually, it starts with a high-level explanation followed by the technical implementation model.

Consequences

    Patterns have their trade-offs, and this section explains what you should look for before implementing them. Whenever possible, each gotcha is completed with a mitigation solution.

Examples

    In this final part, you'll find code snippets explaining how to use the pattern within the modern data engineering tools. Unfortunately, it's not technically possible to share the pattern's implementation in all existing data tools, so this book uses popular open source projects (Apache Spark, Apache Flink, Apache Airflow, PostgreSQL, and Delta Lake). Occasionally, the implementation extends the scope to the managed services in the public cloud. The code snippets are written in Python, SQL, and sometimes Scala or Java if the Python implementation is not available.

At the end of this book, you will find a table summarizing all the described patterns. Also, the book has a GitHub repository (*https://oreil.ly/5eGUD*) that includes a glossary of terms that should give you the definitions of the most frequently used acronyms in the book.

How to Use This Book

It depends on your experience. If you've just started your data engineering journey, you probably haven't seen most of the presented problems yet. In that case, reading this book cover to cover is a good approach.

On the other hand, if you already have some significant experience and some of the problems look familiar, reading the book start to finish may not be the best idea. Instead, you can start by picking the patterns you haven't heard about. To complete the picture, you can later go back to the patterns you know and see if you have implemented them in the same way.

Also, no matter what your level of experience may be, code snippets will help you put the theory into practice and better understand what the pattern implementations can look like in your projects.

Once you've read the book and played with the code snippets, you can consider it a reference book that's almost like a *cookbook* that you can consult whenever you're facing a new data problem to solve (and not because of the flan recipe from Chapter 1).

What Should I Know Prior to Reading This Book?

This book will not be a great resource if you have just started in data engineering and don't have any commercial experience. In my opinion, a minimum of six months of commercial experience with data engineering should help you grasp the ideas more easily. Other than that, the minimum technical knowledge you'll need to get the most out of this book is as follows:

- Familiarity with data engineering concepts, such as extract, transform, load (ETL), extract, load, transform (ELT), data warehousing, data ingestion, and data orchestration.

- Cloud awareness. Even though this book tends to favor open source technologies, there are places where cloud technology is more appropriate (e.g., data security). You don't have to be a cloud expert, but you should at least be able to understand the basics, such as what a managed service is.

- Hands-on experience with data processing logic in Java, Scala, Python, or SQL. Ideally, you have already deployed this logic in production.

If you feel like there are gaps in your knowledge of the required topics, you should be able to easily fill in the gaps by reading *Fundamentals of Data Engineering* by Joe Reis and Matt Housley (O'Reilly, 2022). The book provides a comprehensive overview of the data engineering space that will not only help you understand the content in this book but also better prepare you to deal with the challenges you will face in your day-to-day work.

Glossary and Code Examples

Code examples are available for download on my GitHub page (*https://github.com/bartosz25/data-engineering-design-patterns-book/*). To run them, you'll need your favorite IDE and Docker installed with Docker Compose.

The GitHub repo has the same organizational structure as the book, meaning each chapter has its own directory where you'll find fully working examples of the patterns organized into subdirectories. Each directory has a dedicated *README.md* that will guide you through the demo.

Also, the GitHub repository includes a glossary (*https://oreil.ly/i5UHr*) with the most important terms referred to in the book. It's a complimentary resource that should help you recall some concepts if you haven't heard about them for a while.

This book is here to help you get your job done. In general, if example code is offered with this book, you may use it in your programs and documentation. You do not need to contact us for permission unless you're reproducing a significant portion of the code. For example, writing a program that uses several chunks of code from this book does not require permission. Selling or distributing examples from O'Reilly books does require permission. Answering a question by citing this book and quoting example code does not require permission. Incorporating a significant amount of example code from this book into your product's documentation does require permission.

We appreciate, but generally do not require, attribution. An attribution usually includes the title, author, publisher, and ISBN. For example: "*Data Engineering Design Patterns* by Bartosz Konieczny (O'Reilly). Copyright 2025 Bartosz Konieczny, 978-1-098-16581-9."

If you feel your use of code examples falls outside fair use or the permission given above, feel free to contact us at *permissions@oreilly.com*.

O'Reilly Online Learning

 For more than 40 years, *O'Reilly Media* has provided technology and business training, knowledge, and insight to help companies succeed.

Our unique network of experts and innovators share their knowledge and expertise through books, articles, and our online learning platform. O'Reilly's online learning platform gives you on-demand access to live training courses, in-depth learning paths, interactive coding environments, and a vast collection of text and video from O'Reilly and 200+ other publishers. For more information, visit *https://oreilly.com*.

How to Contact Us

Please address comments and questions concerning this book to the publisher:

O'Reilly Media, Inc.
1005 Gravenstein Highway North
Sebastopol, CA 95472
800-889-8969 (in the United States or Canada)
707-827-7019 (international or local)
707-829-0104 (fax)
support@oreilly.com
https://oreilly.com/about/contact.html

We have a web page for this book, where we list errata, examples, and any additional information. You can access this page at *https://oreil.ly/dataEngDesignPatterns*.

For news and information about our books and courses, visit *https://oreilly.com*.

Find us on LinkedIn: *https://linkedin.com/company/oreilly-media*.

Watch us on YouTube: *https://youtube.com/oreillymedia*.

Acknowledgments

Writing a book for O'Reilly has always been a dream. It turns out that I've made it come true, and although only my name is on the cover, my journey wouldn't have been possible without the support and inspiration I have received from my loved ones and my data community. That's why, before I let you discover the first patterns, I owe a few thank-yous!

First and foremost, thanks to my family. To Sylwia, my wife, who has always been supportive, even when I had serious doubts about writing, freelancing, and programming. To Maja and Arthur, my lovely children, who have reminded me there is a life beyond the screens. Thank you for making the whole book-writing process more enjoyable and less monotonous, even though you unexpectedly shortened some of my miracle morning routines. ;) Also a big thank-you to Jarek and Hania, my parents, whose trust helped me grow and try impossible things, like writing this book!

In addition to my family, I couldn't have written this book without the inspiring people I have met in the data community. To start with, thank you to Jacek Laskowski, who has been a mentor to me since I saw his StackOverflow answers and read his *The Internals of...* books while I was learning Apache Spark. I'm very glad I could meet you in person and learn even more!

Also, a big thank-you to Scott Haines, whose contributions to the data engineering space helped me grasp various stream processing and lakehouse aspects. And I probably never would have tried to write this book without the feedback you shared with me at DAIS 2022. Thank you for that chat and all your involvement in the data community that, I'm sure, has helped many more than just me!

If you're reading this book, it's also thanks to the involvement of tech reviewers. Keith Mascharenas, Laura Uzcategui, Lipi Deepaakshi Patnaik, Matthew Housley, Scott Haines, and William Jamir Silva, thank you so much for your questions and all the technical details that helped me grow as a writer and engineer. I'm sure the readers will now appreciate the book even more! At this time, I'd also like to thank Rahul Arulkumaran, Leszek Michalak, and Jonathan Roussot for their valuable feedback after the first Early Release versions of this book.

Besides the tech reviewers, Aaron Black and Michele Cronin from O'Reilly helped make this book come alive. Thank you, Aaron, for our discussions about the book and your guidance for the proposal writing. Michele, without your involvement, the book wouldn't be here, for sure. I'm very glad that we could collaborate, and I wish all other authors could be supported by a development editor like you!

Finally, I'd like to give a special mention to people who greatly contributed to my professional growth. To start with, thanks to Frank Pavageau, who taught me clean code principles before I knew there was a dedicated book on them! Also, a big thank-you to Jérôme Guibert, who taught me how to leverage automation to make my work easier and more enjoyable! And besides the project knowledge shared by Frank and Jérôme, I've been learning a lot from the data community. Big thank-yous go to Adi Polak, Holden Karau, Itai Yaffe, and Jungtaek Lim, who have inspired and taught me over the years through their content contributions to the data engineering world!

I wish that you, dear reader, can find such inspirational people around you.

## CHAPTER 1

Introducing Data Engineering Design Patterns

Design patterns are well established in the software engineering space, but they have only recently begun getting traction in the data engineering world. Consequently, I owe you a few words of introduction and an explanation of what design patterns are in the context of data engineering.

What Are Design Patterns?

You may be surprised at how many times you rely on patterns in your daily life. Let's take a look at an example involving cooking and one of my favorite desserts, flan; if you like creamy desserts and haven't tried flan yet, I highly recommend it! When you want to prepare flan, you need to get all the ingredients and follow a list of preparation steps. As an outcome, you get a tasty dessert.

Why am I giving this cooking example as the introduction to a technical book about design patterns? It's because a recipe is a great representation of what a design pattern should be: a predefined and customizable template for solving a problem. How does this flan example apply to this definition?

- The ingredients and the list of preparation steps are the *predefined template*. They give you instructions but remain customizable, as you might decide to use brown sugar instead of white, for example.
- There can be a single use or many uses. The flan can be a dessert you'll share with family at teatime, or it can be a product that you'll sell to make a living. This is the *contextualization of a design pattern*. Design patterns always respond to a specific problem, which in this example is the problem of how to share a pleasant dessert with friends or how to produce the dessert to generate business revenue.

- You can decide to prepare this delicious dessert once or many times, if it happens to be your new favorite. For each new preparation, you won't reinvent the wheel. Chances are, you'll rely on the same successful recipe you tried before. That's the *reusability of the pattern*.

- But you must also be aware that preparing and eating flan has some implications for your life and health. If you prepare it every day, you'll maybe have less time for sports practice, and as a result, you might have some health issues in the long run. These are the *consequences of a pattern*.

- Finally, the recipe *saves you time* as it has been tested by many other people before. Additionally, it introduces a common dictionary that will make your life easier when discussing it with other people. Finding a recipe for flan is easier than finding one for caramel custard, which is a less popular name for flan.

Now, how does all this relate to data engineering? Again, let's use an example. You need to process a semi-structured dataset from a continuously running job. From time to time, you might be processing a record with a completely invalid format that will throw an exception and stop your job. But you don't want your whole job to fail because of that simple malformed record. This is our *contextualization*.

To solve this processing issue, you'll apply a set of best practices to your data processing logic, such as wrapping the risky transformation with a `try-catch` block to capture bad records and write them to another destination for analysis. That's the *predefined template*. These are the rules you can adapt to your specific use case. For example, you could decide not to send these bad records to another database and instead, simply count their occurrences.

Turns out that the example of handling erroneous records without breaking the pipeline has a specific name, *dead-lettering*. Now, if you encounter the same problem again, but in a slightly different context—maybe while working on an ELT pipeline and performing the transformations in a data warehouse directly—you can apply the same logic. That's the *reusability of the pattern*. The Dead-Letter pattern is one of the error management patterns detailed in Chapter 3.

However, you shouldn't follow the Dead-Letter pattern blindly. As with eating a flan every day, implementing the pattern has some *consequences* you should be aware of. Here, you add extra logic that adds some extra complexity to the codebase. You must be ready to accept this.

Finally, a data engineering design pattern represents a holistic picture of a solution for a given problem. It then *saves you time* and also introduces a common language that can greatly simplify discussions with your teammates or data engineers you have just met.

Yet More Design Patterns?

If you write software, you've heard about the Gang of Four's design patterns[1] and maybe even consider them as one of the clean code pillars. And now, you're probably asking yourself, aren't they enough for data engineering projects? Unfortunately, no.

Software design patterns are the recipes that you can use to keep an easily maintainable codebase. Since the patterns are standardized ways to represent a given concept, they're quickly understandable by any new person in the project.

For example, a pattern to avoid allocating unnecessary objects is *Singleton*. A newcomer who is aware of the design pattern can quickly identify it and understand its purpose in the code.

Writing maintainable code does indeed apply to data engineering projects, but it's not enough. Besides pure software aspects, you need to think about the data aspects, such as the aforementioned failure management, backfilling, idempotency, and data correctness aspects.

Common Data Engineering Patterns

The failed record management from the previous section is only one example of a data engineering design pattern. The others are part of the book, which follows a typical data flow from data ingestion to final data exposition with monitoring and alerting. Therefore, in the book you will find:

Chapter 2, "Data Ingestion Design Patterns"
> Bringing data to your system will always be the first technical step in your architecture. After all, it guarantees that you have data to work on!

Chapter 3, "Error Management Design Patterns"
> Errors, just like data, are an intrinsic part of data engineering. Errors may result from coding mistakes but may also come directly from data providers, who might not respect their initial engagements, for example, by sharing a dataset without required fields defined.

Chapter 4, "Idempotency Design Patterns"
> A natural consequence of errors is retries that are either automatic or manual. In case of an automatic retry, part or all of your data pipeline will rerun and probably try to rewrite already saved records. If you trigger a pipeline manually, you

---

1 The 23 software engineering design patterns introduced in *Design Patterns: Elements of Reusable Object-Oriented Software* by Erich Gamma et al. (Addison-Wesley Professional, 1994) are colloquially known as the Gang of Four design patterns because of the book's four authors.

start a backfill[2] that will execute one or more past pipelines. Thanks to idempotency, the multiple runs will generate unique outputs.

Chapter 5, "Data Value Design Patterns"
Once you're able to deal with errors and retries, you can take care of the data and generate meaningful datasets for your business users. To do so, you may need to summarize the dataset or combine it with other data sources. All of this creates extra value that is important for your end users.

Chapter 6, "Data Flow Design Patterns"
After providing a direct value to your consumers by exposing an enriched dataset, you can move to the next step and include the dataset generation as part of a data flow. The data flow defines how the pipeline that generates data value interacts with other data components in your organization.

Chapter 7, "Data Security Design Patterns", "Data Security Design Patterns"
After the first six chapters, you should know how to bring the data to your system and how to enhance it to meet your business needs. However, you must also ensure that the dataset is securely stored and that it meets data privacy requirements.

Chapter 8, "Data Storage Design Patterns"
Security is crucial, but leveraging data storage techniques to reduce the latency of processing the data is also important. That's why in this chapter you'll see how to leverage your data storage to improve the user experience.

Chapter 9, "Data Quality Design Patterns"
The bad news is that even though you have implemented all the previous chapters, your data may still be irrelevant to your consumers if you don't get rid of data quality issues, or worse, if you're not even aware of them.

Chapter 10, "Data Observability Design Patterns"
This is the last step in your journey, where you'll define various monitoring metrics that will be important to the data you work on. Alongside the data quality design patterns, the data observability design patterns help make your data trustworthy by alerting you whenever something bad is happening or is about to happen.

---

2 This is known as reprocessing. So as not to confuse you, from this point forward, we'll refer to any task processing past data as *backfilling*, whether the data has already been processed or not. Technically, there is a small difference between reprocessing and backfilling, which you can learn about in the glossary available on GitHub (*https://oreil.ly/Dvu3b*).

Case Study Used in This Book

The design patterns in this book are not tied to one specific business domain. How-ever, understanding them without any business context would be hard, especially for less experienced readers. For that reason, you'll see each pattern introduced in the context of our case study project, which is a blog data analytics platform.

Our project follows common data practices and is divided into the layers presented in Figure 1-1.

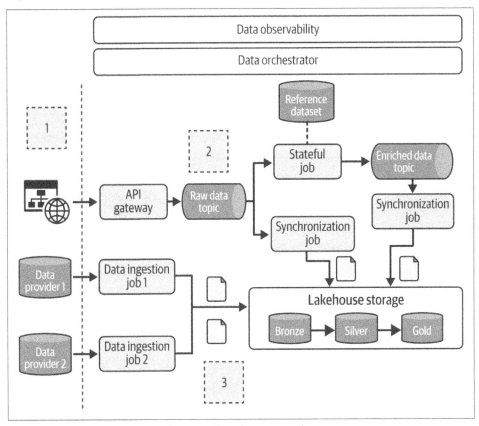

Figure 1-1. Blog analytics platform used in the case study

Figure 1-1 highlights the three most important parts of the project:

Online and offline data ingestion components
> The online part applies to the data generated by users interacting with the blogs hosted on our platform. The offline part, marked in the figure as "Data provider," applies to the static external or internal datasets such as referential datasets,

which are produced on a less regular schedule than the visit events (for example, once an hour).

The real-time layer

This is where you can find streaming job processing events data from a streaming broker. The jobs here may be one of two types. The first is a business-facing job that generates data for the stakeholders, such as a real-time session aggregation. The second type is a technical job that is often a technical enabler for other business use cases. An example here would be data synchronization with the data at-rest storage for ad hoc querying.

The data organization layer

This layer follows a now-common dataset structure that's based on the Medallion architecture[3] principle, in which a dataset may live in one of three different layers: Bronze, Silver, and Gold. Each layer applies to a different data maturity level. The Bronze layer stores data in its raw format, unaltered and probably with serious data quality issues. The Silver layer is responsible for cleansed and enriched datasets. Finally, the Gold layer exposes data in the format expected by the final users, such as data marts or reference datasets.

Why are these three storage layers interesting in the context of this book? Each layer represents a different data maturity level, exactly like the design patterns presented here. The patterns impacting business value will mostly expose the data in the Gold layer, while the others will remain behind, in the Bronze or Silver layer. Problem statement sections for the patterns may reference those layers to help you better understand any issues you encounter.

The schema doesn't present any implementation details on purpose. Focusing on them could shift your focus to the technology instead of the universal pattern-based solutions that are the main topic of the book. But it doesn't mean you won't see any technical details in the next chapters. On the contrary! Each pattern has a dedicated Examples section where you will see different implementations of the presented pattern.

Summary

Now that you've read this chapter, you should understand not only that flan is a great creamy dessert but also that its recipe is a great analogy for the data engineering design patterns that you will discover in the next nine chapters. I know it's a lot, but with a cup of coffee or tea and your favorite dessert (why not flan!), it'll be an exciting learning journey!

---

3 You can learn more about the Medallion architecture in Chapter 4 of *Delta Lake: The Definitive Guide* by Denny Lee et al. (O'Reilly, 2024).

## CHAPTER 2

Data Ingestion Design Patterns

Data engineering systems are rarely data generators. More often, their first stage is data acquisition from various data producers. Working with these producers is not easy; they can be different pipelines inside your team, different teams within your company, or even completely different organizations. Because each producer has dedicated constraints inherited from technical and business environments, interacting with them may be challenging for you.

But you have no choice. You have to adapt. Otherwise, you won't get any data, and as a result, you won't feed your data analytics or data science workloads. Or even worse, you will get some data, share it with your downstream consumers, and a few days later, you'll get some complaints. They may be about an incomplete dataset, inefficient data organization, or completely broken data requiring internal restoration processes and backfilling.

As you can see by now, bringing data to your system is a key task for making your life and your users' lives better. For that reason, this book has to start by covering data ingestion design patterns.

The patterns presented in this chapter address scenarios and challenges you may face while integrating data from external providers or from your other pipelines. It starts by discussing two common data loading scenarios: the full and incremental loads that you'll use to acquire all or part of the dataset, respectively. Next, it discusses a special type of data ingestion called data replication. You'll see there two other patterns to copy the data without and with transformation that may help you address data privacy issues.

Since ingesting the data also covers some topics not closely related to the moving data itself, you'll also learn more about technical parts of data ingestion. First, you need to know when to start the ingestion process, and here, the data readiness section will be helpful. Second, you must also know how to improve the user experience and address one of the biggest data engineering nightmares, the small files problem. That's where the data compaction section will come in handy. In the final section, you'll also learn that data ingestion is not always a predictable process. Hopefully, the External Trigger pattern, which we discuss last in this chapter, will address this uncertainty.

With all the context set up, I can now let you discover the first data ingestion patterns for full and incremental load scenarios!

Full Load

The *full load* design pattern refers to the data ingestion scenario that works on a complete dataset each time. It can be useful in many situations, including a database bootstrap or a *reference dataset* generation.

Pattern: Full Loader

The Full Loader implementation is one of the most straightforward patterns presented in this book. However, despite its simple two-step construction, it has some pitfalls.

Problem

You're setting up the Silver layer for our use case. One of the transformation jobs requires extra information about the device from an external data provider. This device's dataset changes only a few times a week. It's also a very slowly evolving entity with the total number of rows not exceeding one million. Unfortunately, the data provider doesn't define any attribute that could help you detect the rows that have changed since the last ingestion.

Solution

The lack of the last updated value in the dataset makes the Full Loader pattern an ideal solution to the problem.

The simplest implementation relies on two steps, extract and load (EL). It uses native data stores commands to export data from one database and import it to another. This EL approach is ideal for homogeneous data stores because it doesn't require any data transformation.

Passthrough Jobs

Extract and load jobs are also known as *passthrough jobs* because the data is simply passing through the pipeline, from the source to the destination.

Unfortunately, using EL pipelines will not always be possible. If you need to load the data between heterogeneous databases, you will need to adapt the input format to the output format with a thin transformation layer between the extract and load steps. Your pipeline then becomes an extract, transform, load (ETL) job, where you can leverage a data processing framework that often provides native interfaces for interacting with various data stores.

Consequences

Despite this simple task of moving a dataset between two data stores, the Full Loader pattern comes with some challenges.

Data volume. The Full Loader's implementations will often be batch jobs running on some regular schedule. If the data volume of the loaded dataset grows slowly, your data loading infrastructure will probably work without any issues for a long time thanks to these almost constant compute needs.

On the other hand, a more dynamically evolving dataset can lead to some issues if you use static compute resources to process it. For example, if the dataset doubles in size from one day to another, the ingestion process will be slower and can even fail due to static hardware limitations.

To reduce this data variability impact on your data loading process, you can leverage the auto-scaling capabilities of your data processing layer.

Data consistency. The second risk related to the Full Loader pattern is the risk of losing data consistency. As the data must be completely overwritten, you may be tempted to fully replace it in each run with a *drop-and-insert* operation. If you opt for this strategy, you should be aware of its shortcomings.

First, think about data consistency from the consumer's perspective. What if your data ingestion process runs at the same time as the pipelines reading the dataset? Consumers might process partial data or even not see any data at all if the insert step doesn't complete. Transactions automatically manage data visibility, and they're the easiest mitigation of this concurrency issue. If your data store doesn't support transactions, you can rely on a *single data exposition abstraction*,[1] such as view, and manipulate only the underlying technical and hidden structures. Figure 2-1 shows how to perform a switch between two technical tables and keep the data available.

---

1 You can learn more about it in the section on the Proxy pattern in Chapter 4.

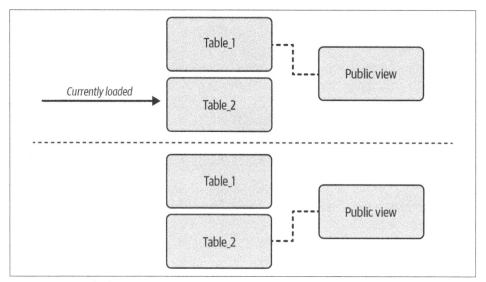

Figure 2-1. Single data exposition abstraction example with a database view

Second, keep in mind that you may need to use the previous version of the dataset if unexpected issues arise. If you fully overwrite your dataset, you may not be able to perform this action, unless you use a format supporting the time travel feature, such as Delta Lake, Apache Iceberg, or Google Cloud Platform (GCP) BigQuery. Eventually, you can also implement the feature on your own by relying on the single data exposition abstraction concept presented in Figure 2-1.

Not Only Ingestion

Although this chapter discusses data ingestion, remember that all the patterns presented here directly impact data analytics and data science workloads, as they load the data into the system.

Examples

Let's see now how to implement the pattern in different technical contexts. First, if you have to ingest a dataset between two identical or compatible data stores, you can simply write a script and deploy it to your runtime service. Example 2-1 demonstrates how to load files from one Amazon Web Services (AWS) S3 bucket to another. The command automatically synchronizes the content of the buckets and removes all objects missing in the source but present in the destination (the --delete argument).

Example 2-1. Synchronization of buckets

```
aws s3 sync s3://input-bucket s3://output-bucket --delete
```

Commands like `aws s3 sync` are a great way to simply move datasets, but sometimes, the load operation may require some fine-tuning, like adding parallel or distributed processing. An example of such an implementation is Apache Spark.

Apache Spark, as a distributed data processing framework, can be seamlessly scaled so that even drastically changing volumes shouldn't negatively impact the data ingestion job as long as you scale your compute infrastructure. Besides, if you use it with a table file format like Delta Lake, you automatically address the consistency issues presented previously, thanks to the transactional and versioning capabilities. The cherry on the cake is that the code for the full data ingestion is pretty easy. Example 2-2 shows how to leverage the Apache Spark read and write API to write JSON records as a Delta Lake table.

Example 2-2. Extract load implementation with Apache Spark and Delta Lake

```
input_data = spark.read.schema(input_data_schema).json("s3://devices/list")

input_data.write.format("delta").save("s3://master/devices")
```

Finally, you can also implement the pattern for databases without the native versioning capability. Let's take an example of Apache Airflow and PostgreSQL. The implementation is more complex because it requires dedicated data ingestion and data exposition tasks.

The data ingestion task writes the dataset to an explicitly versioned table. It can be expressed as a `COPY` statement from Example 2-3, where `${version}` is a parameter provided by Apache Airflow's operator.

Example 2-3. Loading data to a versioned table

```
COPY devices_${version} FROM '/data_to_load/dataset.csv' CSV  DELIMITER ';' HEADER;
```

Next, the exposition task changes the reference of the view exposed to the end users. For that, it can rely on the view update operation in Example 2-4.

Example 2-4. Exposing one versioned table publicly

```
CREATE OR REPLACE VIEW devices AS SELECT * FROM devices_${version}
```

The pipeline may require additional steps, such as retrieving the input dataset and creating versioned tables. I omit them here for brevity's sake, but you'll find the full example in the GitHub repo (*https://oreil.ly/eAG5j*).

Incremental Load

Full load is an easy scenario, but it can be costly to implement for continuously growing datasets. Incremental load patterns are better candidates for them because they ingest smaller parts of a physically or logically divided dataset, often at a higher frequency.

Pattern: Incremental Loader

The first incremental design pattern processes new parts of the dataset, thus its name, the Incremental Loader.

Problem

In our blog analytics use case, most visit events come from a streaming broker in real time. But some of them are still being written to a transactional database by legacy producers.

You need to create a dedicated data ingestion process to bring these legacy visits to the Bronze layer. Due to the continuously increasing data volume, the process should only integrate the visits added since the last execution. Each visit event is immutable.

Solution

The continuously growing dataset is a good condition in which to use the Incremental Loader pattern. There are two possible implementations that depend on the input data structure:

- The first implementation uses a so-called *delta column* to identify rows added since the last run. Typically, for event-driven data like immutable visits, this column will be ingestion time.

- The second implementation relies on *time-partitioned datasets*. Here, the ingestion job uses time-based partitions to detect the whole new bunch of records to ingest. It greatly simplifies and optimizes the process as the data to ingest is already filtered out and logically organized in the storage layer. To ensure that a new partition can be ingested, you can use the Readiness Marker pattern.

 Be Aware of Real-Time Issues

Using *event time* as a delta column is risky. Your ingestion process might miss records if your data producer emits late data (see "Late Data" on page 51) for the event time you already processed.

You can find both implementations in Figure 2-2. As you'll notice, the delta column implementation needs to remember the last ingestion time value to incrementally process new rows. On the other hand, the partition-based implementation doesn't have this requirement because it can implicitly resolve the partition to process from the execution date. For example, if the loader runs at 11:00, it can target the partition for the previous hour.

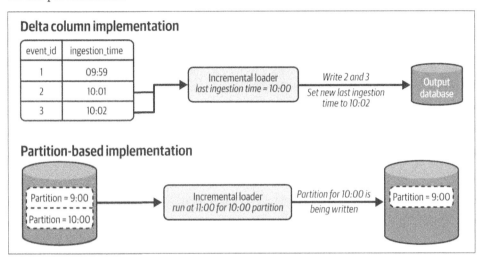

Figure 2-2. Two possible implementations of the Incremental Loader pattern

Consequences

The incremental quality is nice for reducing ingested data volume, but it can also be challenging.

Hard deletes. Using the pattern can be tricky for mutable data. Let's say that instead of the append-only visits, you need to deal with the events that can be updated and deleted. If the ingestion process relies on the delta column, it can identify the updated rows and copy their most recent version. Unfortunately, it's not that simple for deleted rows.

When a data provider deletes a row, the information physically disappears from the input dataset. However, it's still present in your version of the dataset because the *delta column* doesn't exist for a deleted row. To overcome this issue you can rely on *soft deletes*, where the producer, instead of physically removing the data, simply marks it as removed. Put differently, it uses the UPDATE operation instead of DELETE.

Insert-Only Tables

Another answer to the mutability issue could be *insert-only* data-sets. As the name suggests, they accept only new rows via an INSERT operation. They shift the data reconstruction responsibility onto consumers, who must correctly detect any deleted and modified entries. The insert-only tables are also known as append-only tables.

Backfilling. Even these basic data ingestion tasks have a risk of backfilling. The pattern might have a surprisingly bad effect on your data ingestion pipelines in that scenario.

Let's imagine a pipeline relying on the delta column implementation. After processing two months of data, you were asked to start a backfill. Now, when you launch the ingestion process, you'll be doing the full load instead of the incremental one. Therefore, the job will need more resources to accommodate the extra rows.

Thankfully, you can mitigate the problem by limiting the ingestion window. For example, if your ingestion job runs hourly, you can limit the ingestion process to one hour only. In SQL, it can be expressed as `delta_column BETWEEN ingestion_time AND ingestion_time + INTERVAL '1 HOUR'`. This operation brings two things:

- Better control over the data volume. Even in the case of backfilling, you won't be surprised by the compute needs.
- Simultaneous ingestion. You can run multiple concurrent backfilling jobs at the same time, as long as the input data store supports them.

The dataset size problem doesn't happen in the partition-based implementation if your ingestion job works on one partition at a time.

Examples

The script-based example from the Full Loader also applies to the incremental load. The operation from Example 2-5 simply moves all objects with the `date=2024-01-01` prefix key to another bucket. Even though it looks straightforward, there's a catch. If you omit the `date=2024-01-01` prefix from the right side of the command, the ingestion task will flatten the output storage layout.

Example 2-5. Synchronization of S3 buckets

```
aws s3 sync s3://input/date=2024-01-01 s3://output/date=2024-01-01 --delete
```

Sometimes the implementation can't be a simple script. As with the Full Loader, you can rely on your processing and orchestration layers. Example 2-6 is an example of the partition-based implementation with Apache Airflow and Apache Spark. The workflow in Apache Airflow, most commonly known as a DAG, starts with a File Sensor waiting for the next partition to be available. It's a required step to avoid loading partial data and propagating an invalid dataset. The snippet uses a simple verification on the next partition, but Airflow supports sensors for other backends and includes AWS Glue (AwsGlueCatalogPartitionSensor), GCP BigQuery (BigQueryTablePartitionExistenceSensor), or Databricks (DatabricksPartitionSensor). Once the partition is ready, the pipeline triggers the data ingestion job.

Example 2-6. Incremental Loader DAG example

```
next_partition_sensor = FileSensor(
 task_id='input_partition_sensor',
 filepath=get_data_location_base_dir() + '/{{ data_interval_end | ds }}',
 mode='reschedule',
)
load_job_trigger = SparkKubernetesOperator(application_file='load_job_spec.yaml',
 # ... omitted for brevity
)
load_job_sensor = SparkKubernetesSensor(
 # ... omitted for brevity
)

next_partition_sensor >> load_job_trigger >> load_job_sensor
```

The data ingestion job takes the arguments for the input and output locations defined in Example 2-7. The job definition relies on the immutable execution time expressed here as the {{ ds }} macro. If you use these immutable properties, you greatly simplify the backfilling because they will never change. The EventsLoader job uses the specified time expression arguments alongside the Apache Spark API to read and write the dataset.

Example 2-7. Partitioned events loader

```
# ...
 mainClass: com.waitingforcode.EventsLoader
 mainApplicationFile: "local:///tmp/dedp-1.0-SNAPSHOT-jar-with-dependencies.jar"
 arguments:
  - "/data_for_demo/input/date={{ ds }}"
  - "/data_for_demo/output/date={{ ds }}"
```

Since you already learned how to leverage the Apache Spark API in the previous section, let's move directly to the Incremental Loader based on a delta column implementation. The delta column implementation slightly differs from the partitioned version as it removes the sensor step and executes the ingestion job directly (see Example 2-8).

Example 2-8. Incremental Loader for transactional (not partitioned) dataset

```
load_job_trigger = SparkKubernetesOperator(
  # ...
  application_file='load_job_spec_for_delta_column.yaml',
)
load_job_sensor = SparkKubernetesSensor(
  # ...
)

load_job_trigger >> load_job_sensor
```

This job includes an extra filtering operation on top of the delta column to get the rows corresponding to the time range configured for a given job execution. Thanks to the filter, if you need to run a job execution again, it will not take any extra records, and thus it will guarantee consistent data volume. Example 2-9 shows the job adapted to the delta column implementation.

Example 2-9. Data ingestion job with delta column and time boundaries

```
in_data = (spark_session.read.text(input_path).select('value',
   functions.from_json(functions.col('value'), 'ingestion_time TIMESTAMP')))

input_to_write = in_data.filter(
  f'ingestion_time BETWEEN "{date_from}" AND "{date_to}"'
)

input_to_write.mode('append').select('value').write.text(output_path)
```

Pattern: Change Data Capture

The Incremental Loader will not work for all use cases. When you need a lower ingestion latency or built-in support for the physical deletes, the next pattern will be a better choice.

Problem

Unfortunately, the legacy visit events you integrated with the Incremental Loader must evolve. Their ingestion rate is too slow, and downstream consumers have started to complain about too much time spent waiting for the data. To mitigate the issue, your product manager asked you to integrate these transactional records into your streaming broker as soon as possible. The ingestion job must capture each change from the table within 30 seconds and make it available to other consumers from a central topic.

Solution

The latency requirement makes it impossible to use the Incremental Loader. The pattern has some job scheduling and query execution overheads that could make the expected latency difficult to reach.

A better candidate is the Change Data Capture (CDC) pattern. Due to its internal ingestion mechanism, it guarantees lower latency. The pattern consists of continuously ingesting all modified rows directly from the internal database commit log. It allows lower-level and faster access to the records, compared to any high-level query or processing task.

A *commit log* is an append-only structure. It records any operations on the existing rows at the end of the logfile. The CDC consumer streams those changes and sends them to the streaming broker or any other configured output. From that point on, consumers can do whatever they want with the data, such as storing the whole history of changes or keeping the most recent value for each row.

Besides guaranteeing lower latency, CDC intercepts all types of data operations, including hard deletes. So there is no need to ask data producers to use soft deletes for data removal.

Consequences

The latency promise is great, but like any engineering component, it also brings its own challenges.

Complexity. The CDC pattern is different from the two others covered so far as it requires different setup skills. The Full Loader and Incremental Loader can be implemented by a data engineer alone, as long as the required compute and orchestration layers exist. The CDC pattern may need some help from the operations team, for example, to enable the commit log on the servers.

Data scope. Be careful about the data scope you want to target with this pattern. Depending on the client's implementation, you may be able to get the changes made only after starting the client process. If you are interested in the previous changes too, you will need to combine CDC with other data ingestion patterns from this chapter.

Payload. Besides latency, another difference between CDC and the Incremental Loader is the payload. CDC will bring additional metadata with the records, such as the operation type (update, insert, delete), modification time, or column type. As a consumer of this data, you may need to adapt your processing logic to ignore irrelevant attributes.

Data semantics. Don't get this wrong; the pattern ingests data at rest. As a side effect, these static rows become data in motion. Why is this worth emphasizing? Data in motion has different processing semantics for many operations that appear to be trivial in the data-at-rest world.

Let's look at an example of the JOIN operation. If you perform it against static tables orchestrated from your data orchestration layer and you don't get a result, it's because there is no matching data. But if you run the query against two dynamic streaming sources and you don't get a match, it's because the data might not be there *yet*. One stream can simply be later than the other, and the JOIN operation may eventually succeed in the future. For that reason, you shouldn't consider the data ingested from the CDC consumer to be static data.

Examples

There are many ways to implement the pattern. You can create your own commit log reader or rely on the available solutions. One of the most popular open source solutions is Debezium.[2] The framework supports many relational and NoSQL databases and uses Kafka Connect as the bridge between the data-at-rest and data-in-motion worlds. The setup is mostly configuration driven (see Example 2-10).

Example 2-10. Debezium Kafka Connect configuration for PostgreSQL

```
{
  "name": "visits-connector",
  "config": {
    "connector.class": "io.debezium.connector.postgresql.PostgresConnector",
    "database.hostname": "postgres", "database.port": "5432",
    "database.user": "postgres", "database.password": "postgres",
    "database.dbname" : "postgres", "database.server.name": "dbserver1",
    "schema.include.list": "dedp_schema",
    "topic.prefix": "dedp"
  }
}
```

This snippet shows the configuration file for a PostgreSQL database. It defines the connection parameters, all the schemas to include in the watching operation, and finally the prefix for the created topic for each synchronized table. As a result, if there is a dedp_schema.events table, the connector will write all the changes to the dedp.dedp_schema.events topic. Figure 2-3 illustrates this dependency.

---

2 Besides Kafka Connect, Debezium has two other implementations called Debezium Embedded Engine and Debezium Server.

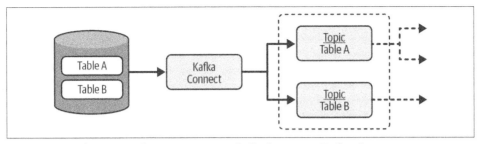

Figure 2-3. Debezium architecture in a nutshell, showing a Kafka Connect consumer leveraging the database commit logs and writing all matching datasets to dedicated Apache Kafka topics

Besides creating a new Kafka Connect task, you need to prepare the database. The PostgreSQL expects the logical replication stream enabled with the `pgoutput` plug-in and a user with all necessary privileges. Now, you certainly understand better why the CDC pattern is more challenging in terms of setup than the Incremental Loader.

The good news is that lake-native formats do support CDC in a simpler way. Delta Lake has a built-in *change data feed* (CDF) feature to stream the changed rows that you can enable either as a global session property or as a local table property with the `readChangeFeed` option. Example 2-11 demonstrates both configuration approaches.

Example 2-11. CDF setup in Delta Lake

```
spark_session_builder
  .config('spark.databricks.delta.properties.defaults.enableChangeDataFeed', 'true')

spark_session.sql('''
  CREATE TABLE events (
    visit_id STRING, event_time TIMESTAMP, user_id STRING, page STRING
  )
  TBLPROPERTIES (delta.enableChangeDataFeed = true)''')
```

Also, with the `enableChangeDataFeed` property, you can configure the throughput limits with the `maxFilesPerTrigger` or `maxBytesPerTrigger`. The tables also support time travel, so you can start reading from a particular version. Example 2-12 shows the most basic reader configuration processing four files each time from the very first table's version.

Example 2-12. CDF usage in Delta Lake

```
events = (spark_session.readStream.format('delta')
 .option('maxFilesPerTrigger', 4).option('readChangeFeed', 'true')
 .option('startingVersion', 0).table('events'))
query = events.writeStream.format('console').start()
```

Other than a different reader configuration, there is a difference in the returned dataset. Example 2-13 shows that a CDF table contains some extra columns compared to the classical table.

Example 2-13. CDF table output

```
+-------------+-------------------+-------------+----------------+--------------------+
|     visit_id|         event_time|_change_type|_commit_version|   _commit_timestamp|
+-------------+-------------------+-------------+----------------+--------------------+
| 1400800256_0|2023-11-24 01:44:00|      insert|              6|2023-12-03 13:28:...|
| 1400800256_1|2023-11-24 01:36:00|      insert|              6|2023-12-03 13:28:...|
| 1400800256_2|2023-11-24 01:44:00|      insert|              6|2023-12-03 13:28:...|
| 1400800256_3|2023-11-24 01:37:00|      insert|              6|2023-12-03 13:28:...|
+-------------+-------------------+-------------+----------------+--------------------+
```

The extra columns in Example 2-13 begin with the _ and mean, respectively, how the row changed, at which version, and when. This example comes from an append-only table and may not be that interesting. However, if you apply some in-place operations like UPDATE, the changes feed will contain rows for both pre- and post-update versions. You can identify them with update_preimage and update_postimage types.

Replication

Another family of data ingestion patterns is *data replication*, the main goal of which is to copy data as is from one location to another. But that's only in a perfect world. In the real world, you will often need to alter the input, for example, because of regulatory compliance.

Data Loading Versus Replication

These two concepts look similar at first glance, but there is a slight difference. Replication is about moving data between the same type of storage and ideally preserving all its metadata attributes, such as primary keys in a database or event positions in a streaming broker. Loading is more flexible and doesn't have this homogeneous environment constraint.

Pattern: Passthrough Replicator

As with data loading, the data replication area has a passthrough mode that you can use by default if you can accept the consequences.

Problem

Your deployment process consists of three separate environments: development, staging, and production. Many of your jobs use a reference dataset with device parameters that you load daily on production from an external API. For a better development experience and easier bug detection, you want to have this dataset in the remaining environments.

The reference dataset loading process uses a third-party API and is not idempotent. This means that it may return different results for the same API call throughout the day. That's why you can't simply copy and replay the loading pipeline in the development and staging environments. You need the same data as in production.

Solution

A data provider which is not idempotent, plus the required consistency across environments, is a great reason to use the Passthrough Replicator pattern. You can set it up either at the compute level or the infrastructure level.

The compute implementation relies on the EL job, which is a process with only two phases, read and write. Ideally, the EL job will copy files or rows from the input as is (i.e., without any data transformation). Otherwise, it could introduce data quality issues, such as type conversion from string to dates or rounding of floating numbers.

The infrastructure part is based on a *replication policy* document where you configure the input and output location and let your data storage provider replicate the records on your behalf.

Consequences

The key learning here is to keep the implementation simple. However, even the simplest implementation possible may have some challenges to address.

Keep it simple.   Remember, you need the data as is. To reduce the interference risk in the replicated dataset, you should rely on the simplest replication job possible, which is ideally the data copy command available in the database.

However, when the command is not available and you must use a data processing framework for a text format like JSON, avoid relying on the JSON I/O API. Instead, use the simpler raw text API that will take and copy lines as they are, without any prior interpretation.

Additionally, if you do care about other aspects, such as the same number of files or even the same filenames, you should avoid using a distributed data processing framework if it doesn't let you customize those parameters.

Security and isolation.   Cross-environment communication is always tricky and can be error prone if the replication job has bugs. In that scenario, there is a risk of negatively impacting the target environment, even to the point of making it unstable. You certainly don't want to take that risk in production, so for that reason, you should implement the replication with the *push* approach instead of *pull*. This means that the environment owning the dataset will copy it to the others and thus control the process with its frequency and throughput.

Even though the push strategy greatly reduces the risk of instability, you can still encounter some issues. You can imagine a use case when you start a job on your cloud subscription and it takes the last available IP address in the data processing subnet. Other jobs will not run as long as the replicator doesn't complete.

PII data. If the replicated dataset stores *personally identifiable information* (PII), or any kind of information that cannot be propagated from the production environment, use the Transformation Replicator pattern, which we discuss next. It adds an extra transformation step to get rid of any unexpected attributes.

Latency. The infrastructure-based implementation often has some extra latency, and you should always check the service level agreement (SLA) of the cloud provider to see if it's acceptable as the solution. Even though the problem announcement discusses a development experience, you might want to implement it for other and more time-sensitive scenarios.

Metadata. Do not ignore the metadata part because it could make the replicated dataset unusable. For example, replicating only the Apache Parquet files of a Delta Lake table will not be enough. The same applies to Apache Kafka, where you should care not only about the key and values but also about headers and the order of events within the partition.

Examples

You can implement the pattern in two ways. The first implementation relies on the code, which can be either a distributed data processing framework or a data copy utility script running on your storage layer that you already saw in the Full Loader pattern. The code-based solution is more error prone, but you can leverage your framework's I/O layer (see Example 2-14).

Example 2-14. JSON data replication with Apache Spark

```
input_dataset = spark_session.read.text(f'{base_dir}/input/date=2023-11-01')
input_dataset.write.mode('overwrite').text(f'{base_dir}/output-raw/date=2023-11-01')
```

The code uses Apache Spark to synchronize semi-structured JSON files. It uses the simplest API possible to copy JSON lines data without any interference in the data itself. However, please notice that the snippet in the example doesn't preserve the files (i.e., the number of files in the source and destination can be different, even though they will both store the same data).

Despite that, Example 2-14 looks simple. Unfortunately, it'll not always be that straightforward for other data stores. Let's see the same extract and load operation for an Apache Kafka topic that requires an extra ordering guarantee within the partitions. Example 2-15 would be a simple extract and load job if it didn't have the write_sorted_events function in the middle. The function is crucial to guaranteeing that the replicated records include the metadata (.option('includeHeaders'...)) and keep the same order as the input records (sortWithinPartitions('offset', ascending=True)).

Example 2-15. Passthrough Replicator with an ordering semantic

```
events_to_replicate = (input_data_stream
  .selectExpr('key', 'value', 'partition', 'headers', 'offset'))

def write_sorted_events(events: DataFrame, batch_number: int):
  (events.sortWithinPartitions('offset', ascending=True).drop('offset').write
  .format('kafka').option('kafka.bootstrap.servers', 'localhost:9094')
  .option('topic', 'events-replicated').option('includeHeaders', 'true').save())

write_data_stream = (events_to_replicate.writeStream
  .option('checkpointLocation', f'{get_base_dir()}/checkpoint-kafka-replicator')
  .foreachBatch(write_sorted_events))
```

Apart from the code-based implementations, there are the infrastructure-based ones. For Apache Kafka topic replication, you could use the MirrorMaker utility,[3] while for the files, it could be the replication mechanism of your cloud provider. In Example 2-16, you can see an example of an S3 bucket replication with Terraform.

Example 2-16. AWS S3 bucket replication

```
resource "aws_s3_bucket_replication_configuration" "replication" {
  role   = aws_iam_role.replication.arn
  bucket = aws_s3_bucket.devices_production.id

  rule {
    id = "devices"
    status = "Enabled"
    destination {
      bucket        = aws_s3_bucket.devices_staging.arn
      storage_class = "STANDARD"
    }
  }
}
```

---

3 Explaining MirrorMaker in depth is beyond the scope of this book. If you are interested in more details, the official documentation (*https://oreil.ly/x0BlQ*) covers it extensively.

Pattern: Transformation Replicator

Even though the Kafka example looks complex, your replication scenario can require even more code effort. This is the case when you use the Transformation Replicator pattern.

Problem

Before releasing a new version of your data processing job, you want to perform tests against real data to avoid surprises during production. You can't use a synthetic data generator because your data provider often has data quality issues and it's impossible to simulate them with any tool. You have to replicate the data from production to the staging environment. Unfortunately, the replicated dataset contains PII data that is not accessible outside the production environment. As a result, you can't use a simple Passthrough Replicator job.

Solution

One big problem of testing data systems is...the data itself. If the data provider cannot guarantee consistent schema and values, using production data is unavoidable. Unfortunately, the production data very often has some sensitive attributes that can't move to other environments, where possibly more people can access it due to less strict access policies.

In that scenario, you should implement the Transformation Replicator pattern, which, in addition to the classical read and write parts from the Passthrough Replicator pattern, has a transformation layer in between.

Transformation is a generic term, but depending on your technical stack, it can be implemented as either of the following:

- A custom mapping function if you use a data processing framework like Apache Spark or Apache Flink
- A SQL SELECT statement if your processing logic can be easily run and expressed in SQL

The transformation consists of either replacing the attributes that shouldn't be replicated (for example, with the Anonymizer pattern) or simply removing them if they are not required for processing.

Consequences

Since you'll be writing some custom logic, the risk of breaking the dataset is higher than with the Passthrough Replicator. And that's not the only drawback of the pattern!

Transformation risk for text file formats. Let's look at a rather innocent transformation example on top of a text file format such as JSON or CSV. You defined a schema for the replicated dataset but didn't notice that the datetime format is different from the standard used by your data processing framework. As a result, the replicated dataset doesn't contain all the timestamp columns and your job of staging fails because of that. Although you should be able to fix the issue very quickly, it causes unnecessary work in the release process.

That's why you should still apply the "keep it simple" approach here. In our example, instead of defining the timestamp columns as is, you can simply configure them as strings and not worry about any silent transformations.

Desynchronization. You need to take special care that the replication jobs implement this pattern to avoid any privacy-related issues. Data is continuously evolving, and nothing guarantees that the privacy fields you have today will still be valid in the future. Maybe new ones will appear or attributes that are not currently considered PII will be reclassified as PII.

To avoid these kinds of issues, if possible, you should rely on a data governance tool, such as a data catalog or a data contract in which the sensitive fields are tagged. With such a tool, you can automatize the transformation logic. Otherwise, you'll need to implement the rules on your own.

Examples

As mentioned previously, there are two possible implementation approaches. The first of them is a *data reduction* approach that eliminates unnecessary fields. It's relatively easy to express. Some databases and compute layers, such as Databricks and BigQuery, support an EXCEPT operator. Example 2-17 shows this operator in action by selecting all rows but ip, latitude, and longitude.

Example 2-17. Dataset reduction with EXCEPT operator

```
SELECT * EXCEPT (ip, latitude, longitude)
```

Additionally, you can leverage your data processing framework to remove irrelevant columns. Example 2-18 shows how to use the PySpark drop function to remove the ip, latitude, and logitude columns from the dataset.

Example 2-18. Dataset reduction with drop function

```
input_delta_dataset = spark_session.read.format('delta').load(users_table_path)
users_no_pii = input_delta_dataset.drop('ip', 'latitude', 'longitude')
```

An alternative way to transform the dataset consists of controlling access to it. For example, your data provider can expose your user to only a subset of permitted columns, such as the ones in Example 2-19.

Example 2-19. Column-level access for user_a on table visits

```
GRANT SELECT (visit_id, event_time, user_id) ON TABLE visits TO user_a
```

Example 2-19 shows how to grant permissions on a subset of fields in AWS Redshift. The user_a will only be able to access the three columns mentioned after the SELECT operation. Although this is more verbose than the EXCEPT-based solution, it adds an extra layer of protection for accessing the private attributes. You'll learn more about this approach in the Fine-Grained Accessor pattern.

However, removing the rows may not always be an option, especially if they are important for the tested data processing job. For these use cases, you will define a *column-based transformation* to alter the sensitive fields (see Example 2-20).

Example 2-20. Column-based transformation

```
devices_trunc_full_name = (input_delta_dataset
  .withColumn('full_name',
      functions.expr('SUBSTRING(full_name, 2, LENGTH(full_name))'))
)
```

Column-based transformations work great for column-targeted operations. If you need to operate at the row level, or if the modification rule is complex, you may need a *mapping function* like the one in Example 2-21. The code leverages the Scala API for Apache Spark because it's more concise than the Python one. The code first calls the as function to convert input rows to a specific type. Later, it applies the transformation logic and exposes an eventually modified row from the transformed attribute.

Example 2-21. Mapping function from a strongly typed Scala Spark API

```
case class Device(`type`: String, full_name: String, version: String) {
  lazy val transformed = {
    if (version.startsWith("1.")) {
      this.copy(full_name = full_name.substring(1), version = "invalid")
    } else {
        this
      }
  }
}
inputDataset.as[Device].map(device => device.transformed)
```

Data Compaction

Even a perfect dataset can become a bottleneck, especially when it grows over time because of new data. As a result, at some point, metadata-related operations like listing files can take even longer than data processing transformations.

Pattern: Compactor

The easiest way to address this issue of a growing dataset is to reduce the storage footprint of the underlying files. The Compactor pattern helps in this task.

Problem

Your real-time data ingestion pipeline synchronizes events from a streaming broker to an object store. The main goal is to make the data available for batch jobs within at most 10 minutes. Since it's a simple passthrough job, the pipeline is running without any apparent issues. However, after three months, all the batch jobs are suffering from the *metadata overhead* problem due to too many small files composing the dataset. As a result, they spend 70% of their execution time on listing files to process and only the remaining 30% on processing the data. This has a serious latency and cost impact as you use pay-as-you-go services.

Solution

Having small files is a well-known problem in the data engineering space.[4] It has been there since the Hadoop era and is still present even in modern, virtually unlimited, object store–based lakehouses. Storing many small files involves longer listing operations and heavier I/O for opening and closing files. A natural solution to this issue is to store fewer files.

That's what the Compactor pattern does. It addresses the problem by combining multiple smaller files into bigger ones, thus reducing the overall I/O overhead on reading.

The implementation varies with the technology. Open table file formats have their dedicated compaction command that often runs a transactional distributed data processing job under the hood to merge smaller files into bigger ones as a part of the new commit. Apache Iceberg performs this via a *rewrite data file* action, while Delta Lake employs the `OPTIMIZE` command.

The compaction works differently on Apache Hudi, which is the third open table file format. A Hudi table can be configured as a *merge-on-read* (MoR) table where the dataset is written in columnar format and any subsequent changes are written in row

---

4 There's a detailed explanation of the problem of having small files in Chapters 4 and 5 of *The Cloud Data Lake* by Rukmani Gopalan (O'Reilly, 2023).

format. As this approach favors faster writes, to optimize the read process, the compaction operation in Hudi merges the changes from the row storage with the columnar storage. This approach differs from Delta Lake and Apache Iceberg as they operate in the homogeneous columnar format only.

The Compactor also works for data stores other than lake-related storage. One of them is Apache Kafka, which is an append-only key-based logs system. In this configuration-based implementation, you only need to configure the compaction frequency. The whole compaction process is later managed, according to the frequency, by the data store. However, in key-based systems, the compaction consists of optimizing the storage by keeping only the most recent entry for a given record key. It still improves the storage footprint, but unlike compaction in table file formats, the operation overwrites the present data.

Consequences

Despite its apparent harmlessness and native support in many data stores, the Compactor can require some significant design effort.

Cost versus performance trade-offs. The compaction job is just a regular data processing job that can be compute intensive on big tables. If you consider only this aspect, you should execute it rarely, such as once a day, ideally outside working hours, and outside the pipeline generating the dataset.

On the other hand, rare execution can be problematic for jobs that work on the not yet compacted data as they will simply not take advantage of this optimization technique. You'll then need to choose your strategy and accept that it may not be perfect from both the cost and performance perspectives.

There is no one-size-fits-all solution, unfortunately. Sometimes, running it once a day will be fine as the not compacted dataset may be small enough to not impact consumers. On the other hand, sometimes it won't be acceptable and you'll even prefer to include compaction in the data ingestion process since penalizing consumers will have a bigger impact than impacting the ingestion throughput.

Consistency. Remember, compaction simply rewrites already existing data. Consequently, consumers may have difficulties distinguishing the data to use from the data being compacted. For that reason, compaction is much simpler and safer to implement in modern, open table file formats with ACID properties (such as Delta Lake and Apache Iceberg) than in raw file formats (such as JSON and CSV).

Cleaning. The compaction job may preserve source files. Consequently, the small files will still be there and will continue impacting metadata actions. For that reason, the compaction job alone won't be enough. You'll have to complete it with a cleaning job to reclaim the space taken up by the already compacted files.

To overcome that side effect, you will need to reclaim this occupied but not used space with commands like VACUUM, which are available in modern data storage technologies like Delta Lake, Apache Iceberg, PostgreSQL, and Redshift. But choose your cleaning strategy wisely, because you may not recover your dataset to the version based on these deleted, already compacted files.

Example

Let's start by seeing how the pattern applies to data lakes and lakehouses using open table file formats like Delta Lake. The format provides a native compaction capability that's available from the programmatic API or as a SQL command. In both cases, you should look for the optimize keyword, as shown in Example 2-22. The code initializes the path-based Delta table object and calls the data compaction operation. As it only reorganizes the files that are available when the job starts, it's a safe and nonconflicting operation for readers and writers.

Example 2-22. Compaction job with Delta Lake

```
devices_table = DeltaTable.forPath(spark_session, table_dir)
devices_table.optimize().executeCompaction()
```

However, the compaction may require an extra VACUUM step to clean all irrelevant (because already compacted) files. Example 2-23 again leverages the Delta table abstraction but this time calls the vacuum() function. The cleaning process applies only to the files that are older than the configured retention threshold. Otherwise, it could lead to a corrupted table state because the vacuum could remove the files that are being written and are not yet committed.

Example 2-23. VACUUM in Delta Lake

```
devices_table = DeltaTable.forPath(spark_session, table_dir)
devices_table.vacuum()
```

Compaction is also available in other data stores, but compared to the Delta Lake example, it can be a bit misleading. Let's take a look at a transactional PostgreSQL database. Compaction there uses only the VACUUM command that reclaims space taken by dead tuples, which are the deleted rows not physically removed from the storage layer. You can trigger it with an explicit command.

This pattern is also present in Apache Kafka. When you create a topic, you can set the log compaction configuration, which is particularly useful when you write key-based records and each new append is a state update. With the compaction enabled, Apache Kafka runs a cleaning process that removes all but the latest versions of each key. The configuration supports properties like log.cleanup.policy (compaction strategy) and `log.cleaner.min.compaction.lag.ms` with `log.cleaner.max. compaction.lag.ms` (compaction frequency). Unlike in the Delta Lake example, Kafka's compaction is nondeterministic. You can't expect it to run on a regular schedule, and as a result, it doesn't guarantee that you'll always see a unique record for each key.

Data Readiness

The different data ingestion semantics covered so far in this chapter are not the only problems you can encounter in this apparently easy data ingestion task. The next problematic question you'll certainly ask yourself is, "When should I start the ingestion process?"

Pattern: Readiness Marker

The Readiness Marker is a pattern that helps trigger the ingestion process at the most appropriate moment. Its goal is to guarantee the ingestion of the complete dataset. Let's see how it achieves this.

Problem

Every hour, you're running a batch job that prepares data in the Silver layer of your Medallion architecture. The dataset has all known data quality issues fixed and is enriched with the extra context loaded from your user's database and from an external API service. For these reasons, other teams rely on it to generate ML models and BI dashboards. But there is one big problem: they often complain about incomplete datasets, and they've asked you to implement a mechanism that will notify them—directly or indirectly—when they can start consuming your data.

Solution

The issue is particularly visible in the logically dependent but physically isolated pipelines maintained by different teams. Because of these isolated workloads, it's not possible for your job to directly trigger downstream pipelines. Instead, you can mark your dataset as ready for processing with the Readiness Marker pattern. Its implementation will depend on the file format and storage organization.

The first implementation uses an event to signal the dataset's completeness. Due to the popularity of object stores and distributed file systems in modern data architectures, this approach can be easily implemented with a *flag file* created after a successful data generation. This feature may be natively available in your data processing layer, as with Apache Spark (which writes a _SUCCESS file for raw file formats) or a new commit log for Delta Lake. If you can't leverage the data processing layer, you can implement the flag file from the data orchestration layer as a separate task executed after successful data processing. You'll see how to implement it in the Examples section.

A different implementation applies to partitioned data sources. If you're generating data for time-based tables or locations, the Readiness Marker can be conventional. Are you perplexed? Let's use an example to better understand the convention. Your job runs hourly and writes data to hourly based partitions. As a result, the run for 10:00 writes data to partition 10, the run for 11:00 to 11, and so on. Now, if your consumer wants to process partition 10, they must simply wait for your job to work on partition 11.

Consequences

The Readiness Marker relies on the pull approach, in which the readers control the data retrieval process. As the implementations are implicit, there are some points to be aware of.

Lack of enforcement. There is no easy way to enforce conventional readiness based on the flag file or the next partition detection. Either way, a consumer may start to consume the dataset while you're generating it.

Because of this implicitness, it's very important to communicate with your consumers and agree upon the conditions that may trigger processing on their side. Additionally, you should clearly explain the risks of not respecting the readiness conventions.

Reliability for late data. If the partitions are based on the event time, the partition-based implementation will suffer from late data issues. To understand this better, let's imagine that you closed the partition from eight, nine, and ten o'clock. This means your consumers have already processed the partitions from eight, nine, and ten o'clock. Unfortunately, you've just detected late data for nine o'clock. As your partitions are based on event time, you decide to integrate this data into the partition from nine o'clock. Very probably, your consumers won't be able to do the same as they may consider the partition to be closed.

That's why you should either consider partitions as immutable parts that will never change once closed or clearly define and share the mutability conditions with your consumers. Besides sharing the partition updates with consumers, you should notify them about new data to eventually process. We're going to address this issue in "Late Data" on page 51.

Examples

For raw files, Apache Spark creates the flag file called _SUCCESS out of the box. Whenever you generate Apache Parquet, Apache Avro, or any other supported format, the job will always write the data files first, and only when this operation completes will it generate the marker file. Let's take a look at this in Example 2-24, where the job converts JSON files into Apache Parquet files and creates a _SUCCESS file under the hood.

Example 2-24. PySpark code generating the _SUCCESS file

```
dataset = (spark_session.read.schema('...').json(f'{base_dir}/input'))
dataset.write.mode('overwrite').format('parquet').save('devices-parquet')
```

As a consumer, you rely on the created _SUCCESS file to implement the Readiness Marker. If you use Apache Airflow, you can define this file as a condition in the File Sensor (see Example 2-25).

Example 2-25. FileSensor waiting for the _SUCCESS file

```
FileSensor(filepath=f'{input_data_file_path}/_SUCCESS, mode='reschedule'
# ...
```

Example 2-25 defines the filepath and also configures an important mode property to reschedule. Thanks to it, the sensor task will not occupy the worker slot without interruption. Instead, it will wake up and verify whether the configured file exists. This is an important point to consider if you want to avoid keeping your orchestration layer busy by only waiting for the data while other tasks may be ready to process it.

By the way, Apache Airflow also simplifies creating a Readiness Marker file if the latter is not natively available from the data processing job. The code from Example 2-26 generates the Readiness Marker file called COMPLETED in the last task called created_readiness_file.

Example 2-26. Creating a Readiness Marker file as a part of the data orchestration process

```
@task
def delete_dataset():
 shutil.rmtree(dataset_dir, ignore_errors=True)

@task
def generate_dataset():
 # processing part, omitted for brevity but available on GitHub

@task
def create_readiness_file():
 with open(f'{dataset_dir}/COMPLETED', 'w') as marker_file:
   marker_file.write('')

delete_dataset() >> generate_dataset() >> create_readiness_file()
```

This code snippet uses the @task decorator, which is a convenient way to declare data processing functions in Apache Airflow. The most important thing to keep in mind here is that the readiness marker should always be generated as the last step in a pipeline (i.e., after performing the last transformation of the dataset).

Event Driven

In ideal data ingestion scenarios, new datasets are available on a regular schedule. You can trigger your pipeline and use the Readiness Marker pattern before you start processing. In less-than-ideal scenarios, it's hard to predict the incoming frequency. Consequently, you must shift your mindset from static ingestion to event-driven ingestion.

Pattern: External Trigger

The Readiness Marker pattern from the previous section relies on *pull semantics*, in which the consumer is responsible for checking whether there is new data to process. But the event-driven nature of a dataset favors *push semantics*, in which the producer is in charge of notifying consumers about data availability.

Problem

Let's say the backend team of your organization releases new features at most once a week, between Monday and Thursday. Each release enriches your reference datasets, where you keep all the features available on your website at any given moment. So far, the refresh job for this dataset has been scheduled for once a day. It has been reloading data even when there were no changes, which led to some wastage of compute resources.

With the goal of reducing costs, you want to change the scheduling mechanism and run the pipeline only when there is something new to process. As the backend team sends a notification event to a central message bus whenever it publishes a new feature, you think about implementing a more event-driven approach.

Solution

Unpredictable data generation is often caused by the event-driven nature of the data. This problem can be solved with a time-scheduled job that copies the whole dataset or runs very often to check whether there is something new to process. However, this wastes compute resources and adds an unnecessary operational burden. A better approach is to address this issue with an event-driven External Trigger pattern.

> **Not Only Trigger**
>
> If for whatever reason you don't have a job to trigger, you can run the ingestion process directly in the notification handler. We'll therefore talk about *event-driven data ingestion.*

The pattern consists of three main actions:

1. Subscribing to a notification channel. The first step sets up the connection between the external world (event-driven producers) and your pipelines. From now on, whenever something new happens, you'll have the ability to handle it.

2. Reacting to the notifications. This is the events handler, and the role of this step is to analyze the event and decide whether it should result in triggering a pipeline in the data orchestration layer or starting a job in the data processing layer. Depending on the message bus technology, your handler can subscribe to particular events, such as data creation in a given table. If this filtering feature is not possible, the handler will need to implement it on its own.

3. Triggering the ingestion pipeline in the data orchestration or data processing layer. Here, the handler starts data ingestion either by triggering a workflow to orchestrate or directly triggering a job. For the sake of simplicity, one event should trigger one ingestion pipeline. However, it's also possible to start multiple ones, for example, when the same dataset is the input data source for various workloads.

You'll find these three main actions in Figure 2-4, where the trigger arrow is the reaction to the subscribed notification channel.

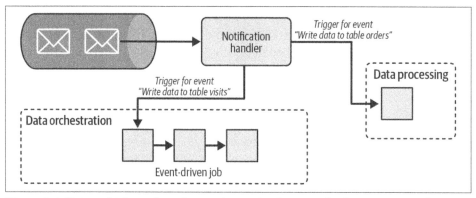

Figure 2-4. External trigger for a data orchestration layer and a data processing layer

Consequences

Even though this event-driven character sounds appealing because it reduces resource waste, it also has some consequences in your data stack.

Push versus pull. The External Trigger component can implement pull or push semantics. The difference is the key in understanding the pattern's impact on your system. The pull-based trigger continuously checks whether there are new events to process, while the push-based trigger does nothing as long as the event producer doesn't notify it about something new to process.

The pull-based trigger is a long-running job, so it's a process that stays up and checks at short, regular intervals whether there is new data to process. Although it's a technically valid implementation, it's not the most optimized since the job may spend most of its time pulling zero messages from the notification source.

A better alternative for this pattern is the push-based trigger, where the data source informs the endpoint(s) about new messages present in the bus. Each notification message starts a new consumer instance which finishes after reacting to the event.

Execution context. There is a risk that the external trigger may become *just* a ping mechanism that calls a data orchestrator endpoint. Although this simplistic approach is tempting, you should keep in mind that the triggered data ingestion pipeline will need to be maintained like any other. Hence, if you simply trigger it, you may not have enough context to understand why it has been triggered and what it's supposed to process.

For these reasons, it's important to enrich the triggering call with any appropriate metadata information, including the version of the trigger job, the notification envelope, the processing time, and the event time. They will be useful in day-to-day monitoring, when you will need to investigate the reasons for any eventual failures.

Error management. The events are the key elements here, and without them, you won't be able to trigger any work. For that reason, you should design the trigger for failure with the goal in mind to keep the events whatever happens. Typically, you'll rely here on the patterns described in the next chapter, such as the Dead-Letter pattern.

Examples

The pattern is easy to implement in the cloud. AWS, Azure, and GCP provide serverless function services that enable this event-driven capability. Therefore, they're great candidates for the triggers. Besides, most of the data orchestrators expose an API that you can use to start a pipeline. Let's see how to connect an AWS Lambda function with Apache Airflow. First, take a look at the pipeline definition in Example 2-27.

Example 2-27. Externally triggered DAG definition

```
with DAG('devices-loader', max_active_runs=5, schedule_interval=None,
 default_args={'depends_on_past': False,}) as dag:
# the pipeline just copies the file from the trigger,
# I'm omitting the content for brevity, it's available on GitHub
```

Compared to the previous DAGs, the one in Example 2-27 has the `schedule_interval` set to `None`. This means the Airflow scheduler will ignore it in the planning stage, and the only way to start the pipeline is with an explicit trigger action. It'll be the responsibility of the Lambda function that runs whenever a new object appears in the monitored S3 bucket (see Example 2-28).

Example 2-28. AWS Lambda handler to trigger the DAG

```
def lambda_handler(event, ctx):
  payload = {
   'event': json.dumps(event),
   'trigger': {
   'function_name': ctx.function_name, 'function_version': ctx.function_version,
   'lambda_request_id': ctx.aws_request_id
   },
   'file_to_load': (urllib.parse.
   unquote_plus(event['Records'][0]['s3']['object']['key'],encoding='utf-8')),
   'dag_run_id': f'External-{ctx.aws_request_id}'
}

trigger_response = requests
   .post('http://localhost:8080/api/v1/dags/devices-loader/dagRuns',
   data=json.dumps({'conf': payload}), auth=('dedp', 'dedp'), headers=headers)

if trigger_response.status_code != 200:
    raise Exception(f"""Couldn't trigger the `devices-loader` DAG.
    {trigger_response} for {payload}""")
else:
    return True
```

As you can see, the function is relatively straightforward. You may be wondering, where is the resiliency part? AWS Lambda implements it at the infrastructure level with *failed-event destinations*, where the service sends any records from the failed function's invocations. You can also configure the batch size for stream data sources or concurrency level.

Explicitness of Code Snippets

Code snippets, unless specified otherwise, are written with readability in mind. That's one of the reasons why in Example 2-28 you see hardcoded credentials. As a general rule, hardcoding credentials directly in your code is a bad practice, as they may easily leak. To mitigate this issue, you can use one of the data security design patterns from Chapter 7.

Summary

When you started reading this chapter, you probably considered data ingestion to be a necessary but not technically challenging step. Hopefully, this chapter has proven to you that the opposite is correct.

You've learned that even this simple operation of moving data from one place to another comes with some challenges. Without a Readiness Marker, you may ingest incomplete data as a customer or get bad press among users if you are the provider. Without the Compactor pattern, your virtually unlimited lakehouse will become a performance bottleneck pretty fast just because of API calls.

Also, even though you've learned about data ingestion relatively early in this book, remember this step is not reserved for the front doors of your system or for simple EL pipelines. Most of the patterns discussed here are great candidates for the extract step in the ETL and ELT pipelines, so you may even use them in more business-oriented jobs. That's another reason to not underestimate their importance.

Finally, I have good news and bad news. The good news is that you now have a list of templates you can apply to ingest the data in both pure technical and business contexts. The bad news is that it's just the beginning. After ingesting the data, you will process it, and there, too, things can go wrong. Hopefully, the next chapter will give you some other recipes for building more efficient data engineering systems!

## CHAPTER 3

Error Management Design Patterns

Our new Constitution is now established, and has an appearance that promises permanency; but in this world nothing can be said to be certain, except death and taxes.

—Benjamin Franklin

That's what Benjamin Franklin, one of the Founders of the United States, wrote in a letter to French physicist Jean-Baptiste Le Roy in 1789. If Franklin had been a data engineer in our day, he probably would have written something like this:

In this world, nothing can be said to be certain, except errors and data quality issues.

Sad but true, but your data engineering life will rarely be a bed of roses. Remember that data is dynamic and your expectations from today will not remain the same for the whole lifecycle. That's why you will need to expect the worst and adapt accordingly.

Besides, keep in mind that you're processing data generated by others. You directly inherit their data or software engineering issues, such as unreliable networks that lead to late delivery or temporary crashes that cause retried deliveries and subsequent duplicates in the dataset.

The design patterns presented in this chapter focus on managing errors, which is the next logical step in a data engineering project after the data ingestion cycle explained in Chapter 2. Design patterns address issues you need to deal with as a data and infrastructure consumer. You'll find here patterns discussing poor upstream data, such as unprocessable records, late data, and even duplicates. You'll also find patterns addressing hardware issues, like streaming job failures.

With all this context set up, it's time to discover the first group of data-related error management design patterns!

Unprocessable Records

Data quality is a recurrent problem in data projects, and that's why the first issue you'll have to deal with is unprocessable records. Often, they cause fatal failures that stop the data processing job. However, maintaining this *fail-fast* approach won't always be possible, especially for long-running streaming jobs.

Pattern: Dead-Letter

An easy solution is to ignore the bad records and continue processing the correct ones. It's easy to do if you can simply skip the invalid events and thus lose them forever. If this isn't an option, you can opt for another approach and save the bad records elsewhere for further investigation.

Problem

Your stream processing job writes visit events from an Apache Kafka topic to an object store. Bad luck: recently, data producers have started to generate unprocessable records and your job has started failing. For three consecutive days, you have been solving the issue manually by relaunching the job and altering the processed offsets in the checkpoint files. But you're tired. Instead of continuing this tedious action, you are looking now for a better solution to mitigate the issue. The solution should keep the pipeline running even for the occasional failed records and give you an opportunity to investigate the errors later.

Transient Versus Nontransient Errors

While processing the data, you'll face two kinds of errors. The first are *transient errors* that are often temporary and will eventually recover automatically in the future. One example is a short database unavailability mitigated with automatic connection retries.

Another type is *nontransient errors* that by definition are not temporary and will never recover by themselves. One example is unprocessable records, also known as *poison pill messages*. They are fatal issues that stop the application and require your manual intervention.

Solution

If your job can't process one particular record but can continue processing the others, it can be a breath of fresh air during a hard daily maintenance routine. The Dead-Letter pattern makes it possible.

The pattern starts by identifying places in the code where your job can fail. It can be a custom mapping function or even an error-safe transformation fully managed by your data processing framework. Next, you need to add some safety controls over the likely fail spots that have been identified. If you're using the mapping function, the most common safety control will be a `try-catch` block. If you're using the error-safe transformation, it will rely on an `if-else` condition. Additionally, you should include the failed message as the metadata to help you better understand the failure at the post-analysis stage. For that, you can leverage the Metadata Decorator pattern.

After identifying the places and decorating your processing part, you need to configure a different output for the erroneous events. The destination can be of the same or a different type than for the successfully processed records. While choosing a destination, you should consider the following:

- Resiliency, so that you don't need to think about a dead-letter strategy for your dead-letter storage.

- Monitoring ease, because it's the key success factor of this implementation. After all, you want to know when your job starts dealing with erroneous records and, especially, how many of them have been written recently. By analyzing these two metrics you should be able to better understand whether the errors are only occasional issues or whether the whole system is going down.

- Writing performance, since writing the unprocessed records to an extra place will incur some cost in the overall job execution time.

Good candidates for the dead-letter stores are object stores in the cloud or streaming brokers since they're highly available, fast, and easy to monitor.

Finally, you can complete the error handling part of the pattern with the replay pipeline that ingests the failed records into the main data flow. This is an optional step if you don't worry about past data.

Overall, an architecture implementing the Dead-Letter pattern should contain the error handling logic, the dead-letter storage, the monitoring layer, and eventually, the replay pipeline (see Figure 3-1).

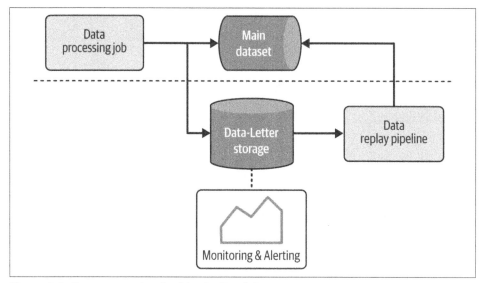

Figure 3-1. Components involved in the Dead-Letter pattern

The Dead-Letter pattern, even though it's often quoted in the context of stream processing, is also widely supported in batch workloads. The difference between stream processing and batch workloads comes from the data perception. Streaming operates on one record at a time and thus can write an individual record to dead-letter storage. Batch works on a bunch of data, and very often, it will write a subset of the erroneous records at once to dead-letter storage. You will see examples of both processing modes in the Examples section.

Consequences

Despite its beneficial impact on daily maintenance efforts, ignoring errors can have some serious consequences that you are going to discover in this section.

Snowball backfilling effect. The good thing about the fail-fast approach is its simplicity for the whole system. In this approach, if your pipeline stops, consumers won't get new data and probably won't run. On the other hand, if your job doesn't follow the fail-fast strategy, consumers will continue processing data that might be partial. Things become even more complicated when it comes to using the optional replay pipeline.

If you decide to run the replay pipeline, the ingested records can belong to the partitions already processed by your downstream consumers. That would require a backfilling action on their part and start a *snowball backfilling effect*, where their downstream consumers must reprocess the data as well. Figure 3-2 shows the beginning of the snowball backfilling effect.

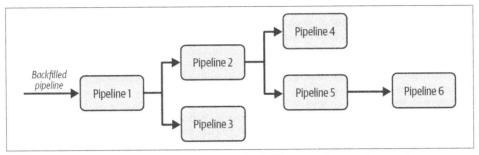

Figure 3-2. Snowball backfilling effect where backfilling Pipeline 1 triggers the same process for all downstream consumers

Mitigating this issue is not easy because each solution comes with its own trade-offs. You can avoid replaying the failed records and thus not trigger the backfilling run. This is the simplest approach, but it has the downside of losing the dead-letterred data. That's why you can decide to trigger the backfilling process. In that configuration, your dataset will be complete but might become inconsistent if you have downstream consumers who don't run or simply can't run a similar backfilling process.

Dead-lettered records identification. Integrating the dead-lettered records with the main data store has another implication: you may want to distinguish them from the rows added in the normal ingestion pipeline. It can be useful to implement a filtering condition skipping replayed records in the downstream consumers or to simply track the origin of each row.

Many solutions exist that you should adapt to your use case. You can add a boolean column or an attribute called `was_dead_lettered` to indicate each record produced by the Dead-Letter replay job. Or you can use more complete metadata to annotate those records with the job name, version, and replay time. This last approach fits perfectly with the data decoration patterns.

Ordering and consistency. The pattern can break data consistency. Let's learn more about this with an example of Internet of Things (IoT) sensors sending events every minute. One of your consumers builds sessions on top of that data, and the closing rule is based on the five-minute inactivity window. If, for whatever reason, events land in dead-letter storage for five consecutive minutes, the consumer will close the session. As a result, the session will be partial and inconsistent with reality.

This is also true for the ordered data delivery requirement. In that case, any replayed failed delivery will break the ordering consistency. Let's take a look at a quick example of three records to be delivered exactly in this order: 10:00, 10:01, and 10:02. If only the first and last records are correctly written and you decide to replay the failed one, your output data store will return 10:00, 10:02, and 10:01.

Error-safe functions. Error-safe functions greatly reduce the risk of runtime issues in the code because instead of throwing a runtime exception in case of an error, they return a NULL value. Moreover, all this logic is fully managed by your framework or database. However, these error-hiding functions make the Dead-Letter pattern implementation more challenging.

When you use error-safe functions, instead of capturing the exception, you'll need to compare the output value with the input. If the input is present but the function returns a NULL value, it might represent a processing error and thus an unprocessable record.

Moreover, to use error-safe functions, you need to understand their error-safety semantics, which may differ from one function to another. That's why implementing the Dead-Letter pattern on top of them, although possible, is challenging.

Error or failure? Although the pattern keeps the processing job up, it hides errors. Therefore, it can hide a fatal failure that should stop the pipeline. For that reason, you should complete the code implementation with an appropriate alerting layer that, in case of too many dropped events, could stop the job to avoid propagating potentially wrong data to your system.

Examples

The Dead-Letter pattern is often quoted in the context of stream processing because it allows the pipeline to run despite erroneous records. For that reason, let's see first how to implement it with an Apache Flink job in Example 3-1. The implementation relies on a feature called *side outputs*, which are additional destinations where you can write processed records.

Example 3-1. Dead-Letter component for Apache Flink

```
# source omitted for brevity

invalid_data_output: OutputTag = OutputTag('invalid_visits', Types.STRING())
visits: DataStream = data_source.map(MapJsonToReducedVisit(invalid_data_output),
  Types.STRING())
```

Example 3-2 shows what happens after the output declaration step. The job interacts with the side output in the mapping function called map_rows that implements the dead-letter logic as the try-catch block. As a result, the function will write any rows intercepted in the except part to the side output object. In the end, the job captures all side output entries by calling the get_side_output function and writes them to a dedicated Apache Kafka topic.

Example 3-2. Side output writing and reading in Apache Flink

```
# MapJsonToReducedVisit snippet w/ reference to the side output
def map_rows(self, json_payload: str) -> str:
try:
  evt = json.loads(json_payload)
  evt_time = int(datetime.datetime.fromisoformat(evt['event_time']).
  yield json.dumps({'visit_id': evt['visit_id'], 'event_time': evt_time,
                    'page': evt['page']})
except Exception as e:
  yield self.invalid_data_output, _wrap_input_with_error(json_payload, e)

kafka_sink_valid_data: KafkaSink = ...
kafka_sink_invalid_data: KafkaSink = ...

visits.get_side_output(invalid_data_output).sink_to(kafka_sink_invalid_data)
visits.sink_to(kafka_sink_valid_data)
```

But streaming is not the only place where you can implement the Dead-Letter pattern. Let's see now how to adapt it to Apache Spark SQL and Delta Lake with an error-safe CONCAT data transformation, which will never fail but will eventually return null if there is any issue, such as a missing value for one of the concatenated columns. Example 3-3 shows the first building block with the SQL query composed of the following:

- A subquery with the transformation logic using the CONCAT function. The function is one of the error-safe transformations because if any of the combined columns is null, it returns null without throwing an exception.
- The top-level query that validates the concatenation result.

Example 3-3. Dead-Letter pattern for error-safe transformations: the query

```
spark_session.sql('''
 SELECT type, full_name, version, name_with_version,
  WHEN (full_name IS NOT NULL OR version IS NOT NULL)
    AND name_with_version IS NULL THEN false ELSE true
  END AS is_valid
 FROM (SELECT type, full_name, version, CONCAT(full_name, version) AS name_w_version
FROM devices_to_load)''')
```

Example 3-4 shows the second part. Here, the code starts with the .persist() invocation that prevents the query from being executed twice. Next, it applies a filter on top of the cached dataset to write correctly and incorrectly transformed results in two different places.

Example 3-4. Dead-Letter pattern for error-safe transformations: the writing

```
devices_to_load_with_validity_flag.persist()

(devices_to_load_with_validity_flag.filter('is_valid IS TRUE')
.drop('is_valid').write.mode('overwrite')
.format('delta').save(f'{base_dir}/output/devices-table'))

(devices_to_load_with_validity_flag.filter('is_valid IS FALSE')
.drop('is_valid').write.mode('overwrite')
.format('delta').save(f'{base_dir}/output/devices-dead-letter-table'))
```

This example shows that implementing the pattern without explicit failures in declarative languages like SQL is challenging. After all, you need to write a custom `try-catch` logic, and in the end, you get a very verbose query that might be hard to maintain over time.

Duplicated Records

Capturing unprocessable records is only the first step in the data error management quest. The next part concerns delivery semantics. It's very rare to see records delivered exactly once because achieving this outcome is very challenging in distributed systems. More often, you'll work with a more relaxed environment where records can arrive at least once. That's fine, but what if your data logic must process each occurrence only once?

Pattern: Windowed Deduplicator

Data deduplication is the most common answer to ensuring that your data logic processes each occurrence only once. But how to do that for both batch and streaming pipelines? The key is to consider the data to be limited. For streaming jobs, the limits will be time-based windows, while the batch jobs will reduce the scope to the currently processed dataset.

Automatic Retries

Exactly-once processing works only if you don't encounter runtime errors. Otherwise, the restarted job execution may reprocess already processed records, despite the deduplication logic. This is often an accepted trade-off between automated transient errror managent and deduplication.

Problem

Your batch job needs to process visit events synchronized from the streaming layer to an object store. The job exposes the data directly to the business users, and hence, it must guarantee exactly-once processing for each distinct record. The problem is, the streaming layer often has duplicated events due to the automatic retries of the data producers.

Solution

Duplicated data can often lead to inconsistent results and mislead end users. If you want to avoid degrading the quality of the dataset, use the Windowed Deduplicator pattern.

The first step requires identifying the deduplication attributes that guarantee the uniqueness of each record. Once you get them, you need to define the deduplication scope. For batch jobs, it'll often be the currently processed dataset. Even though it's possible to extend it by including datasets processed in the past, you must be aware that it will require more compute power and eventually be slower.

When it comes to streaming jobs, by definition, they work on an unbounded set of records. It's therefore difficult to reason in terms of completed datasets, like for batch workloads. Instead, the pattern simulates them by creating time-based windows where the job will retain already processed keys composed of deduplication attributes.

Windows in Batch

Batch processing doesn't imply an explicit window that you might define from code. Instead, it relies on an implicit global window which encompasses the whole processed dataset. The pattern's name doesn't relate to the underlying implementation details but to this dataset consideration in terms of windows.

Regarding code implementation, to eliminate duplicates, batch jobs will either use a DISTINCT expression or a WINDOW function alongside the condition on the row_number(). Streaming jobs will be different because they will need to store already processed records for the deduplication window duration. This involves then keeping some state about the past, thus the name of this store, the *state store*. Consequently, the streaming logic will be more complex than for the batch systems. It will require interacting with the state store to verify whether a record has already been seen or not. The interaction is present in Figure 3-3.

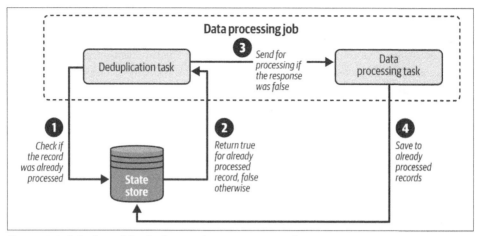

Figure 3-3. Windowed Deduplicator for a streaming job

State Stores

There are three different types of state stores. They're all trade-offs between performance and data consistency:

Local
Here, the state data lives only in memory. It's the fastest solution, but it might not be a good choice for production systems if you can't accept losing the state in case of failure.

Local with fault-tolerance
Here, the state still primarily lives in memory, which makes the access fast. But additionally, the job persists it to a remote storage for fault tolerance reasons. However, the persistence action has a cost in terms of processing time or consistency. If it occurs at each iteration, such as after updating a value in a window or microbatch, consistency should be fine but the job will be slower. In the opposite implementation, you will sacrifice consistency for time.

Remote
Here, the state is only present in a remote data store. Although it natively brings fault tolerance, it might negatively impact the latency and/or the overall cost of the pipeline.

Consequences

You may be surprised, but exactly-once processing doesn't guarantee exactly-once delivery or perfect deduplication. The next two points will shed some light on this.

Space versus time trade-off. This gotcha is valid for streaming pipelines because they're long-running applications on top of incremental datasets. Put differently, you don't have all the data at once, and you don't know if in a few minutes, you won't see any duplicates. For that reason, the implementation uses a time-based deduplication window and looks for duplicates only within the specified period.

As a consequence, a short window will probably miss some duplicates, but on the other hand, it will have a small impact on resources. If you extend the window duration, you'll need more resources since there will be more unique keys to persist and manage in the state store.

Idempotent producer. Correctly deduplicating the data doesn't guarantee exactly-once delivery for processed records. Very often, it will not be possible because of transient errors and their automatic solutions, such as retries. You should be aware of that and look for an idempotency pattern from Chapter 4 if you want to ensure exactly-once delivery.

Examples

Let's see how to first implement the pattern with batch pipelines. Apache Spark provides a `dropDuplicates` function that automatically takes care of duplicates. The function from Example 3-5 deduplicates the records, with the columns list defined in the parameter. If the parameter is missing, it'll use all the columns from the schema.

Example 3-5. Deduplication with `dropDuplicates`

```
dataset = (session.read.schema('...').format('json').load(f'{base_dir}/input'))

deduplicated = dataset.dropDuplicates(['type', 'full_name', 'version'])
```

However, that kind of native deduplication is not widely available. If you rely on a data processing framework, you'll probably have it. If not, you'll need to design the solution on your own. Thankfully, you can easily leverage grouping for that. In plain SQL, you can combine it with a `WINDOW` function. The `WINDOW`-based deduplication shown in Example 3-6 groups all rows by the columns from the `PARTITION BY` expression and filters out all but the first position (`position = 1`).

Example 3-6. Deduplication with a `WINDOW` function

```
SELECT type, full_name, version FROM (
 SELECT type, full_name, version,
   ROW_NUMBER() OVER (PARTITION BY type, full_name, version ORDER BY 1) AS position
 FROM duplicated_devices
) WHERE position = 1
```

This window-based approach will also work for streaming pipelines, but yet again, your data processing framework may help you by providing a high-level abstraction for deduplication. This is the case with Apache Spark, where the dropDuplicates function is also available for streaming data sources. Example 3-7 demonstrates how to declare the dropDuplicates function in that context. First, you need to interpret your input data and extract a time-based column. In our example, it'll be visit_time.

Example 3-7. Deduplication with dropDuplicates *in streaming data preparation*

```
event_schema = StructType([StructField("visit_id", StringType()),
  StructField("visit_time", TimestampType())])
deduplicated_visits = (input
  .select(F.from_json("value", event_schema).alias("value_struct"), "value")
  .select("value_struct.visit_time", "value_struct.visit_id", "value")
# see part 2...
```

After preparing the input dataset, you need to configure how long the job will remember already seen records. Example 3-8 shows how to configure it with a feature called a watermark on top of the visit_time column. The *watermark* has two responsibilities in our job. First, it defines the late data arrival boundary, meaning that records that are older than the current watermark value will not integrate into the pipeline. Since it's a building block of the Late Data Detector pattern described in the next section, I won't detail it here. Second, the watermark in the deduplication context also controls how long the job remembers the given key. Once again, all remembered entries older than the watermark will be automatically removed. Keep in mind that the streaming jobs are long running and that having that kind of control prevents their states from growing indefinitely.

Example 3-8. Deduplication with dropDuplicates *in streaming data expiration*

```
# ...part 2
.withWatermark("visit_time", "10 minutes")
.dropDuplicates(["visit_id", "visit_time"])
.drop("visit_time", "visit_id"))
```

Late Data

If you think that you have seen the worst errors with unprocessable and duplicated records, beware because you haven't heard about late data! Although it sounds very innocent, it has a serious impact on your data pipelines.

Pattern: Late Data Detector

In the context of late data, the first aspect you have to deal with is late data detection. It can help in many situations, such as completing already processed partitions or controlling the state in stateful jobs, as you saw before for deduplication in stream processing.

Problem

Most of the time, visitors to your blogging platform (as shown back in Figure 1-1 from Chapter 1) generate visit events in near real time so that your system can get them within 15 seconds of their creation. However, sometimes the users lose their network connection, and as a result, they buffer the visits locally before flushing them once the connection is restored. Your data processing jobs should detect these late events in order to apply a dedicated strategy for each use case, such as ignoring them.

Solution

The first step when dealing with data arrival issues is their detection with the Late Data Detector pattern. Since the problem is related to the time, the pattern requires defining one time-based attribute to track late data. The attribute should describe when a given event happened. Otherwise, it might be impossible to classify the incoming records as being late or on time.

Event and Processing Time

Data processing has two time concepts: event time and processing time. The event time indicates when a given action happened, while the processing time indicates when the data pipeline interacted with it. Naturally, the processing time will never be late.

In the next step, you need to define a latency aggregation strategy that will apply individually to each partition in your input data store. To avoid a situation in which your processing layer doesn't move on, the latency aggregation strategy must be monotonically increasing. Put differently, the tracked event time must move forward and can never go back. For that reason, the most common aggregation strategy uses the MAX function, taking the greatest event time for each partition. Using the MIN function here would lead to a stuck-in-the-past situation in which your job may never move forward.

After defining the partition-based logic, you need to decide on an additional aggregation strategy that will calculate a single event time for all partitions to represent overall progress. Unlike in the previous step, where the MAX function is recommended to ensure monotonicity, for this global event time, you can opt to use the following:

- The MIN function if your job needs to follow the slowest upstream dependency. This approach guarantees you're going to consider more data as being on time. However, if your processing logic performs some buffering based on the event time, you'll buffer more since the event time follows the slowest partition.

- The MAX function that follows the fastest upstream dependency. This approach risks skipping records coming from the slowest dependencies, but on the other hand, it reduces the buffer size and thus its storage pressure.

- The MIN and MAX combined at different levels. This approach is possible only if you interact with multiple partitioned data sources. In that case, besides the first aggregation on top of each individual data source, you'll have another aggregation on top of all data sources. You can decide to apply the MIN function to each source and MAX to all sources, or the opposite.

Figure 3-4 shows how to apply the MIN and MAX functions on top of a single data source where each partition returns the MAX event time seen so far. At the bottom of the schema, you can see an example of the combined approach where each data source applies a different aggregation strategy, and in the end, the overall progress is represented with the MIN function.

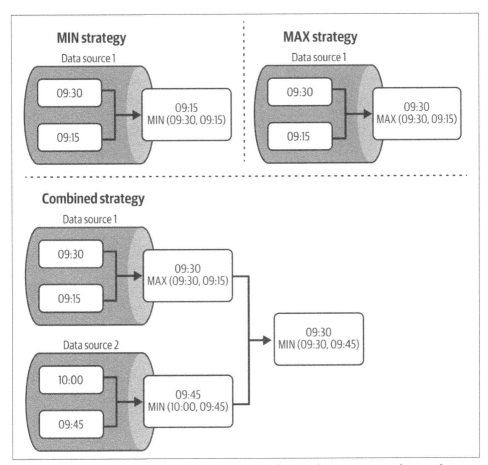

Figure 3-4. Different aggregation strategies applied to a job processing with a single partitioned data source and two partitioned data sources

But the implementation doesn't stop there. Using event time alone would mean you won't accept any data producer issues, such as lost connectivity or a slower network. Unfortunately, this will rarely happen, and your data producers may encounter some difficulties with punctuality in delivering data on the go. For that reason, to allow some extra unexpected latency, the pattern requires an allowed lateness attribute. The Late Data Detector pattern subtracts the allowed lateness value from the workflow's tracked event time as MAX(event time) - allowed lateness. The result of this calculation is called the *watermark*, and it defines the minimum event time to consider an event as on time.

To understand the watermark and the overall Late Data Detection pattern better, let's look at an example. Table 3-1 illustrates data flowing to a streaming system. As you'll notice, in the first row, there is no prior observation to define the watermark.

Consequently, the pipeline accepts all the records and defines a new output watermark. The output watermark, by the way, is the same as the watermark candidate here.

This is not the case in the second row, where new data generates a watermark candidate. However, the candidate doesn't need to be taken into account. Simply speaking, if the candidate value is lower than the current input watermark, it's ignored. Otherwise, it would mean that the job, instead of moving forward, will be moving back.

Table 3-1. Watermark of 30 minutes

Event times	Input watermark	Watermark candidate	Output watermark	Ignored records
10:00, 10:05, 10:06	-	MAX(10:00, 10:05, 10:06) − 30′ = 9:36	MAX(9:36) = 9:36	-
9:20, 9:31, 10:07	9:36	MAX(10:07) − 30′ = 09:37	MAX(9:36, 9:37) = 9:37	9:20, 9:31

What to do once you detect an event as being late? The simplest thing to do is ignore it. However, if even the late records are valuable data assets, you'll need to write them to the system with the Late Data Integrator pattern presented next.

Consequences

Even though the pattern only detects late data, it has some implementation gotchas.

Late data capture. Some of the data processing frameworks either don't support late data detection or don't support late data capture. For example, Apache Spark Structured Streaming has a built-in capability to detect and ignore late events, but it doesn't expose an API to capture them easily. That's not the case with Apache Flink, which provides more flexibility for both capturing and detecting late events.

MIN strategy, stuck-in-the-past situations, and stateful jobs. You learned about this very quickly in the previous section. The partition-based event time tracker doesn't use the MIN function in order to avoid a stuck-in-the-past situation. Let's take a look at an example of a stateful job to help us understand why it's problematic and why even though using this function would technically be possible, you should avoid doing so.

A stateful job accumulates events for a streaming job in a state store, as you discovered in the "Pattern: Windowed Deduplicator" on page 46. For example, it could count the number of visits for a user visiting a website. The challenge with this stateful accumulation is to know when to stop. Put differently, you should define when the accumulated state is complete. Often, you'll use the current watermark for that. Thus, by emitting each counter, you'll say, "For this user, there shouldn't be more new data."

If you used the MIN strategy to track partition event times, it would imply the following consequences:

Open-close-open infinite loop
> This is the semantic implication for the workloads storing some event time–based state. Let's imagine that your watermark moved to 10:30, and you decided to emit all accumulated states older than this time. However, after 10 minutes, you integrated some late records that moved the watermark back to 9:00. Therefore, you will have to reopen all states that are already emitted and thus considered completed.

Stuck in the past
> This is the most serious implication. If your pipeline is getting late data over and over again, the watermark may never make any progress. Consequently, your eventual event time–based state will grow because you will not be able to determine the buffered items as completed with regard to the watermark.

To help you avoid the issues from the previous list, the Late Data Detector should be monotonically increasing, which means it should never decrease as is the case with the MIN function. That's why, although technically possible, this function is not commonly used for tracking event time at the partition level.

Max strategy and event skew. The max-based strategy also has a gotcha. In highly skewed environments, it can be too aggressive and consequently drop many records.

Let's imagine the following example with multiple data sources. Four out of five data sources for our pipeline encounter some network issues, and they deliver the data 40 minutes later than the single fully working source. Since the watermark is based on the MAX function, records coming from the late data sources will be considered late, and the consumer will miss them.

Unfortunately, there is no silver bullet for this issue. The best mitigation strategy should rely on appropriate late events monitoring and the possibility of reintegrating late records whenever there is a high event skew. The next two patterns, Static Late Data Integrator and Dynamic Late Data Integrator, will address the replaying aspect.

Examples

The Late Data Detector pattern is mostly present in stream processing. For that reason, let's take a look at the implementation of two major frameworks from that area. To start with, let's use an example from Apache Spark Structured Streaming.

Example 3-9 shows late data detection in Structured Streaming with the withWatermark function. As you can see, it accepts two parameters, one that defines the event time attribute for time tracking and another for the allowed lateness. In our example, the configuration means that the job accepts data that's up to one hour late.

Example 3-9. Late data detection in a stateful job

```
visits_events = (input_data.selectExpr('CAST(value AS STRING)')
  .select(F.from_json('value', 'visit_id INT, event_time TIMESTAMP, page STRING')
  .alias('visit')).selectExpr('visit.*'))

session_window: DataFrame = (visits_events
  .withWatermark('event_time', '1 hour')
  .groupBy(F.window(F.col('event_time'), '10 minutes')).count())
```

To understand what the code is doing, let's analyze Table 3-2. It shows the buffered and emitted windows for each event time received with incoming records. As you can see, the job ignores the event of 01:50 as it happened earlier than the current watermark (02:15). At the same time, the two windows for three o'clock are pending in the state store. The job emits them only after processing the record from 04:31 since it's the first time the watermark can move on.

Table 3-2. The impact of the watermark on the late data for the event time of 2023-06-30

Event time w/o seconds	Current to new watermark (w/o seconds)	Buffered windows	Emitted windows
03:15	1970-01-01T00:00 to 2023-06-30T02:15	[03:10-03:20]	[]
03:00	02:15 to 02:15	[03:00-03:10, 03:10-03:20]	[]
01:50	02:15 to 02:15	[03:00-03:10, 03:10-03:20]	[]
03:11	02:15 to 02:15	[03:00-03:10, 03:10-03:20]	[]
04:31	02:15 to 03:31[a]	[04:30-04:40]	[03:00-03:10, 03:10-03:20]

[a] Technically, Apache Spark Structured Streaming rounds the watermark up to the upper bound of the window. The example here uses a simplified version to facilitate understanding.

Apache Spark Structured Streaming handles all late data on your behalf. This is great as it means you don't need to worry about it. However, in some scenarios, you may need to capture the late records to, for example, write them into a separate storage for reprocessing or further analysis. Although it can be hard to achieve with Apache Spark, it's relatively simple in Apache Flink, which gives access to the current watermark value from the execution context (see Example 3-10).

The first step is to create a timestamp assigner instance that will extract the event time value from the incoming records. In our example, this is the role of the VisitTimestampAssigner. Next, we also have to declare a watermark-aware data processor function. In our example, it's represented by the VisitLateDataProcessor class. As you can see in Example 3-10, the processor compares the extracted event time with the current watermark, and depending on the outcome, it writes the record to a different storage.

Example 3-10. Timestamp assigner and records processor in Apache Flink

```
class VisitTimestampAssigner(TimestampAssigner):
  def extract_timestamp(self, value: Any, record_timestamp: int) -> int:
    event = json.loads(value)
    event_time = datetime.datetime.fromisoformat(event['event_time'])
    return int(event_time.timestamp())

class VisitLateDataProcessor(ProcessFunction):

  def __init__(self, late_data_output: OutputTag):
    self.late_data_output = late_data_output

  def process_element(self, value: Visit, ctx: 'ProcessFunction.Context'):
    current_watermark = ctx.timer_service().current_watermark()
    if current_watermark > value.event_time:
        yield (self.late_data_output, json.dumps(VisitWithStatus(visit=value,
          is_late=True).to_dict()))
    else:
        yield json.dumps(VisitWithStatus(visit=value, is_late=False).to_dict())
```

After declaring the late data handling logic, we need to integrate it with the data processing job. That's the part shown in Example 3-11. You can see there that we allow records to be late (out of order) by at most five seconds. Later comes the processing logic, which is not relevant here, and finally, the side output definition. A *side output* in Apache Flink is a structure you can use to send records to a different storage location than the one configured mainly for the pipeline.

Example 3-11. Using a timestamp assigner and data processor in Apache Flink

```
watermark_strategy = (WatermarkStrategy
  .for_bounded_out_of_orderness(Duration.of_seconds(5))
  .with_timestamp_assigner(VisitTimestampAssigner()))

data_source = env.from_source(source=kafka_source,
  watermark_strategy=watermark_strategy, source_name="Kafka Source"
).uid("Kafka Source").assign_timestamps_and_watermarks(watermark_strategy)

late_data_output: OutputTag = OutputTag('late_events', Types.STRING())
visits: DataStream = (data_source.map(map_json_to_visit)
  .process(VisitLateDataProcessor(late_data_output), Types.STRING()))
kafka_sink_valid_data: KafkaSink = ...
kafka_sink_late_visits: KafkaSink = ...

visits.get_side_output(late_data_output).sink_to(kafka_sink_late_visits)
visits.sink_to(kafka_sink_valid_data)
```

Pattern: Static Late Data Integrator

You already know that you can ignore late data. It'll make your life easy as neither you nor the downstream consumers will need to backfill the jobs impacted by the late data. However, late data may also be valuable, and if it represents a significant percentage of your dataset, losing it won't be an option. If you were an ecommerce store, you wouldn't want to miss half of your orders, would you? That's only one scenario where you'll need to integrate late data after capturing it.

Problem

One of your daily jobs generates various statistics from the websites that refer your blog posts. The statistical results are considered to be approximate for 15 days because that's the maximum delay allowed to integrate late data. Records older than 15 days are skipped.

Your batch only processes the current day and consequently ignores any late data that's not older than the allowed 15 days. You would like to adapt the job and include late data as part of the daily pipeline without having to run 15 individual jobs separately each day.

Solution

A fixed delay for late data ingestion is a perfect scenario where you can leverage the Static Late Data Integrator pattern.

Easy Solution for You, but Not for Others

In fact, the easiest solution to the problem is using processing time–based partitions. However, if you do care about the event time somewhere in your system, using the processing time solution simply moves the problem somewhere else. Let's look at an example to help us understand this better.

Let's imagine that your processing time partition for nine o'clock has the following distribution: 80% of the data for nine o'clock, 10% for eight o'clock, and 10% for seven o'clock. One of the downstream consumers uses event time–based partitions. Hence, even though your pipeline doesn't need to deal with late data, it generates late data that will need to be handled by other processes in the system (see Figure 3-5).

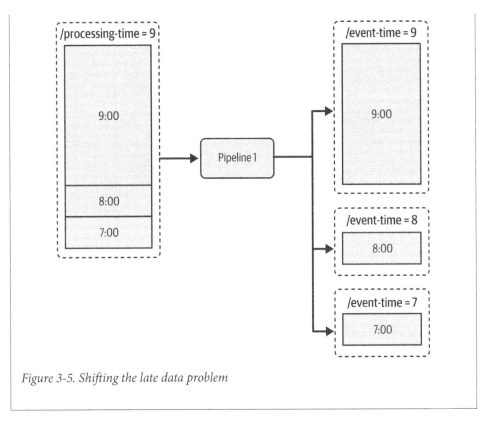

Figure 3-5. Shifting the late data problem

You start the implementation by defining a so-called *static lookback window* (i.e., how far to look back in the past for late data in a given job execution). It's called static because the duration will never change, even though your dataset will receive some late data after the allowed window duration. For example, if your pipeline is about to execute on the dataset from 2024-12-31 and your lookback window is set to 14 days, the current run will reprocess past partitions between 2024-12-17 and 2024-12-30 in addition to the current day. If, for whatever reason, you get some late data for 2024-12-15, it will be ignored.

After defining the lookback window, you need to place the late data integration process in your pipeline. Figure 3-6 shows three different configurations.

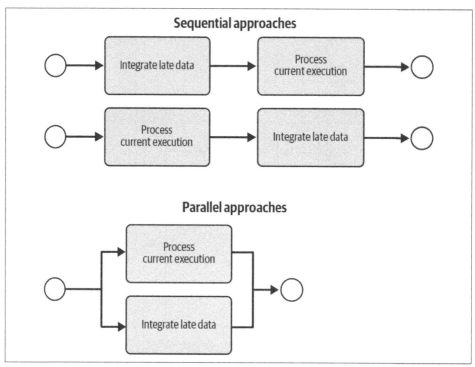

Figure 3-6. Strategies to include late data integration in pipelines

Which strategy you should choose? There is no one-size-fits-all solution, and your choice will depend on the category of the data processing job and the delivery constraints. Here are some hints to help you make a choice:

- For stateful pipelines where the results generated by one execution depend on the results generated by the previous executions, you should opt for the sequential strategy where the late data ingestion is handled as the first step. After all, you need a valid history to generate the current dataset.

- For stateless pipelines, you can use and switch between all three strategies. But if you want to deliver current data first, you should opt for either the second or the third approach, in which late data is handled at the same time or after the current execution time.

Consequences

Although the pattern introduces some data correctness fixes, it does so with an increased complexity cost.

Snowball backfilling effect.   The biggest problem you may encounter here is the snowball effect. If you are a data provider and your data consumers care about consistency, they'll inevitably need to replay all partitions with the late data, just as you have done. If they have consumers too, those consumers will also need to run backfilling for these partitions...and in the end, the whole operation may become very compute-intensive. Unfortunately, there is not much you can do here besides notifying your direct consumers of all backfilling actions and letting them decide what to do on their end.

Overlapping executions and backfilling.   Due to the static nature of the lookback window, you shouldn't backfill your jobs as you would backfill jobs without the static lookback window. To understand this better, let's take a look at an example of a pipeline with a four-day lookback window that already executed on 2024-10-10, 2024-10-11, and 2024-10-12.

If you replay all three executions, you will generate overlapping runs (see Table 3-3).

Table 3-3. Overlapped backfilling examples

Execution date	Executed dates
2024-10-10	2024-10-09, 2024-10-08, 2024-10-07, 2024-10-06
2024-10-11	2024-10-10, 2024-10-09, 2024-10-08, 2024-10-07
2024-10-12	2024-10-11, 2024-10-10, 2024-10-09, 2024-10-08

For that reason, before starting a backfill, you need to take the lookback window duration into account. As a result, in the previous example, it would be enough to restart only the 2024-10-12 execution.

Pipeline trigger.   With the Static Late Data Integrator, your backfilling jobs must be part of the main pipeline. You can't start separated pipelines as part of the lookback window–based backfilling because it'll lead to the same problem explained in the section on overlapping executions and backfilling.

Figure 3-7 depicts both valid and invalid approaches.

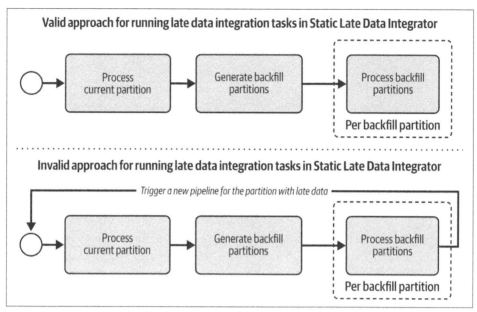

Figure 3-7. Valid and invalid approaches for integrating late data in the Static Late Data Integrator pattern

Waste of resources.   Fixed periods from the lookback window may not contain late data every time. If you are worried about running the job for a partition without new late data to integrate, you can add a control task to run the integration task only when there is late data, or you can use the Dynamic Late Data Integrator pattern.

Time requirement.   If your dataset is not partitioned by time or doesn't have any time concept, you cannot really detect and thus integrate late data. Time partitions from the Static Late Data Integrator pattern are time boundaries that each incoming record is comparing against.

Examples

Let's see how to implement the Static Late Data Integrator pattern in Apache Airflow with a feature called Dynamic Task Mapping. In a nutshell, the feature lets you create tasks dynamically from a data provider function. Since the execution time will change with each new run, Dynamic Task Mapping is a perfect fit for generating late data integration tasks for the static lookback window duration.

The pipeline from our example, which is fully available on GitHub (*https://oreil.ly/ VCas8*), copies files from an input location to an output location. The workflow runs daily, and after copying the file for the current day, the pipeline backfills two previous dates by subtracting the lookback window size from the execution date (see Example 3-12).

Example 3-12. Generation of backfilling tasks with a static lookback window of two days

```
@task
def generate_backfilling_runs():
 dr: DagRun = get_current_context()['dag_run']
 backfilling_dates = []
 days_to_backfill = 2
 start_date_to_backfill = (dr.execution_date
  datetime.timedelta(days=days_to_backfill))
 for days_to_add in range(0, days_to_backfill):
  date_to_backfill = start_date_to_backfill + datetime.timedelta(days=days_to_add)
  backfilling_dates.append(date_to_backfill.date().strftime('%Y-%m-%d'))
 return backfilling_dates
```

So generated `backfilling_dates` are later passed to the `integrate_late_data` task. Under the hood, thanks to the Dynamic Task Mapping expressed in Example 3-13 with the `expand(...)` method, Apache Airflow will create one integration task for each date. As you'll notice, other than the expand call, the code doesn't differ a lot from the code you would write without the late data integration.

Example 3-13. Generating tasks for each of the backfilled dates from an expand *method*

```
@task
def integrate_late_data(late_date: str):
 copy_file(late_date)

# ....
integrate_late_data.expand(late_date=generate_backfilling_runs())
```

Dynamically created tasks integrate with regular ones. In our case, we're loading the current day before backfilling two previous dates, which gives us the workflow in Example 3-14.

Example 3-14. Workflow with tasks created dynamically

```
backfilling_runs_generator = generate_backfilling_runs()
(file_to_load_sensor >> load_current_file() >> backfilling_runs_generator >>
  integrate_late_data.expand(late_date=backfilling_runs_generator))
```

Pattern: Dynamic Late Data Integrator

The Static Late Data Integrator is a simple form of late data inclusion because it relies on some fixed period of time. However, having a static tolerance period is not always possible, and sometimes you may need a more dynamic approach that will just load the partitions impacted by the late data.

Problem

The Static Late Data Integrator pattern that you implemented to handle the last 15 days of data is not enough anymore. Your product owner wants to enrich the statistics with all late data, even beyond the initial 15-day window. Now you need to adapt your pipeline to this new business requirement and avoid blindly replaying only the two previous weeks.

Solution

To handle variability and integrate only the partitions with late data, you can use the Dynamic Late Data Integrator pattern.

The implementation leverages a lookback window that is dynamic, which means that all the backfilled partitions really contain late data. To make this happen, the dynamic approach requires an additional data structure to store the last execution time, and eventually,[1] the last update time for each partition. You can find an example of this structure in Table 3-4.

Table 3-4. Data structure (aka state table) for Dynamic Late Data Integrator

Partition	Last processed time	Last update time
2024-12-17	2024-12-17T10:20	2024-12-17T03:00
2024-12-18	2024-12-18T09:55	2024-12-20T10:12

Based on this table, you can perform a query to get the partitions to backfill (see Example 3-15).

Example 3-15. Query to get the list of late partitions

```
SELECT partition FROM state_table WHERE
`Last update time` > `Last processed time` AND `Partition` < `Processed partition`
```

---

1 The last update time is already stored at the partition level. However, having it in a single place alongside the last processed time simplifies understanding of the pattern and may be helpful in day-to-day maintenance.

However, adding the state table is not enough. You also need to define a place in your pipeline where you will run the query. Typically, after you successfully process your data, you will need to update the last processed time (see Figure 3-8).

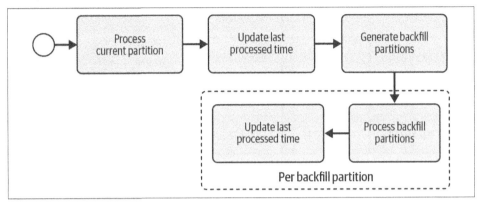

Figure 3-8. Interaction with state table integrated with the main pipeline

Even though you've created the state table and integrated it into the pipeline, one question remains: how can you get the last update time for the partitions? Some data stores provide this fine-grained level of detail out of the box. In this category, you'll find BigQuery, which exposes an `INFORMATION_SCHEMA.PARTITIONS` view with the `last_modified_timestamp` attribute for each partition, or Apache Iceberg, which includes a `last_updated_at` column for the partitions metadata table. For the data stores without this information, you'll need to find a way to generate it from existing data, as we demonstrate in the code in the Examples section.

Not Whole Partitions

If you can isolate the entities impacted by the late data, you don't need to backfill full partitions. Instead, you can only overwrite the data generated for the impacted entities. This approach optimizes resources usage but also is more challenging to implement.

Consequences

The Dynamic Late Data Integrator pattern solves the resources waste issue and fixes the lookback window, but it also has its own shortcomings.

Concurrency. If your pipeline supports concurrent executions, dynamic late data integration may generate duplicated late data integration runs. Figure 3-9 shows what could happen in a pipeline running four different jobs in parallel, with late data in each processed partition. As you'll notice, partitions for 2024-12-10 and 2024-12-11 would be executed more than once.

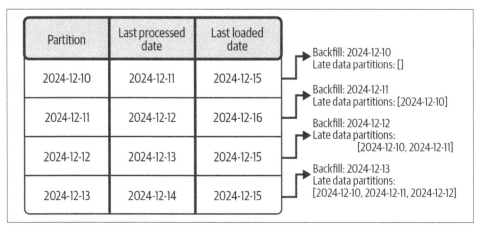

Figure 3-9. Late data integration concurrency problem

To avoid this issue, you need to add an extra column to the state table that will keep the partition status either as already processed or as being processed. Consequently, the query retrieving the partitions to backfill should add this column as an extra filtering condition to ignore the partitions already planned for late data integration. The new query looks like the one in Example 3-16.

Example 3-16. Query to get the partitions to backfill in the concurrent Late Data Integrator pattern

```
SELECT partition FROM state_table WHERE
`Last update time` > `Last processed time` AND
`Partition` < `Processed partition` AND
`Is processed` = false
```

In addition to this query change, you will need to adapt the pipeline with the following adjustments:

- Each pipeline needs to start with the task that updates the `Is processed` column of the currently processed partition. That way, you can avoid having the next execution generate the current partition as the one to backfill. Also, this task should run only if the execution of the previous run succeeded. In our example, this task for 2024-12-11 would start only if the same task successfully completed for the run of 2024-12-10.

- The task that generates the partitions to backfill should now also update all retrieved partitions as having been processed. In addition, it should run only if its previous execution succeeded. This dependency on the past runs helps avoid race conditions and triggering the same partitions in two different runs.

- The task updating the last processed time should additionally set the `Is processed` flag to false. That way, if the partition gets new late data, it can still be replayed.

After applying all these changes, you can extend the execution mode, and instead of executing the late data integration tasks as part of the main pipeline, you can trigger complete late data integration pipelines. Both execution modes are depicted in Figure 3-10, where only the processes in the lighter boxes can run in parallel.

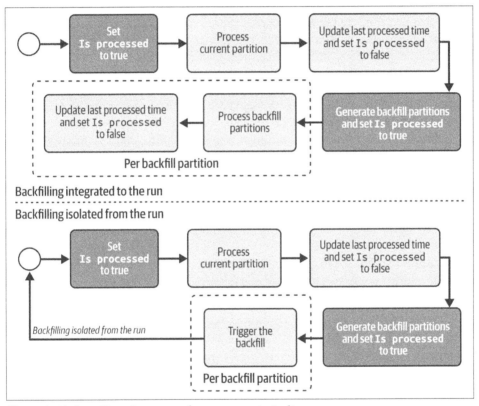

Figure 3-10. Late Data Integrator for concurrent pipelines

It's worth noting that if the task that generates partitions to backfill fails, its future executions will not run due to the dependency on the previous run. Consequently, the pipeline will get stuck in a long in-progress state requiring your manual intervention to unblock it.

You'll find a complete example of a concurrent pipeline protected against duplicated executions in the GitHub repo (*https://oreil.ly/33qRC*).

Stateful pipelines and very late data. By addressing the issue of a fixed lookback window, the Dynamic Late Data Integrator pattern brings up another challenge which is exclusively related to stateful pipelines. Let's imagine a pipeline implementing the Incremental Sessionizer pattern with the last successful run having taken place on 2024-10-20. There hasn't been any late data so far, but the next day's execution spots late data ingested for the partition of 2024-09-21. Since your job is stateful, you will need to regenerate all executions from 2024-09-21 to 2024-10-20 to guarantee the correctness of your dataset.

As you can see, it might not be enough to consider a lookback window to be dynamic because this can lead to heavy backfills when you get very late records. If this is problematic, you will need to define the accepted lookback window even for dynamically created lookback windows.

Scheduling complexity. The dynamic lookback window version involves creating backfilling pipelines dynamically. Depending on your storage layer, getting the last modification time for each partition might not be easy. This step can involve dealing with the internal details of a storage technology or even implementing the update tracking table on your own.

Examples

As an example, we're going to use yet again the Dynamic Task Mapping of Apache Airflow. Since you discovered this feature in the Static Late Data Integrator pattern, I'll omit this part and directly cover the challenge you may face when the last update partition time is not natively available. Thankfully, in our example for Delta Lake, we can get the partition information after some coding effort to use exclusive Scala classes.

The Scala API for Delta Lake provides a `DeltaLog` class that has a `getChanges` method. The results are all the created or deleted files from the table version you specify. Once you get these files, you can simply get the latest Delta Lake version for each partition (see Example 3-17).

Example 3-17. Extracting modified partitions from a Delta Lake version

```
val deltaLog = DeltaLog.forTable(sparkSession, jobArguments.tableFullPath)
val partitionsChangeVersions: Iterator[(String, Long)] = deltaLog.getChanges(0)
 .flatMap {
 case (version, actions) => {
  val changedPartitionsInVersion: Set[String] = actions.map {
   case addFile: AddFile if addFile.dataChange =>
     Some(addFile.partitionValues.map(e => s"${e._1}=${e._2}").mkString("/"))
   case removeFile: RemoveFile if removeFile.dataChange =>
     Some(removeFile.partitionValues.map(e => s"${e._1}=${e._2}").mkString("/"))
```

```
  case _ => None}.filter(_.isDefined).map(_.get).toSet

  changedPartitionsInVersion.map(partition => (partition, version))
 }
}
val lastVersionForEachPartition: Map[String, Long] = partitionsChangeVersions
 .toSeq.groupBy(pair => pair._1).mapValues(pairs => pairs.map(_._2).max)
lastVersionForEachPartition
```

The next part consists of getting the partitions to backfill (see Example 3-18).

Example 3-18. Method to get partitions to backfill where the last processed version is lower than the last written version

```
val partitionsToBackfill = sparkSession.read.format("delta").load(TablePath)
 .select("partition", "isProcessed", "lastProcessedVersion").as[PartitionState]
 .filter(state => state.lastProcessedVersion.isDefined)
 .filter(state => {
  (!lastVersionPerPartition.contains(state.partition) ||
  lastVersionPerPartition(state.partition) > state.lastProcessedVersion.get) &&
  !state.isProcessed && state.partition < currentPartition
 })
partitionsToBackfill.map(_.partition).collect()
```

As you'll notice, for Delta Lake, we reason in terms of table versions, which is a simpler concept than update time. Next, the job writes partitionsToBackfill as a timestamped file to avoid race conditions in case of concurrent executions. Consequently, each job execution will use its own late data integration file to create backfilling tasks dynamically via Dynamic Task Mapping and the function from Example 3-19.

Example 3-19. Reading a configuration file and triggering past executions

```
@task
def generate_backfilling_arguments():
  context = get_current_context()
  current_partition_date = context['ds']
  dag_run: DagRun = context['dag_run']
  dag_run_start_time: str = dag_run.start_date.isoformat()

  def _run_id_for_event_time(event_time: str) -> str:
   return f'backfill_{event_time}_from_{current_partition_date}_{dag_run_start_time}'

  configuration = read_backfilling_configuration(current_partition_date)
  return list(map(lambda partition: {
   'execution_date': partition['event_time'],
   'trigger_run_id': _run_id_for_event_time(partition['event_time'])
  }, configuration['partitions']))
```

If your job can run concurrently, you'll need to add dependency constraints on the previous execution. Therefore, some tasks in the pipeline, despite overall concurrency, will run sequentially.

Apache Airflow achieves this sequential execution with the task-level depends_on_past attribute. If it's set, the orchestrator blocks any execution for a given task as long as its previous execution doesn't succeed. In our case, it guarantees that there will only be one job generating partitions to backfill. Example 3-20 shows our pipeline with the default allowed concurrency and sequential execution enforced on the key tasks for the Dynamic Late Data Integrator pattern.

Example 3-20. A pipeline configured with the default concurrency and custom sequentiality on some tasks

```
with DAG('devices_loader', max_active_runs=5,
  default_args={'depends_on_past': False, ...},
) as dag:
  processing_marker = SparkKubernetesOperator(
    task_id='mark_partition_as_being_processed', depends_on_past=True # ...
  )
  backfill_creation_job = SparkKubernetesOperator(
    task_id='get_late_partitions_and_mark_them_as_being_processed',# ...
    depends_on_past=True
  )
  # ...
```

Filtering

An error in data engineering tasks does not always mean a technical failure. Errors also include human mistakes, like incorrectly implementing filters, which might lead to partial or bad data being exposed to end users.

Pattern: Filter Interceptor

One of the most common data operations is filtering. It lets you select only the records that are relevant to a given business use case. Despite this popularity, it's often hard to know what particular condition has filtered out most of the rows, which, as a result, would give you the ability to detect errors due to aggressive and possibly buggy filtering conditions. The pattern presented here provides more insight.

Problem

One of your batch jobs uses a distributed data processing framework. Recently, you released a new version to production and noticed a sudden spike of filtered data volume to 90% from 15%. You're wondering if the change comes from the data or from software regression, and you can't find this out by simply looking at the execution plan. The framework performs many optimizations, and one of them collapses the filtering expressions into a single one.

Solution

Ideally, you should address this issue with physical query execution plan analysis. However, this might lack precision, especially when the engine performs some optimizations such as combining all filter conditions into one execution step. In that case, the plan will contain the number of filtered rows for all filters and not the statistics for each condition. The Filter Interceptor pattern overcomes that.

The implementation is relatively straightforward in data processing frameworks with a programmatic API. Instead of simply expressing your filtering condition, you must wrap it with a counter logic that you increment if the condition evaluates to true. At the end of the job execution, after completing your business logic, you must explicitly gather all filter counters.

The implementation requires a bit more effort in declarative languages like SQL. The solution here consists of using a subquery or a temporary table that exposes filtering conditions as columns. Let's take an example of a query with the two filter expressions a IS NOT NULL and b != "abc". The implementation would include them as new columns storing the validation results (*a_is_not_null*, *b_is_not_abc*) in a subquery table. These columns would later be used in the main query as filtering predicates. As you can see, it's not as easy as just wrapping the filtering logic with the programmatic API. If this is confusing, you'll find an example in the Examples section.

Stay Pragmatic

Remember to use the right tool for the job. If the programmatic API is better for what you're trying to do, use it, even though you have been writing only SQL queries so far! The opposite is true as well.

Consequences

The pattern gives you some extra insight into job execution but doesn't do it for free.

Runtime impact. Wrapping the filtering condition will impact the job execution time and resources. However, the impact should be small. Counters from the implementation are rather simple data structures living locally in each task, and exchanging them across the network to get the final result shouldn't be costly. The impact can be greater for the SQL example, where you might need to create a temporary table before executing the queries to correctly extract the filtering stats and really filter out the data before writing to another table.

Declarative languages. As you already know, sometimes it's better to code even though you get used to working only with SQL. The Filter Interceptor is one of the examples where declarative languages are less powerful than the programmatic API. The programmatic API, besides providing some flexibility, helps you write code that is easier to grasp and maintain over time.

Streaming. The implementation is not only challenging for declarative languages but also for streaming jobs. Although it's easier than for SQL, it may require transforming your stateless job into a stateful one, hence adding some additional state management overhead to count the number of filters applied so far for each input record.

Also, since streaming data is continuously arriving, you should define some time boundaries for the interceptor statistics. Otherwise, you may not be able to relate the statistics to the current time and may not know what filters are currently the most active in the queries. For example, the filtering statistics could rely on time-based processing windows so that you can get trends over time and have a single view of the whole job history.

Examples

The Solution section already gave you an idea of how to implement the pattern with the programmatic API of a data processing framework. Let's now learn what it means to concretely implement it with Apache Spark SQL. Depending on your language, you can implement it with either `filter` programmatic functions (Scala API) or `mapInPandas` (PySpark). The former, because it's easier, is present in the GitHub repo (*https://oreil.ly/oVpyu*). Let's then focus here on a more complex implementation.

To start with, we're defining a class that wraps a filtering condition and an Apache Spark accumulator together as a `FilterWithAccumulator` class. The accumulator will increment at each false evaluation of the filter. You can find both declarations in Example 3-21.

Example 3-21. Filter Interceptor in PySpark: accumulators and filtering functions

```
@dataclasses.dataclass
class FilterWithAccumulator:
 name: str
 filter: Callable[[Any], bool]
 accumulator: Accumulator[int]

filters_with_accumulators = {
 'type': [
  FilterWithAccumulator('type is null', lambda device: device['type'] is not None,
   spark_context.accumulator(0)),
  FilterWithAccumulator('type is too short (1 chars or less)',
   lambda device: len(device['type']) > 1, spark_context.accumulator(0))
```

```
    ],
    # ...
}
```

Next comes Example 3-22 with the data processing step. As you can see, it relies on the `mapInPandas` transformation that calls a `filter_null_type` function. This custom function iterates all previously declared filters and evaluates each of them, and in the case of a false result, it increases the associated accumulator.

Example 3-22. Filter Interceptor in PySpark: the job

```
def filter_null_type(devices_iterator: Iterator[pandas.DataFrame]):
 def filter_row_with_accumulator(device_row):
  for device_row_attribute in device_row.keys():
   for filter_with_accumulator in filters_with_accumulators[device_row_attribute]:
    if not filter_with_accumulator.filter(device_row):
     filter_with_accumulator.accumulator.add(1)
     return False
  return True

 for devices_df in devices_iterator:
  yield devices_df[devices_df.apply(lambda device:
   filter_row_with_accumulator(device), axis=1) == True]

valid_devices = input_dataset.mapInPandas(filter_null_type, input_dataset.schema)
valid_devices.write.mode('append').format('delta').save(output_dir)
```

Finally, to get the filtering statistics, you need to check the accumulators' value by iterating the list (see Example 3-23).

Example 3-23. Filter Interceptor in PySpark: getting the values

```
for key, accumulators in filters_with_accumulators.items():
 for accumulator_with_filter in accumulators:
  print(f'{key} // {accumulator_with_filter.name} //
      {accumulator_with_filter.accumulator.value}')
```

That was for the programmatic API. As you saw, the pattern relies on a wrapper for the filter function. The same solution applies to the SQL version, but this time, with additional aliases (see Example 3-24).

Example 3-24. SQL queries for Filter Interceptor

```
spark_session.sql('''SELECT * FROM (
  SELECT
    CASE
      WHEN (type IS NOT NULL) IS FALSE THEN 'null_type'
      WHEN (LEN(type) > 2) IS FALSE THEN 'short_type'
```

```
   WHEN (full_name IS NOT NULL) IS FALSE THEN 'null_full_name'
   WHEN (version IS NOT NULL) IS FALSE THEN 'null_version'
   ELSE NULL
 END AS status_flag,
 type, full_name, version
FROM input)''').createTempView('input_with_flags')


spark_session.sql('''SELECT COUNT(*), status_flag FROM input_with_flags WHERE
status_flag IS NOT NULL GROUP BY status_flag''').createTempView('grouped_filters')

(spark_session.sql('SELECT type, full_name, version FROM input_with_flags
  WHERE status_flag IS NULL')
 .write.mode('append').format('delta').save(f'{base_dir}/devices-valid-sql-table'))
```

Example 3-24 starts with a table creation query, which returns all input columns plus a computed filter alias based on an `if-elseif-elseif-...else` statement. The job later uses the results of that table to count the number of filtered rows for each condition and to create a new user-facing table with all valid records.

Fault Tolerance

Let's finish this chapter with a form of protection that ensures recoverability for continuous data processing workflows, such as streaming ones. The challenge with these workflows is to know when to start after stopping the job. Without a proper progress tracking mechanism, you'll end up reprocessing already processed data.

Pattern: Checkpointer

The fatal error is particularly critical in stream processing. Remember, these applications are working on continuously arriving events that are often stored in an append-only log. Put differently, you can't simply restart them as batch pipelines since the dataset doesn't have any particular organizational structure, such as partitions, that could help you figure out what to process next.

Problem

You're processing the visit events in streaming. The job counts the number of unique visits in 10-minute windows. You're worried that any fatal failure will stop the job and make it reprocess the data from the beginning. To mitigate that risk, you're looking for a solution that will persist the results as the query moves on.

Solution

To avoid reprocessing past data, your job must keep track of the most recent position in the consumed data source, as well as the computed state. The Checkpointer pattern implements this tracking mechanism.

Checkpointing consists of recording the data processing process in a more persistent storage than the job's environment, which may change when you restart it. Two approaches exist here, depending on your consumer's logic.

Data processing framework based

If you rely on a data processing framework, the progress information may be recorded in the environment managed by the framework itself. Apache Spark Structured Streaming and Apache Flink are great examples here as they store the progress metadata in a resilient object store with full progress tracking management.

Data store based

On the other hand, if you are using the data store SDK, you may be interacting with the data store layer for the checkpoint information. An example here is Apache Kafka SDK, which persists the checkpoint data to an Apache Kafka topic (`__consumer_offsets`), or Amazon Kinesis Client Library (KCL), which writes checkpoints to an Amazon DynamoDB table.

Two implementations also exist for the checkpointing operation itself. The first one is configuration driven, where you only configure the checkpointing frequency and delegate the execution to your library. That's how Apache Spark Structured Streaming and Apache Flink work.

The second implementation relies on an intentional checkpointing action from your code. Here, after reading and processing the records, you'll be responsible for confirming this operation to avoid getting the same data in the next execution. An example here is an Apache Kafka custom consumer with the commit methods.

Consequences

Although the pattern provides an extra fault tolerance mechanism, it doesn't do it for free. Latency is the biggest drawback here.

Delivery guarantee versus latency trade-off. Position tracking is not an expensive operation in terms of latency. It only accumulates some numbers for each input partition in memory and persists them once in a while to a persistent storage. However, the pattern also applies to the state in cases of stateful applications such as user sessions (cf. the Stateful Sessionizer pattern). Tracking the state may have a more significant latency impact as the state will probably be many times bigger than those numeric positions.

For that reason, once again, you'll need to balance the latency requirements and the processing guarantee. The more frequent the checkpoints are, the slower the job will be due to checkpoint creation overhead. When you opt for less frequent checkpoints, the job will spend less time dealing with the metadata, but on the other hand, in the case of failure, you may have more data to reprocess.

Exactly-once feeling. The pattern gives you the exactly-once delivery feeling, but it's just an impression. The first reason for this is the distributed character of the job. There could be multiple tasks working in parallel and in an asynchronous manner. If one of them fails in the middle of the work before triggering the checkpoint, the restart will involve retries and reprocessing of the already successful records.

To achieve exactly-once delivery, you'll need to apply one of the idempotency patterns presented in the next chapter. The checkpointing alone will not be enough.

Delivery Modes

Exactly once is a delivery mode where the producer delivers records only one time to the data store. It's the perfect scenario that you can achieve with the idempotency patterns from Chapter 4. Two other available modes are impacted by checkpointing:

At least once
> This happens when you perform the checkpoint after processing (and thus writing) the data; you can generate duplicates in case of retries.

At most once
> This occurs when you create the checkpoint before processing; it involves losing the data in the case of processing failures.

Examples

Because this pattern works for streaming pipelines, let's focus on two slightly different implementations. The first solution comes from Apache Spark Structured Streaming and is present in Example 3-25. As you can see, the code defines the checkpoint storage in the `checkpointLocation` attribute. After starting the job, Apache Spark will write all processed offsets to the metadata files located under `{base_dir}/check point`.

Example 3-25. Checkpoints in Apache Spark Structured Streaming

```
write_query = (input_stream_data.writeStream.outputMode('update')
    .option('checkpointLocation', f'{base_dir}/checkpoint')
    .foreachBatch(synchronize_visits_to_files).start())
```

The written files are named after each executed job's iteration. Example 3-26 shows an example of the type of file you can find under the checkpoint location.

Example 3-26. Checkpointed metadata for fault tolerance

```
$ cat /tmp/dedp/ch03/fault-tolerance/micro-batch/checkpoint/offsets/18
# omitted two irrelevant lines
{"visits":{"1":1276,"0":1224}}
```

Checkpointer in Apache Spark writes offsets at a job's iteration. This regularity adds overhead, but it provides a stronger guarantee and incurs less risk of processing duplicates in case of restart. Apache Flink, which is another stream processing framework, works a bit differently. It doesn't follow the job iteration's mode and instead is based on time.

Example 3-27 shows checkpoint configuration in Apache Flink.

Example 3-27. Time-based checkpointing with Apache Flink

```
checkpoint_interval_30_sec = 30000
env.enable_checkpointing(checkpoint_interval_30_sec, mode=EXACTLY_ONCE)

(env.get_checkpoint_config().enable_externalized_checkpoints(RETAIN_ON_CANCELLATION))
```

Even though the snippet is short, it may be confusing because of various configuration parameters. The easiest to explain is the RETAIN_ON_CANCELLATION mode. This property simply asks Flink to keep the checkpointed files after a job's failure. By default, the checkpoint location is tied to the job instance and Flink removes it whenever the job restarts. When it comes to the EXACTLY_ONCE checkpoint mode, it impacts stateful operations, such as windowed counters. The configuration from the snippet guarantees that each input record reflects the state once. In the case of our counter, it means that any restart will not lead to counting an element twice.

Asynchronous Progress Tracking

Apache Spark 3.4.0 has introduced support for asynchronous checkpoints that are not synchronized with microbatches. At the time of writing this book (2024), the feature is still experimental, and the open source version doesn't support state store.

Summary

Errors are inevitable. They may come from buggy code, poor quality of the ingested data, or just temporary hardware issues. Error management design patterns are there to help you deal with the inevitable.

At the beginning of the chapter, you discovered three patterns that are adapted to data quality issues. You learned about using the Dead-Letter pattern to handle unprocessable records gracefully, the Windowed Deduplicator pattern to reduce the risk of duplicates, and the Late Data Detector pattern with Integrator to identify and process late data.

Next, you discovered the Filter Interceptor that can help you better understand how your code behaves in a filtering operation. Finally, you saw that failures can be critical for long-running applications and that thankfully, modern data processing services manage fault tolerance on your behalf with the Checkpointer pattern.

But as we've already mentioned a few times, error management doesn't guarantee exposing perfectly valid data. Even though they may give a feeling of an exactly-once delivery, which is the holy grail in delivery semantics, processing retries or backfills can still have a negative impact. But it's less serious when your pipelines are idempotent—and if you don't know what that means, the next chapter will shed some light on it!

## CHAPTER 4

Idempotency Design Patterns

Each data engineering activity eventually leads to errors—you already know that from the previous chapter. Thankfully, correctly implemented error management design patterns address most of the issues. Yes, you read that correctly: most, not all. But why?

Let's take a look at an example of an automatic recovery from a temporary failure. From the engineering standpoint, that's a great feature as you don't have anything to do besides configuring the number of attempts to retry. However, from the data perspective, this great feature brings a serious challenge for consistency. A retried task or job might replay already successful write operations in the target data store, leading to duplication in the best-case scenario. You read that right: duplication is the best-case scenario because duplicates can be removed on the consumer's side. But let's imagine the contrary. The retried item generates duplicates that cannot be removed because you can't even tell they represent the same data! Welcome to your nightmare and bad publicity for your dataset.

Hopefully, you can mitigate these issues with the idempotency design patterns presented in this chapter. But before you see how they apply to data engineering, let's recall the idempotency definition. The best example to explain it is the `absolute` function. You know, it's the simple method that returns a positive number even if the input argument is a negative number. Why is it idempotent? Because no matter how many times you invoke the function, you always get the same result. In other words, `absolute(-1) == absolute(absolute(absolute(-1)))`.

Idempotency in a data engineering context has the same purpose. It's a way to ensure that no matter how many times you run a data processing job, you'll always get consistent output without duplicates or with clearly identifiable duplicates. By the way, avoiding duplicates will not always be possible. If you generate the data to a messaging system that doesn't support transactional producers, retries can still generate duplicated entries. However, thanks to idempotent processing, your consumers will be able to identify those records as such.

In this chapter, you'll discover various idempotency approaches in data engineering. You'll learn what to do if you can fully overwrite the dataset or when you only have its subset available. You'll also learn how to leverage databases to implement an idempotency strategy. Finally, you'll see a design pattern to keep the dataset immutable but idempotent.

And one last thing before you see the patterns: I'd like to leave here a special mention of Maxime Beauchemin, who made idempotency popular in 2018 with his state-of-the-art article "Functional Data Engineering: A Modern Paradigm for Batch Data Processing" (*https://oreil.ly/Bz_6J*).

Overwriting

The first idempotency family covers the data removal scenario. Removing existing data before writing new data is the easiest approach. However, running it on big datasets can be compute intensive. For that reason, to handle the removal, you can use data- or metadata-based solutions.

Pattern: Fast Metadata Cleaner

Metadata operations are often the fastest since they don't need to interact with the data files. Instead, they operate on a much smaller layer that describes these data files. Because of that, we often say that the metadata part operates on the logical level instead of the physical one. The next pattern you're going to see leverages metadata to enable fast data cleaning.

Problem

Your daily batch job processes between 500 GB and 1.5 TB of visits data events. To guarantee idempotency, you define two steps. The first action removes all rows added to the table by the previous run with a DELETE operation. The second task inserts processed rows with an INSERT operation.

The workflow ran fine for three weeks, but then it started suffering from latency issues. Over the past several weeks, the table has grown a lot and the DELETE task's performance has degraded considerably. You're looking now for a more scalable and idempotent pipeline design for this continuously growing table and the daily batch job.

Solution

DELETE is probably the first operation that comes to mind for data removal. Unfortunately, it may perform poorly on big volumes of data as it's often a two-step action. A DELETE has to first identify the rows to delete and later overwrite the all identified data files. Thankfully, faster alternatives relying on the metadata operations exist. DROP TABLE and TRUNCATE TABLE are two such operations and are the building blocks of the Fast Metadata Cleaner pattern.

TRUNCATE TABLE table_a = DELETE FROM table_a

Semantically, the TRUNCATE TABLE command does the same thing as DELETE FROM without conditions. In both cases you'll get all records removed. However, under the hood, TRUNCATE is different as it doesn't do the table scan. For that reason, it's classified as a *metadata operation*.

But how can truncating or dropping a table replace physical deletes? It all boils down to changing your perceptions. Instead of considering the dataset as a single monolithic unit, you can think about it as multiple physically divided datasets that together form a whole logical data unit. Put differently, you can store the dataset in multiple tables and expose it from a single place, like a view. Figure 4-1 shows a high-level example of such an incremental workload in which weekly tables compose the final yearly dataset.

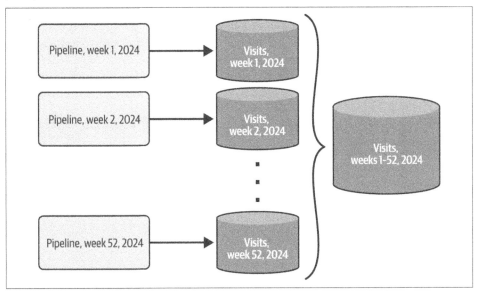

Figure 4-1. Physically isolated dataset in weekly tables and a common data exposition view for all the weeks in each year

To achieve idempotency, the Fast Metadata Cleaner pattern relies on dataset partitioning and data orchestration. You need to define the partitioning carefully since it directly impacts the *idempotency granularity*. What does that mean? As you saw in Figure 4-1, the whole visits dataset is composed of 52 weekly (aka partitioned) tables. The idempotency granularity is one week. In other words, this granularity defines at the same time the units on top of which you can apply the metadata operations to clean the table. It has an important consequence for backfilling, but I'll let you discover it in the next section.

Next, you have to adapt the data orchestration to the idempotency granularity. The adaptation consists of adding these extra steps:

- Analyze the execution date and decide whether the pipeline should start a new idempotency granularity or continue with the previous one. For example, you can use the Exclusive Choice pattern to analyze current execution context and decide what to do next. If you deal with weekly tables and the analysis finds that the pipeline's execution day is Monday, the pipeline will follow the initialization branch. Otherwise, it can go directly to the data insertion part.

- Create the idempotency environment. Here, you'll leverage two metadata operations, namely, TRUNCATE TABLE or DROP TABLE. The solution using TRUNCATE will often be preceded with a task to create the idempotency context table, whereas the approach leveraging DROP will be followed by the table's creation. Using DROP has another implication, but we need to move on to understand it better.

- Update the single abstraction exposing the idempotency context tables. It could be, for example, a view built as a union of the weekly tables. However, the DROP-based approach may result in an error if a user tries to access the view while you are dropping one of the tables. If this is an issue, you can mitigate it with an optional step that removes the table from the view before dropping it from the database.

Overall, a pipeline using TRUNCATE or DROP for our weekly visits idempotency tables could look like the one in Figure 4-2.

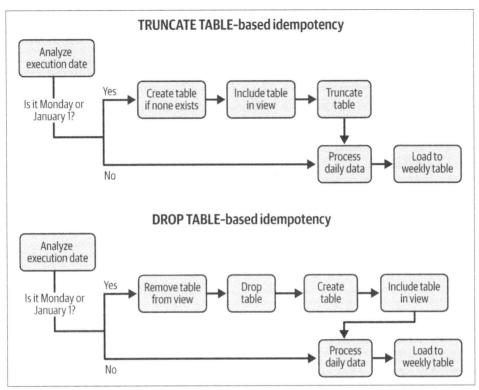

Figure 4-2. Fast Metadata Cleaner pattern example on top of weekly tables for TRUNCATE TABLE and DROP TABLE commands

Besides incremental and partitioned datasets, the Fast Metadata Cleaner pattern applies to the full datasets. In that case, you can simplify the workflow and run the table's re-creation step at each load or use the alternative Data Overwrite pattern presented in the next section. Figure 4-3 shows an example of the Fast Metadata Cleaner pattern adapted to a fully loaded table.

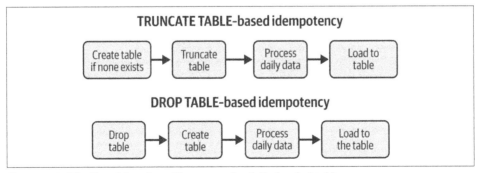

Figure 4-3. The Fast Metadata Cleaner and a fully loaded table

Consequences

These *fast* and *data removal* keywords sound fantastic, but despite its bright side, the pattern has some gotchas you should be aware of.[1]

Granularity and backfilling boundary. The pattern defines an idempotency granularity that is also a *backfilling granularity*. In other words, if you replay the pipeline, you have to do it from the task that creates a partitioned table. Otherwise, you'll end up with an inconsistent dataset.

For example, if you partition the data on a weekly basis and you need to backfill for only one day, you have no choice but to rerun the whole week. This doesn't mean you'll have to reprocess full pipelines for other days, though. If only one day generated an invalid dataset, it's enough to replay only the data loading step for the remaining days.

Another limitation related to granularity is the issue of fine-grained backfills, for example, for one data provider, user, or customer. The Fast Metadata Cleaner pattern will not help here because the metadata operations always work on whole tables.

Metadata limits. Also be aware of the limits of your data store. The pattern relies on creating dedicated partitions or tables, but unfortunately, it often won't be possible to create them indefinitely. For example, modern data warehouses like GCP BigQuery and AWS Redshift have, respectively, limits of 4,000 partitions and 200,000 tables. Both numbers are huge, but if you need to apply this pattern in multiple pipelines operating on different tables, you can reach these high quotas very quickly.

To overcome these limitation issues, you can add a *freezing* step to transform the mutable idempotent tables into immutable ones, thus reducing the partition scope. For example, weekly tables could turn into monthly or yearly tables if there are no possible changes after a freezing period.

Also, the Fast Metadata Cleaner pattern works only on the databases supporting metadata operations. Among them, you will find data warehouses, lakehouses, and relational databases. On the other hand, they may be difficult to implement on top of object stores, where you will rely on the Data Overwrite pattern.

Data exposition layer. The final point is about access. The dataset is not living in a single place anymore, and your end users may not want to know the internal details of the design and may instead prefer to access the data from a single point of entry. To

---

1 You may think that the name Fast Metadata Cleaner implies the availability of the metadata operations, and you'd be right. We don't need to go too far into detail here, but this is a potential consequence.

overcome that issue, you can use a solution similar to a database view, such as a logical structure grouping multiple tables and exposing them as a single unit.

Schema evolution.   Another challenge is schema evolution. If your idempotency tables get a new optional field, you'll need a separate pipeline to update the schema of already existing tables. Doing that in the Fast Metadata Cleaner pattern would automatically involve reprocessing the data, which is less effective.

However, there is another scenario in which you evolve the schema and add a new required field. In that case, you can include the new field in the Fast Metadata Cleaner pattern because replaying past runs will automatically trigger processing and thus add the new field.

Examples

The pattern heavily relies on a data orchestration layer. It's not surprising that you're going to see an example with Apache Airflow, this time coordinating a pipeline writing data to a PostgreSQL table. The key part of the pipeline from Example 4-1 is the `BranchPythonOperator`. This task verifies the execution date and, depending on the outcome, goes to the data processing or follows the weekly table management.

Example 4-1. Idempotency router with `BranchPythonOperator`

```
def retrieve_path_for_table_creation(**context):
  ex_date = context['execution_date']
  should_create_table = ex_date.day_of_week == 1 or ex_date.day_of_year == 1
  return 'create_weekly_table' if should_create_table else "dummy_task"


check_if_monday_or_first_january_at_midnight = BranchPythonOperator(
  task_id='check_if_monday_or_first_january_at_midnight',
  provide_context=True,
  python_callable=retrieve_path_for_table_creation
)
```

Example 4-2 shows the weekly table management part. The workflow starts by creating a weekly table suffixed with the week number retrieved from Apache Airflow's execution context. The next task uses `PostgresViewManagerOperator`, which is a custom operator that refreshes the visits view with the new weekly table.

Example 4-2. Table management branch

```
create_weekly_table = PostgresOperator(# ...
  sql='/sql/create_weekly_table.sql'
)
recreate_view = PostgresViewManagerOperator(# ...
  view_name='visits',
```

```
sql='/sql/recreate_view.sql'
)
```

The next tasks in the pipeline are common for both branches and consist of loading the input dataset to the weekly table. We're omitting them here for brevity, but you can find the full example in the GitHub repo (*https://oreil.ly/noVUs*).

Pattern: Data Overwrite

If using a metadata operation is not an option (for example, because you work on an object store that doesn't have the TRUNCATE and DROP commands), you have no other choice but to apply a data operation. Thankfully, there is also a dedicated pattern for this category.

Problem

One of your batch jobs runs daily. It works on the visits dataset stored in event time–partitioned locations in an object store. The pipeline is still missing a proper idempotency strategy because each backfilling action generates duplicated records. You've heard about the Fast Metadata Cleaner pattern, but you can't use it because of the lack of a proper metadata layer. That's why you're looking for an alternative solution.

Solution

When the metadata layer is unavailable or using it involves a lot of effort, you can rely on the data layer and the Data Overwrite pattern.

The implementation depends on the technology, but typically, it relies on a native dataset replacement command. Your technical stack will drive the available solutions here, and the following will also apply:

- If you use a data processing framework, you may simply need to set an option while configuring your data writer. For this, Apache Spark uses a save mode and Apache Flink uses the write mode properties. Once you've configured your data writer, the data processing framework will do the rest (i.e., cleaning the existing files before writing). This configuration-driven solution can be extended to a selective overwriting if the output data store supports the conditions. That's the case with Delta Lake, where you can overwrite only a part of the dataset that matches the filtering condition specified in a replaceWhere option.
- If you work directly with SQL, you have multiple choices:
  — First, you can use a combination of DELETE FROM and INSERT INTO operations. It's a simple approach known by many engineers working with databases.

— A more concise alternative to DELETE and INSERT leverages the INSERT OVERWRITE command. This alternative overwrites the whole table with the records from the INSERT part of the statement. However, besides the conciseness, there is also a semantical difference. INSERT OVERWRITE doesn't support selecting rows to overwrite, whereas the combination of DELETE and INSERT operations does.

— Finally, for the SQL part, you can also use the data loading commands available in your data store. Some of them, such as LOAD DATA OVERWRITE in Big-Query, support data overwriting natively. The others should be preceded with a TRUNCATE TABLE command.

Not Only List of Columns

Although it's a commonly shared belief, the INSERT command doesn't need explicitly defined values. You can also insert records from another table by issuing a SELECT statement that will match the list of columns to insert. For example, INSERT INTO visits (id, v_time) SELECT visit_id, visit_time FROM visits_raw would add all visits present in the visits_raw table, without having to declare them explicitly.

Running the overwriting command doesn't guarantee your data will disappear, though. If you use a data store–supporting time travel feature, thus making it possible to restore the dataset to one of its past versions, the data blocks will still be there after you execute the overwrite. They will only be deleted after the configured retention period or after running the vacuum operation to reclaim unused space if the command is supported. Among the examples of data stores not deleting data on the way, you'll find table file formats, GCP BigQuery, and Snowflake.

Consequences

Even though the pattern operates on the data layer directly and has wider support than the Fast Metadata Cleaner, it has some drawbacks.

Data overhead. Since there is a data operation involved, the pattern can perform poorly if the overwritten dataset is big and not partitioned. In that case, the overwrite will be slower over the course of days, as there will be more and more data to process.

You can try to mitigate this overhead by applying some storage optimizations, like partitioning. They should reduce the volume of data to overwrite and hence make the replacement action faster. Storage strategies are also a design patterns family you'll discover later in this book.

Vacuum need. A `DELETE` operation might not remove the data immediately from the disk. This happens with table file formats and relational databases, where deleted data blocks, albeit not accessible by users with `SELECT` queries, still exist on disk. To reclaim the space occupied by these dead rows, you will need to run a vacuum process that will remove them for real.

Examples

Many modern data engineering solutions, including Databricks and Snowflake, provide a native implementation of the pattern with the `INSERT OVERWRITE` operation. The command truncates the content of the table or partition(s) before inserting new data. Example 4-3 replaces all rows in the `devices` table with the rows from the `devices_staging` table. Typically, this implementation is very flexible as you can extend this simple `SELECT` statement to more complex expressions involving joins or aggregations.

Example 4-3. `INSERT OVERWRITE` example

```
INSERT OVERWRITE INTO devices SELECT * FROM devices_staging WHERE state = 'valid';
```

Besides this pure SQL capability, the implementations of the pattern might rely on a separate data loading component. That's the case with BigQuery, which supports a `writeDisposition` in the jobs feature. The load job from Example 4-4 ingests devices data from the CSV file into the `devices` table. It sets the `--replace=true` flag to remove all existing data before writing the new data to save. This attribute is a shortcut for the `WRITE_TRUNCATE` distribution introduced previously.

Example 4-4. Loading data with a prior table truncation in BigQuery

```
bq load dedp.devices gs://devices/in_20240101.csv ./info_schema.json --replace=true
```

But if you're not using any of these tools, no worries because Apache Spark also implements the pattern. It's as configuration based as BigQuery because it lets you set a *save mode* option. The overwrite mode from Example 4-5 behaves exactly like Big-Query's `replace` flag (i.e., it drops all existing data before writing). Although it looks simple, you must be aware of one thing: the save mode by itself is not transactional (i.e., everything depends on the target data format). Thankfully, the modern table file format addresses that issue because the delete is a new commit in the log and the data files remain untouched.

Example 4-5. Overwriting data in PySpark

```
input_data.write.mode('overwrite').text(job_arguments.output_dir)
```

Updates

Removing a complete dataset to guarantee idempotency is an easy approach. Unfortunately, some types of datasets are not good candidates for full replacement. This is the case with updated incremental datasets, in which each new version generated by your data provider contains only a subset of modified or updated data. If you try to rewrite the whole dataset, you'll have to do some preparation work to keep only the most recent version of each entity. Thankfully, an easier approach exists, and you'll discover it in this section.

Pattern: Merger

If your dataset identity is static (i.e., there is no risk of modifying the identity of the rows), and your dataset only supports updates or inserts, then the best approach is to merge changes with the existing dataset. But that's only a theory because in real life, there are some extra considerations you should take into account.

Problem

You're writing a pipeline to manage a stream of changes synchronized from your Apache Kafka topic via the Change Data Capture pattern. Your new batch pipeline must replicate all changes to the existing dataset stored as a Delta Lake table. The table must fully reflect the data present at a given moment in the data source, so it cannot contain duplicates.

Solution

If you don't have the complete dataset available—for example, if you're working with the incremental changes streamed from a database in our problem statement—you need to consider combining changes with an existing dataset. In a nutshell, that's what the Merger pattern does.

Simpler Overwrite

Idempotent processing for fully available datasets is easier with one of the overwriting patterns (see "Overwriting" on page 80) because they simply delete and replace a dataset. The Merger pattern, on the other hand, requires you to interact with the data to combine new and existing rows. To keep things simple, the Merger pattern in this section is presented in the context of incremental datasets that can't be easily managed with a delete-and-replace approach.

The most important part of the implementation is the first step, when you define the attributes you're going to use to combine the new dataset with the old one. You can use a single property—such as the user ID—if it guarantees uniqueness across the dataset. If that's not the case, you can use multiple attributes, such as the visit ID and visit time for a website visit event.

Next, you need to find a way to combine datasets in your processing layer. Nowadays, most widely used solutions—including data processing frameworks, table file formats, and data warehouses—support the MERGE (aka UPSERT) command, which is the best way to implement the Merger pattern.

Once you find the right execution method, you need to define the behavior for each of the possible scenarios, which are as follows:

Insert
> In this mode, the entry from the new dataset doesn't exist in your current dataset. Therefore, it's a new record you have to add.

Update
> Here, both datasets store a given record, but it's very likely that the new dataset will provide an updated version of the record.

Delete
> This is the trickiest case because the Merger pattern doesn't support deletes. As you saw before, if a record is missing from the dataset you want to merge, nothing will happen. For that reason, deletes are only possible if they're expressed as soft deletes (i.e., updates with an attribute marking a given record as removed). That way, you can detect the change and apply a hard or soft delete to your data. If you need a refresher, review our discussion of soft deletes in the Incremental Loader pattern.

Overall, the MERGE statement covering all three scenarios could look like the statement in Example 4-6.

Example 4-6. Implementation of soft deletes for the Merger pattern

```
MERGE INTO dedp.devices_output AS target
USING dedp.devices_input AS input
ON target.type = input.type AND target.version = input.version
WHEN MATCHED AND input.is_deleted = true THEN
DELETE
WHEN MATCHED AND input.is_deleted = false THEN
UPDATE SET full_name = input.full_name
WHEN NOT MATCHED AND input.is_deleted = false THEN
INSERT (full_name, version, type) VALUES (input.full_name, input.version, input.type)
```

You might be surprised to see the is_deleted flag used for the INSERT statement. However, it's important to use it here because otherwise, you could insert removed records during the first execution of the Merger pattern and consequently never get rid of them. Figure 4-4 shows what happens if you remove this flag for the first run of a job relying on the Merger pattern.

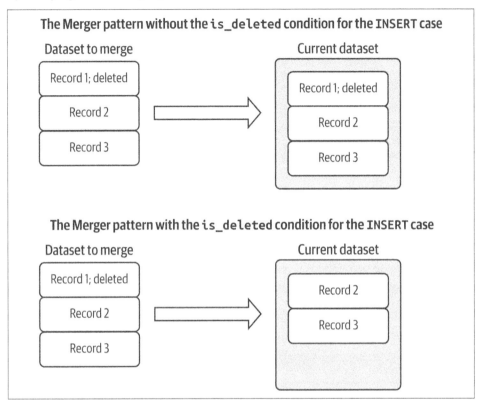

Figure 4-4. What happens during the first run of the Merger pattern with different `is_deleted` *conditions for the* INSERT *case*

Consequences

Despite its apparent simplicity, the pattern hides some gotchas and trade-offs, especially due to the character of the dataset (incremental or full).

Uniqueness.   This is the first and most important requirement. Your data provider, or your data generation job, must define some immutable attributes you can use to safely identify each record. Otherwise, the merge logic will simply not work because instead of updating a row in case of backfilling, it might insert a new one, leading to inconsistent duplicates.

I/O.   Unlike the Fast Metadata Cleaner, Merger is a data-based pattern. It works directly at the data blocks level, which makes it more compute intensive. However, modern databases and table file formats optimize this reading part by searching for the impacted records in the metadata layer first. The optimization helps to skip processing irrelevant files.

Incremental datasets with backfilling. You need to be aware of a shortcoming of the Merger pattern in the context of backfilling. Let's take a look at an example to help us better understand this issue. Table 4-1 shows how a job implementing the Merger pattern changed a dataset over time. As you can see, the job correctly integrated the updated and softly deleted rows, and at this point in time, the dataset is consistent.

Table 4-1. Incremental dataset loading with the Merger pattern (U stands for update, and D stands for delete)

Ingestion time	New rows	Output table rows
07:00	A	A
08:00	A–U, B	A–U, B
09:00	B–D, C	A–U, C
10:00	M, N, O	A–U, C, M, N, O

Now, let's imagine that you need to replay the pipeline from 08:00. Since the dataset is incremental, the backfill will start from the most recent version, which is the one containing the following rows: A–U, C, M, N, and O. As you can see, some of them are missing in the parts of the table written after 08:00. Consequently, during backfilling, your consumers won't see the same data as during the normal run. Table 4-2 shows the output rows available to consumers while the backfilled table slowly returns to normal after backfilling the last period.

Table 4-2. Incremental dataset after backfilling with the Merger pattern

Ingestion time	New rows	Current rows	Output table rows
08:00	A–U, B	A–U, C, M, N, O	A–U, B, C, M, N, O
09:00	B–D, C	A–U, B, C, M, N, O	A–U, C, M, N, O
10:00	M, N, O	A–U, C, M, N, O	A–U, C, M, N, O

To mitigate this issue, you may need to implement a restore mechanism outside the pipeline that will roll back the table to the first replayed execution. It's relatively easy to do if the database natively supports this versioning capability, for example, via a time travel feature that's available in table file formats. But since it transforms the stateless Merger pattern into a stateful one, you'll learn more about this solution in the Stateful Merger pattern.

Backfilling for Data Provider's Mistakes

If your data provider has introduced some errors into the dataset, you don't need to replay your pipeline. Instead, simply ask for a dataset with the fixed errors so that you can process it as a new dataset increment. The MERGE operation will apply the correct values for invalid rows. This solution works as long as the identity of the rows doesn't change (i.e., you can still match the rows from the invalid version with the rows from the new valid dataset).

Examples

Let's see the pattern in action with Apache Airflow and a SQL query loading new devices. For simplicity's sake, the pipeline consists of only one task executing a SQL query. The query starts with the operations present in Example 4-7.

Example 4-7. The first part of the Merger pattern query

```
CREATE TEMPORARY TABLE changed_devices (LIKE dedp.devices);
COPY changed_devices FROM '/data_to_load/dataset.csv' CSV  DELIMITER ';' HEADER;
# ...
```

The part from Example 4-7 is responsible for loading the new file into a temporary table that will be automatically destroyed at the end of the transaction. An important thing here is the table creation statement based on the LIKE operator. It avoids declaring all attributes of the target table here, which might potentially lead to metadata desynchronization if you managed the two schemas in different places.

Next, the query declares the MERGE operation relevant to the pattern itself (see Example 4-8).

Example 4-8. The second part of the Merger pattern query

```
# ...
MERGE INTO dedp.devices AS d USING changed_devices AS c_d
  ON c_d.type = d.type AND c_d.version = d.version
  WHEN MATCHED THEN
    UPDATE SET full_name = c_d.full_name
  WHEN NOT MATCHED THEN
    INSERT (type, full_name, version) VALUES (c_d.type, c_d.full_name, c_d.version)
```

Example 4-8 demonstrates the expected changes for our dataset. First, the query manages new rows with the WHEN NOT MATCHED THEN section, followed by an INSERT statement. Second, if the file has some updates, then the WHEN MATCHED THEN branch is responsible for applying the changes. The query doesn't handle the deletes because the input file is incremental (i.e., it only brings new records or changed attributes for existing ones). Deletes are not expected for this query.

If you are interested in the code using soft deletes, you can check out the the GitHub repo (*https://oreil.ly/_v8NA*).

Pattern: Stateful Merger

As you learned in the previous section, the Merger pattern lacks some consistency for datasets during the backfillings. If consistency is important to you, you should try the alternative pattern presented in this section.

Problem

You managed to synchronize changes between two Delta Lake tables with the help of the Merger pattern. Unfortunately, one week later, you detected an issue in the merged dataset and your business users asked you to backfill the dataset. As they care about consistency, they want you to restore the dataset to the last valid version before triggering any backfilling. The Merger pattern is not adapted for that, which is why you are looking for a way to extend it and support your response to these kinds of demands in the future.

Solution

Whenever you need to restore a dataset, the Merger pattern won't be enough because it focuses only on the merge action. But there is an alternative called a Stateful Merger pattern that provides data restoration capability via an extra state table.

This extra state table involves some changes in the pipeline. The workflow now has an additional step in the beginning to restore the merged table if needed and another at the end to update the state table. Figure 4-5 illustrates what the Stateful Merger pattern looks like with these additional tasks.

Figure 4-5. The workflow of the Stateful Merger pattern

To better understand the logic, let's start with the last task. Once the merge operation from the middle completes, it creates a new version of the merged table. The completion also triggers another task that retrieves the created table version and associates it with the pipeline's execution time. For example, if the execution at 09:00 creates version 5 and the execution at 10:00 writes version 6, the state table will look like Table 4-3.

Table 4-3. State table after running the pipeline at 09:00 and 10:00

Execution time	Table version
08:00	4
09:00	5
10:00	6

Knowing what the table looks like, we can now better grasp the role of the restoration step from the beginning of the workflow. The first thing to keep in mind is that the restore process will happen only when the pipeline runs in the backfilling mode. Otherwise, it will do nothing.

How do you implement this backfilling detection logic? If your data orchestrator provides a context for the execution, and from this context, you can learn about the execution mode (backfilling or normal run), you can simply analyze this context metadata. If that's not the case, you need to implement some logic leveraging the state table. The high-level logic consists of the following:

1. Getting the version of the table created by the previous pipeline's run. If this version is missing, it means you'll run the pipeline for the first time or backfill the first pipeline's execution. In that case, you can clean the table with the help of the TRUNCATE TABLE command and move directly to the merge operation.

2. Comparing the current dataset version with the dataset version created by the previous pipeline's execution. Here, two things can happen:

   a. If the two versions are the same, there is nothing to restore as the pipeline is running in the normal mode. If we stay with our example from Table 4-3, the new run for 11:00 would detect the same version for the most recent execution and the previous execution at 10:00. In both cases, the version will be 6, which means the pipeline is performing the normal run scenario.

   b. If the two versions are different, it means the pipeline has entered into the backfilling scenario. If we stay with our example from Table 4-3, the run at 09:00 would detect a difference between the previous and the most recent version (4 versus 6), meaning that the pipeline should restore the table before applying the merge.

Does this work? Let's assume our state table looks like Table 4-4.

Table 4-4. A state table after four executions of a daily job

Execution time	Version
2024-10-05	1
2024-10-06	2
2024-10-07	3

Execution time	Version
2024-10-08	4

Let's see what happens in each scenario:

- The next pipeline runs. The execution time is 2024-10-09, and the version created by the previous run (2024-10-08) is the same as the most recent version of the table. The pipeline doesn't need to restore the table and can move directly to the merge operation.
- The pipeline runs 2024-10-05 for the second time. There is no version created for 2024-10-04, so before proceeding to the merge operation, the restore task needs to truncate the table.
- The pipeline runs 2024-10-07 for the second time. The version created by the run from 2024-10-06 is different from the most recent version of the table, so the restore task needs to roll back the table to version 2. Once the pipeline for 2024-10-07 completes, it will update its version and the state table will look like Table 4-5.

Table 4-5. State table after backfilling 2024-10-07

Execution time	Version
2024-10-05	1
2024-10-06	2
2024-10-07	5
2024-10-08	4

After backfilling 2024-10-07, your data orchestrator will also backfill 2024-10-08. However, in that context, the most recent version is equal to the version created by the previous (already backfilled) run. Consequently, the workflow falls back into the normal run scenario.

Consequences

Even though the Stateful Merger pattern addresses the backfilling issue of the Merger pattern, it also brings its own gotchas.

Versioned data stores. The presented implementation of the Stateful Merger pattern requires your data store to be versioned (i.e., each write should create a new version of the table). That's the only way you can track the state and restore the table to a prior version.

If you don't work on a database with versioning capabilities, such as table file formats, you should slightly adapt the implementation to your use case. In that scenario, the pipeline will be composed of the steps in Figure 4-6.

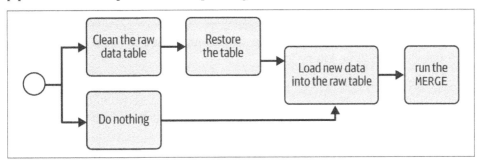

Figure 4-6. The Stateful Merger pattern adapted to a data store without versioning capabilities

Instead of versioning the table, the pipeline loads all raw data into a dedicated raw data table with a column storing the execution time. The backfilling detection logic verifies whether the raw data table has some records for the execution times in the future (see Example 4-9).

Example 4-9. Query verifying the pipeline's mode

```
SELECT CASE WHEN COUNT(*) > 0 THEN true ELSE false END
FROM dedp.devices_history WHERE execution_time > '{{ ts }}'
```

When the query returns true, it means the pipeline should first remove all rows matching the `WHERE execution_time >= '{{ ts }}'` condition. That way, the raw data stores all rows corresponding to the last valid version. Next, the workflow rebuilds the table by querying the `devices_history` table with the help of the Windowed Deduplicator pattern. In the end, the input data for the current execution time is loaded to the `devices_history` table and merged with the restored main table.

You can find a full example of PostgreSQL relying on this alternative approach in the GitHub repo (*https://oreil.ly/dyzsm*).

Vacuum operations. Even though versioned datasets, such as tables in Delta Lake or Apache Iceberg, enable implementing the state table, they also hide a trap. After the configured retention duration, they remove files that are not used anymore by the dataset. Consequently, some of the prior versions will become unavailable at that moment.

You can mitigate the issue a bit by increasing the retention period, but that would increase your storage costs as well. Or you can accept the fact that the pipeline cannot be backfilled beyond the retention period.

Metadata operations. Besides the vacuum, there are other operations that can run against your table. One of them is compaction, which you discovered while you were learning about the Compactor pattern.

Compaction doesn't overwrite the data but only combines smaller files into bigger ones. But despite this no-data action, it also creates a new version of the table. As a result, if you always use the previous version from the state table in the restore action, you will miss the operations made between two merge runs.

To overcome this issue, assuming the versions increase by 1, you could change the logic and, instead of reading the previous version, read the version corresponding to the current execution time and subtract 1 (see Example 4-10).

Example 4-10. Changed logic for retrieving the version to restore

```
version_to_restore = version_for_current_execution_time - 1
```

To better understand this change, let's suppose we have the state table and dataset history in Figure 4-7.

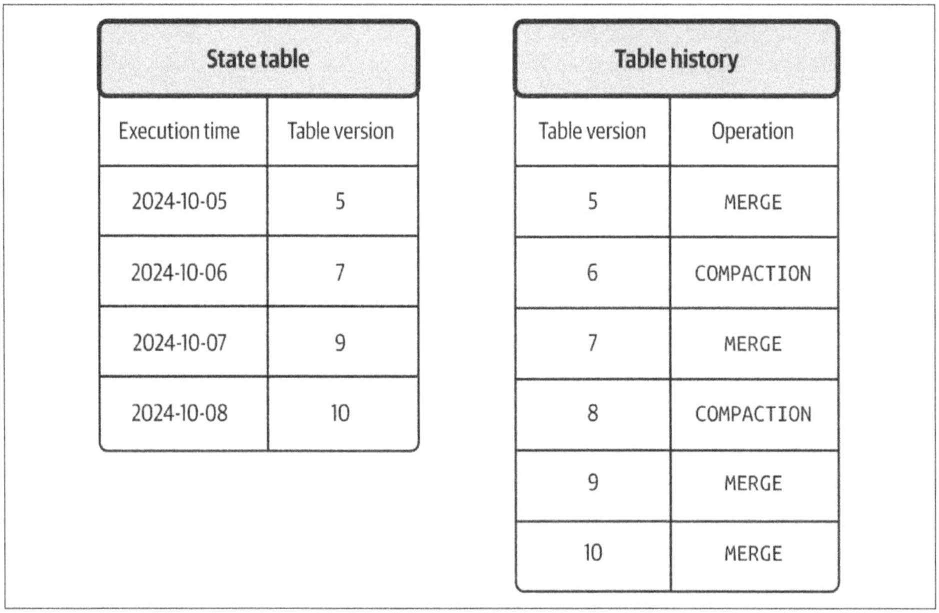

State table			Table history	
Execution time	Table version		Table version	Operation
2024-10-05	5		5	MERGE
2024-10-06	7		6	COMPACTION
2024-10-07	9		7	MERGE
2024-10-08	10		8	COMPACTION
			9	MERGE
			10	MERGE

Figure 4-7. State table for a table with no-data operations, such as compaction

If you want to backfill the pipeline executed on 2024-10-07, the version for this execution time is 9, so the version to restore will be 8. As you can see in the table history, this version corresponds to the compacted table between the runs of 2024-10-07 and 2024-10-08. The same logic will also work for the pipeline executed on 2024-10-08, where the restored version will be 9, meaning the one created by the previously executed pipeline on 2024-10-07.

Examples

Let's see how to implement the Stateful Merger pattern on top of Delta Lake and orchestrated from Apache Airflow. The first snippet shows the declaration of the state table. The table from Example 4-11 has two fields, one for the job's execution time and another for the corresponding Delta table version created.

Example 4-11. State table definition

```
CREATE TABLE IF NOT EXISTS `default`.`versions`
(execution_time STRING NOT NULL, delta_table_version INT NOT NULL)
```

Next comes the data restoration task. It implements the logic presented in the Solution section where, depending on the current and previous version, the table was either backfilled or not. The restoration task starting with Example 4-12 first retrieves the last table version created by the MERGE operation alongside the table version written at the previous execution time.

Example 4-12. Reading of current and past versions

```
last_merge_version = (spark.sql('DESCRIBE HISTORY default.devices')
    .filter('operation = "MERGE"')
    .selectExpr('MAX(version) AS last_version').collect()[0].last_version)

maybe_previous_job_version = spark.sql(f'''SELECT delta_table_version FROM versions
  WHERE execution_time = "{previous_execution_time}"''').collect()
```

After the restoration task comes the part that will evaluate the retrieved versions and, depending on the outcome, trigger table truncation or table restoration. Example 4-13 shows both steps in the exact same order.

Example 4-13. Data restoration action

```
if not maybe_previous_job_version:
  spark.sql('TRUNCATE TABLE default.devices')
else:
  previous_job_version = maybe_previous_job_version[0].delta_table_version
  if previous_job_version < last_merge_version:
    current_run_version = (spark_session.sql(f'''SELECT delta_table_version FROM
```

```
versions WHERE execution_time = "{currently_processed_version}"''')
    .collect()[0].delta_table_version)
version_to_restore = current_run_version - 1
(DeltaTable.forName(spark, 'devices').restoreToVersion(previous_job_version ))
```

After eventually restoring the table, the pipeline executes the MERGE operation. The outcome of this operation creates a new commit version in the table, but this version is retrieved only in the next task and written to the state table. It's worth noting that there is a MERGE too because in the case of backfilling, the writer updates the previous value, and in the case of the normal run, it inserts it. Example 4-14 summarizes this logic.

Example 4-14. State table update after successful MERGE

```
last_version = (spark.sql('DESCRIBE HISTORY default.devices')
    .selectExpr('MAX(version) AS last_version').collect()[0].last_version)
new_version_df = (spark.createDataFrame([
  Row(execution_time=current_execution_time, delta_table_version=last_version)]))

(DeltaTable.forName(spark_session, 'versions').alias('old_versions')
 .merge(new_version.alias('new_version'),
  'old_versions.execution_time = new_version.execution_time')
 .whenMatchedUpdateAll().whenNotMatchedInsertAll().execute())
```

You can find the full snippet alongside the data orchestration part in the GitHub repo (*https://oreil.ly/qD8bn*).

Database

The previous patterns discussed in this chapter require some extra work on your part. You need to either adapt the orchestration layer or use a well-thought-out writing operation. If this sounds like a lot of work, sometimes you can take shortcuts and rely on the databases to guarantee idempotency.

Pattern: Keyed Idempotency

The first pattern in this section uses key-based data stores and an idempotent key generation strategy. This mix results in writing data exactly once, no matter how many times you try to save a record.

Problem

Your streaming pipeline processes visit events to generate user sessions. The logic buffers all messages for a dedicated time window per user and writes an updated session to a key-value data store. As for other pipelines, you want to make sure this one is idempotent to avoid duplicates in case a task retries.

Solution

In the context of a key-based database, idempotency applies to the key generation logic on the data processing side. In our problem, it'll result in generating the same session ID for all visits events of a given user, thus writing it only once. By the way, that's a simple explanation of what the Keyed Idempotency pattern does.

When it comes to the actual implementation, you should start by finding immutable properties for the key generation. Depending on how lucky you are, your input dataset may already have unique attributes for your use case. For example, if you need to get the most recent activity for a user, you'll simply use the user ID as the key.

However, the key may not always be available. To understand this, let's take a look at an example of user session activity from website visits, which we first introduced in "Case Study Used in This Book" on page 5. The input dataset contains only the user ID and visit time, so you can't rely on the user ID to create a session key as each new session would always replace the previous sessions. Instead, you could use the combination of the user ID and the first visit time to generate an idempotent key. Although this is a valid solution, it hides a trap depicted in Figure 4-8. As you can see, our job stopped because of an unexpected runtime error, and after the restart, the session ID changed because of late data written to the input data store.

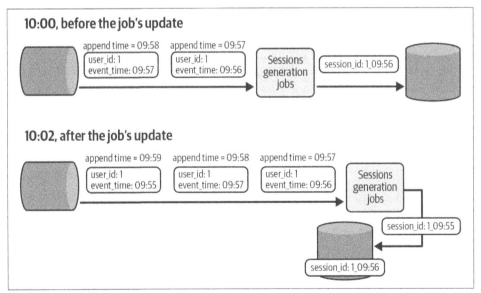

Figure 4-8. Late data impact on key generation; the late record for 09:55 creates a new session for the job restarted after an update

In the context of idempotent key generation for a user session, the event time attribute is mutable (i.e., the value may change between runs). For that reason, it's safer to use an immutable value, like an *append time*, which is the time a given entry was physically written to the streaming broker. Then, even if there are late events, the key won't be impacted by them and will remain the same. You'll find an example of this in Apache Kafka, where the property is indeed called append time. Other streaming brokers have the same attribute but call it by a different name. For example, Amazon Kinesis Data Streams uses the term *approximate arrival timestamp* for that property.

The same attribute, albeit named differently, exists in data-at-rest stores. It is often referred to as *added time, ingestion time,* or *insertion time* and is often implemented with a default value corresponding to the current time. If you apply this to our example, you'll see that for both batch and streaming cases, you're going to use the data from 10:09 to generate the session key. That way, you keep the key consistent across runs, even when late data arrives. Moreover, you'll be able to emit partial and consistent results as they'll share the same ID in the final state. Example 4-15 shows a WINDOW expression that retrieves the first recorded user activity to get attributes for the idempotent session key. The sorting is ascending, meaning that it will not be impacted by new data added to the table.

Example 4-15. Window operation using ingestion time

```
SELECT ... OVER (PARTITION BY user_id ORDER BY ingestion_time ASC, visit_time ASC)
```

The examples from this part have covered a key-based data store since it's the easiest one to explain. However, the key generation strategy also works for data containers, like files. For example, if you need to generate a new file from a daily batch job, you can name the file with the execution time. Consequently, a job running on 20/11/2024 would write a file named *20_11_2024*, and a job running the next day would write a file named *21_11_2024*, and so forth. Replaying a pipeline would always create one file. By the way, the example applies to partitions or even tables, if you can afford to create a table every day. The one requirement here is to use immutable attributes, exactly like for key generation in the context of a key-value store.

Consequences

Despite its simplicity, this pattern has some gotchas mostly related to the databases.

Database dependent.   Even though your job generates the same keys every time, it doesn't mean the pattern will apply everywhere. You might already deduce that it works well for databases with key-based support, such as NoSQL solutions (Apache Cassandra, ScyllaDB, HBase, etc.).

For other scenarios, the pattern is either not applicable or applicable with some extra effort or trade-offs. The first, more demanding implementation is a relational database. If you try to insert a row with the same primary key, you'll get an error instead of overwritting it as for a key-value store. That's why here, the writing operation becomes a MERGE instead of INSERT, which adds some extra complexity on the expression itself, exactly like in the Merger pattern presented previously.

Regarding the trade-offs, the best illustration here is Apache Kafka. It does support keys to uniquely identify each record, but as an append-only log, so it does it without deduplicating the events at insertion time. Instead, uses an asynchronous compaction mechanism that runs after writing the data. As a result, for some time, your consumers can see duplicated entries. They share the same keys, though, so it should be easier to distinguish them from new records.

Mutable data source. The compaction from the last example introduces the second gotcha. Besides duplicated entries, compaction can be configured to remove events that are too old. In that context, if you restart the job and the compaction deleted the first event used for the key creation, you'll take the next record from the log and logically break the idempotency guarantee. On the other hand, since the data has changed, using a different key does make sense as the record's shape will be different.

Examples

Now, let's see the Keyed Idempotency pattern in action with an Apache Spark Structured Streaming job transforming Apache Kafka visit events into sessions and writing them to a ScyllaDB table. The output table from Example 4-16 defines a unique key composed of the session_id and user_id fields. They are a guarantee for our idempotent session generation based on the following data source definition.

Example 4-16. ScyllaDB table for the sessions

```
CREATE TABLE sessions (
  session_id BIGINT,
  user_id BIGINT,
  pages LIST<TEXT>,
  ingestion_time TIMESTAMP,
PRIMARY KEY(session_id, user_id));
```

Next comes the logic for grouping the visits. Example 4-17 first extracts the value and timestamp attributes from each Kafka record. Next, the job builds the visit structure from the value's JSON and uses some of the attributes in the watermark definition. The timestamp column corresponds to the append time and naturally is a part of the key generation logic presented in the snippet.

Example 4-17. Visits grouping with append time (timestamp column)

```
(input_data.selectExpr('CAST(value AS STRING)', 'timestamp').select(F.from_json(
    F.col('value'), 'user_id LONG, page STRING, event_time TIMESTAMP')
```

```
  .alias('visit'), F.col('timestamp'))
.selectExpr('visit.*', 'UNIX_TIMESTAMP(timestamp) AS append_time')
.withWatermark('event_time', '10 seconds').groupBy(F.col('user_id')))
```

Finally, there is the idempotent key generation logic based on the append time. The first part, depicted in Example 4-18, handles the expired state and generates the final output with respect to the idempotent key.

Example 4-18. Idempotent ID generation logic

```
def map_visit_to_session(user_tuple: Any,
    input_rows: Iterable[pandas.DataFrame],
    current_state: GroupState) -> Iterable[pandas.DataFrame]:
  session_expiration_time_50_seconds_as_ms = 50 * 1000
  user_id = user_tuple[0]
  # ommitted for brevity
  if current_state.hasTimedOut:
    min_append_time, pages, = current_state.get
    session_to_return = {
      'user_id': [user_id],
      'session_id': [hash(str(min_append_time))],
      'pages': [pages]
  }
  else:
    # ...
    # accumulation logic explained below
```

The output is a session identified by the user, and session IDs get it directly from the accumulated state. The state accumulates in the second part of the code, presented in Example 4-19. The mapping function reads all records in each window and gets the earliest append time among them. It later sets this value to the first version of the session state. Whenever there are other visits for the same entity, the logic follows the if current_state.exists branch. However, as the append time in our Apache Kafka topic is guaranteed to be increasing, we can simply take the same append time as the one computed in the first iteration.

Example 4-19. Append time accumulation in the state

```
else:
  # ...
  data_min_append_time = 0
  for input_df_for_group in input_rows:
    # ...
    data_min_append_time = int(input_df_for_group['append_time'].min()) * 1000
    if current_state.exists:
      min_append_time, current_pages, = current_state.get
      visited_pages = current_pages + pages
      current_state.update((
```

```
    min_append_time, visited_pages
  ,))
else:
  current_state.update((data_min_append_time, pages,))
```

The same solution can be implemented on top of other streaming brokers, and the only difference is the attribute name. If we take a look at the previously mentioned Amazon Kinesis Data Streams, it's enough to adapt the reading part as depicted in Example 4-20, where the approximate arrival timestamp column gets renamed to the `append_time` from the previous example. You could also avoid the renaming and use the approximate arrival timestamp in Example 4-18.

Example 4-20. Input part adapted to Amazon Kinesis Data Streams

```
(spark_session.readStream.format("kinesis") # ...
  .load().selectExpr("CAST(data AS STRING)",
        "approximateArrivalTimestamp AS append_time"))
```

Apache Kafka and a Timestamp Attribute

You can define the append time externally with an Apache Kafka producer. However, in the context of the pattern, it's a bit riskier and less reliable than using the mechanism fully controlled by the broker. To see what strategy is set on your topic, you can verify the `log.message.timestamp.type` attribute.

Pattern: Transactional Writer

In addition to the key uniqueness you saw in the previous pattern, transactions are another powerful database capability that can help you implement idempotent data producers. Transactions provide all-or-nothing semantics, where changes are fully visible to consumers only when the writer confirms them. This confirmation step is more commonly known as *commit*, but with all that said, we're already covering the implementation a bit too much. Before delving into details, let's see where transactions can help.

Problem

One of your batch jobs leverages the unused compute capacity of your cloud provider to reduce the total cost of ownership (TCO). Thanks to this special runtime environment, you have managed to save 60% on the infrastructure costs. However, your downstream consumers start complaining about data quality.

Whenever the cloud provider takes a node off of your cluster, all the running tasks fail and retry on a different node. Because of this rescheduling, the tasks write the data again and your consumers see duplicates and incomplete records. You need to fix this issue and ensure that your job never exposes partial data.

Solution

The best way to protect your consumers from the incomplete data issue is to leverage the transactions with the Transactional Writer pattern. It relies on the native database transactional capacity so that any of the in-progress but not committed changes will not be visible to downstream readers.

From a broader perspective, the implementation consists of three main steps. In the first step, the producer initializes the transaction. Depending on your processing layer, this step can be explicit or implicit. In the explicit mode, you need to call a transaction initialization instruction, such as START TRANSACTION or BEGIN. In the implicit mode, your data processing layer handles the transaction opening on your behalf.

After the initialization, you write the data. While you're producing new records, the changes are added to the database but remain private to your transaction scope. Only in the end, when you have finished writing the data, do you need to change the new records' visibility to make them publicly available to consumers. That's where the *commit* step happens. If there is an issue, instead of publishing the data, you need to discard it by calling the action that is the opposite of the commit step, which is *rollback*. Figure 4-9 summarizes all of these actions.

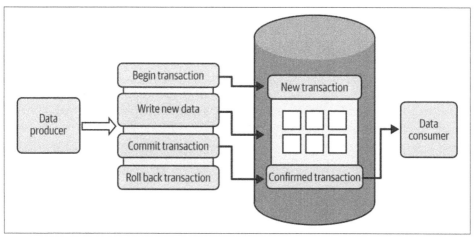

Figure 4-9. High-level view of a producer using the Transactional Writer pattern, in which the data is available to the consumer only after the commit step

However, life is not that rosy. From a low-level point of view, there are two implementations that you will use, depending on your processing model. The first one is for standalone jobs or ELT workloads processing datasets at the data storage layer directly, for example, in a data warehouse like BigQuery, Redshift, or Snowflake.

Here, the transaction is usually declarative and fully managed by the data store, and so, despite the fact that it's under the hood, the processing can be distributed.

A different implementation applies to distributed data processing jobs, which are often implemented with the ETL paradigm. In this mode, multiple tasks work in parallel to write a dataset to the same output. Knowing that, you can deduce two possible implementations of the Transactional Writer pattern:

- The transaction is local (i.e., task based). Each task performs an isolated transaction. This works well as long as you don't encounter any job retries, but we'll let you discover this point in "Consequences" on page 108.

- The whole job is transactional. In this mode, the job initializes the transaction before it starts running the tasks, and it commits the transaction once all the tasks complete their work. This provides a stronger guarantee than the local transaction but is also more challenging to achieve. For example, with Apache Spark and Delta Lake, the transaction is committed when the writer creates a new entry in the commit log directory. But if this step fails, data files will still be there and will need to be moved aside.

The idempotency comes from the all-or-nothing transactions semantics. In case of any error, the producer doesn't commit the transaction, which leads to either an automatic rollback or orphan records in the data storage layer that are not visible to the readers. However, if you backfill the data producer, the writing job will initialize a new transaction and thus insert the processed records again. Idempotency is then guaranteed only for the current run.

Read Uncommitted Isolation Level

Despite transactions on the writer's side, a reader might still see records from uncommitted transactions if it sets its transaction isolation level to read uncommitted. In the database world, this side effect is known as *dirty reads* because the records from uncommitted transactions might be rolled back.

Among the client libraries and data stores supporting transactions, you'll find modern table file formats (Delta Lake, Apache Iceberg, and Apache Hudi), streaming brokers (Apache Kafka), data warehouses (AWS Redshift and GCP BigQuery), and even relational database management systems (PostgreSQL, MySQL, Oracle, and SQL Server).

As you have seen, not all of the aforementioned technologies integrate perfectly with the distributed data processing tools. Table file formats are pretty well covered by major tools (Apache Flink and Apache Spark), whereas Apache Kafka transactional producers are only available for Apache Flink.

Consequences

A transactional producer is easier to implement than all of the patterns in this section as it's often just a matter of calling appropriate commands in the processing logic. Despite that, there are some pitfalls.

Commit step. Unlike a nontransactional write, a transactional one involves two extra steps, which are opening and committing the transaction, alongside resolving data conflicts at both stages.

The steps may have an impact on the overall data availability latency. For example, each file produced in a raw data format like JSON or CSV is immediately visible to consumers. On the other hand, the files generated in a transactional file format like Delta Lake become visible once the producer generates a corresponding commit log-file. Put differently, consumers will have to wait for the slowest task to complete before being able to access the transactional data.

But this coordination overhead is necessary to provide transactional capability and therefore to expose only complete datasets.

Distributed processing. Distributed data processing frameworks' support for transactions is not global. For example, the already mentioned Apache Kafka is not supported in Apache Spark, despite its popularity among data engineers. This greatly reduces the application of the pattern, unfortunately.

Idempotency scope. Remember, the idempotency is limited to the transaction itself! For example, if a distributed data processing framework uses local (i.e., task-based) transactions without any further coordination to store already committed tasks, any job restart will rewrite the data from committed transactions.

The same side effect applies to the backfilling scenarios where reprocessing the data will result in a new transaction eventually adding the same records.

Examples

First, let's take a look at an example of the Transactional Writer for a batch pipeline. The pipeline needs to load data from two datasets and apply each of them individually on the target table (see Example 4-21).

Example 4-21. Two visually separated operations within the same transaction

```
CREATE TEMPORARY TABLE changed_devices_file1 (LIKE dedp.devices);
COPY changed_devices_file1 FROM '/data_to_load/dataset_1.csv'
  CSV  DELIMITER ';' HEADER;
MERGE INTO dedp.devices AS d USING changed_devices_file1 AS c_d
-- ... ommitted for brevity

CREATE TEMPORARY TABLE changed_devices_file2 (LIKE dedp.devices);
COPY changed_devices_file2 FROM '/data_to_load/dataset_too_long_type.csv'
  CSV  DELIMITER ';' HEADER;
MERGE INTO dedp.devices AS d USING changed_devices_file1 AS c_d
-- ... ommitted for brevity

COMMIT;
```

As you can see in Example 4-21, one of the files stores rows with values that are too long for some columns. Because these two merge operations are visually separated, you may be thinking the first one will succeed while the second will fail. And you're right! That's the result, but we must add an important aspect here: none of them will commit. Put differently, the database won't accept the partial success because the SQL runner doesn't reach the commit stage. The same logic works for table file formats where the written files are not considered to be readable as long as there is no corresponding commit file.

And you may be surprised to hear that Apache Kafka, which is more often quoted in a stream processing context, also works that way for the transactions. The producer initializes the transaction by sending a special message to the partition, and once it reaches the commit step, it generates a new metadata event confirming the pending transaction. You can then implement the Transactional Writer pattern natively with the Kafka producers or from a distributed data processing framework like Apache Flink (see Example 4-22).

Example 4-22. Transactional data producer with Apache Flink

```
kafka_sink_valid_data = (KafkaSink.builder().set_bootstrap_servers("localhost:9094")
  .set_record_serializer(KafkaRecordSerializationSchema.builder()
    .set_topic('reduced_visits')
    .set_value_serialization_schema(SimpleStringSchema())
    .build())
  .set_delivery_guarantee(DeliveryGuarantee.EXACTLY_ONCE)
  .set_property('transaction.timeout.ms', str(1 * 60 * 1000))
  .build())
```

Example 4-22 shows a configuration for a transactional Kafka writer. Two important attributes here are the delivery guarantee and the transaction timeout. The delivery guarantee is quite obvious as it involves using transactions for data delivery. The timeout parameter, although harder to understand at first glance, is also important.

The exactly-once delivery relies on Apache Flink's checkpointing mechanism, which can take some time. If the timeout is too short and the checkpoint takes longer than the timeout parameter, Flink will be unable to commit the transaction due to its expiration.

Immutable Dataset

So far, you have seen patterns working on mutable datasets. This means that you can alter the datasets in any way, including total data removal. But what do you do if you cannot delete or update the existing data? A dedicated pattern exists for that category too.

Pattern: Proxy

This pattern is inspired by one of the best-known engineering sayings: "We can solve any problem by introducing an extra level of indirection." Hence its name, the Proxy.

Problem

One of your batch jobs generates a full dataset each time. Since you only need the most recent version of the data, you have been overwriting the previous dataset so far. However, your legal department has asked you to keep copies of all past versions, and consequently, your current mutable approach doesn't hold anymore. You need to rework the pipeline to keep each copy but expose only the most recent table from a single place.

Solution

The requirement expects the dataset to be immutable and thus written only once. To achieve this, you can implement the Proxy pattern. As the proxy in network engineering, it's an intermediate component between the end users and the real physical storage.

How does it work? First, you must guarantee the immutability by loading the new data into a different location each time. A good and easy solution is to use time-stamped or versioned tables. They're like regular tables, except that their names are suffixed with a version or a timestamp to distinguish them. An important point is that all writing permissions should be removed from these tables after creating them. Consequently, they will be writable only once.

You can achieve the writable-once semantics more easily if your storage layer sits on top of an object store. You can additionally enhance the access controls with a locking mechanism. The locking approach is also known as *write once read many* (WORM) and is supported by all major object store services. For AWS S3, you'll use Object Lock; for Azure Blob , you'll use immutability policies; and for GCP, you'll rely on object holds or bucket locks.

After implementing the writable-once semantics, you need to create a single data access point, which is the proxy. Most of the time, it'll be a passthrough view that exposes the most recent table without any data transformations in the SELECT statement. This approach works for most data warehouses and relational databases, plus some NoSQL stores, such as OpenSearch (via aliases), Apache Cassandra, ScyllaDB, and even MongoDB.

If your data store doesn't support a specific view, you'll have to create a similar structure on your own. It can be a manifest file referencing the location or explicitly listing the files that should be processed by consumers. From a responsibility standpoint, it's better to isolate the manifest creation from the data processing job. That way, if for whatever reason the manifest creation fails, you won't have to reprocess the data, which most of the time will be a much slower operation.

Creating manual immutable tables and defining manifest files are only two ways to implement the Proxy pattern. The last alternative strategy applies to table file formats like Delta Lake and Apache Iceberg, plus some data warehouses like GCP BigQuery. Even though you can create one table per write for these data stores, a simpler implementation is possible. Remember, when you overwrite the table, the data is still there to guarantee time travel capability. Consequently, each write produces a new version of the table under the hood and keeps old data on disk available for querying or restoration if needed. However, sometimes, this solution may have limited and not configurable retention capabilities, like seven days for BigQuery at the moment of writing.

It's worth noting that it's not possible to remove write permissions for the natively versioned data stores presented in the previous paragraph, but thanks to the underlying storage system, permissions management is not required for this solution. As you can see, the Proxy pattern heavily relies on your database capabilities. Figure 4-10 summarizes the three possible implementations covered in this section.

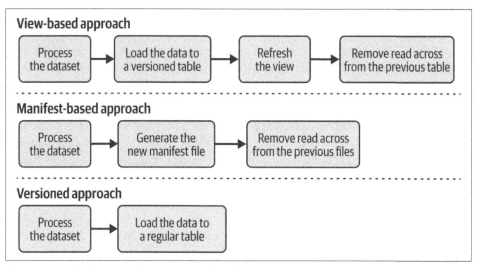

Figure 4-10. Implementation scenarios for the Proxy pattern

Consequences

At first glance, the pattern looks simple and familiar. However, it hides some important consequences.

Database support. Not all databases have this great view feature, which will be an immutable access point to expose underlying changing datasets. Although it can be replaced with a manifest file, that makes the reading process more cumbersome.

Immutability configuration. You can enforce immutability at the data orchestration level by configuring the output of the triggered writing task. But that won't be enough. You'll need some help, maybe from the infrastructure team, to enforce immutability on the data store too. You can do this by creating locks on object stores and removing writing permissions from the table, once it gets created.

Examples

Let's see how to implement the Proxy pattern with Apache Airflow and PostgreSQL. The pipeline is composed of the two steps that are defined in Example 4-23.

Example 4-23. The Proxy pattern's pipeline

```
load_data_to_internal_table = PostgresOperator(
  sql='/sql/load_devices_to_weekly_table.sql'
)
refresh_view = PostgresOperator(# ...
  sql='/sql/refresh_view.sql'
)
```

```
load_data_to_internal_table >> refresh_view
```

Example 4-23 starts by loading the data into a hidden internal table. Since this step is a simple COPY command you saw previously in this chapter, let's move directly to the refresh_view.sql query in Example 4-24.

Example 4-24. View refresh

```
{% set devices_internal_table = get_devices_table_name() %}
CREATE OR REPLACE VIEW dedp.devices AS
  SELECT * FROM {{ devices_internal_table }};
```

The view refresh is also based on a SQL operation that is simple but hides an important detail, which is the generation of the internal table name. Remember, if the pipeline's instance reruns, it can't rewrite the previous dataset. Instead, it must write the new dataset to a different table. That's where the get_devices_table_name function comes into play. Example 4-25 shows how the function leverages Apache Airflow's context to create unique table names.

Example 4-25. Generation of a unique table name

```
def get_devices_table_name() -> str:
  context = get_current_context()
  dag_run: DagRun = context['dag_run']
  table_suffix = dag_run.start_date.strftime('%Y%m%d_%H%M%S')
  return f'dedp.devices_internal_{table_suffix}'
```

The function in Example 4-25 uses the pipeline start time to compute a unique suffix for the internal table and guarantee that each load goes to its dedicated storage space.

Other aspects to keep in mind for the Proxy pattern are the permissions. The implementation should also ensure the user doing the manipulation can only create tables. Otherwise, the user could, even accidentally, delete previously created internal tables and, as a consequence, break the immutability guarantee provided by the Proxy pattern.

Summary

Always expecting the worst is probably not the best way to go through life, but it's definitely one of the best approaches you can take to your data engineering projects. As you know from the previous chapter, errors are inevitable and it's better to be prepared. The backbone of this preparation consists of the error management design patterns. However, they mitigate the impact of failure on the processing layer only.

To complete the cycle of handling error management, you need idempotency and typically the design patterns described in this chapter. To start, you saw data overwriting patterns that automatically replace the dataset, either by leveraging fast metadata operations like TRUNCATE or DROP or simply by physically replacing the dataset files.

The overwriting patterns are good if you have the whole dataset available in each operation. If that's not the case and your input is an incremental version, you can use the Merger pattern detailed in "Updates" on page 89. Even though the combination operation looks costly at first glance, modern data storage solutions optimize it by leveraging the metadata (statistics) too!

These overwriting and update pattern categories mostly rely on the data orchestration layer. If you don't have one, maybe because your job is a streaming job, no worries as you can always rely on the database itself for idempotency. That's the next category, where you can use either idempotent row key generation or transactions to ensure unique record delivery, even under retries.

Finally, sometimes, your data must remain immutable (i.e., you must be able to write it only once). This scenario isn't supported by the patterns presented so far. Instead, you should opt for the Proxy pattern shown in "Immutable Dataset" on page 110 and use an intermediary layer to expose the data.

These last two chapters on error management and idempotency talked mostly about a technical aspect of data engineering. Even though they help to improve business value, error management and idempotency don't generate meaningful datasets alone. Instead, you should leverage the data value design patterns that we cover in the next chapter!

## CHAPTER 5

Data Value Design Patterns

It may be an unpopular opinion, but data sitting somewhere in your storage is not a real asset. Most of the time, after it's ingested into your system, it'll be poor and have various quality issues. Let's take an example of the visit events ingested to the streaming broker from our use case architecture.

The data producer for the streaming layer is a web browser, which means it can get any valuable technical information about the browser version, language, or operating system of the user. That would be enough if you wanted to analyze the technical part of each visit in your system. But what if you need to know more, like what the visitors using a specific browser have in common? Each visit event is ingested as a distinct item without any explicit relationship, so correlating the data is impossible without extra effort.

This is a typical scenario where data value design patterns are helpful. Their purpose is to augment the dataset to improve its usefulness for end users. How? There are different solutions that you're going to learn about in this chapter.

You'll see how to add extra value by either combining two datasets or computing the individual attributes with the Data Enrichment and Data Decoration patterns, which are both covered in the next sections. That said, they're great for extending the context, but they won't help if you have a huge volume of data and need an overview, as in the example quoted previously. That's why next, you'll see the Data Aggregation or Sessionization patterns. To complete the picture, you'll also learn about the data ordering patterns you'll use in situations where the order of the records matters most.

Are you curious about how to solve our web browser issue and many others? Let's see the data value design patterns in action!

Data Enrichment

Very often, raw data will be poor because of technical constraints. Events are the best examples here. They're a perfect representation of time and space attributes, but frequently, they lack an extended context. Sure, they can identify the author of the event, but they'll rarely be capable of providing extra information, such as the last connection date or a user profile score in the context of our visits example. Data enrichment patterns overcome this limitation and make data more useful for different stakeholders.

Pattern: Static Joiner

If your enrichment dataset has a static nature, which is by far the easiest situation, you'll opt for the Static Joiner pattern presented here.

Problem

The datasets developed by your team are extensively used by business stakeholders. In a new project, you've been asked to create a dataset to simplify understanding of the dependency between the registration date of a user and day-to-day activity.

Unfortunately, your raw dataset doesn't include the user context. You can find it only in a static user reference dataset. To answer the business demand, you want to find a way to bring the reference data to the user's activity.

Solution

The at-rest character of the joined dataset presents the perfect condition for using the Static Joiner pattern. Surprisingly, despite the at-rest nature of this data, the pattern also works for streaming pipelines.

The implementation requires a list of attributes from both datasets that may be used to combine the datasets. In our example, it could be any field identifying a user in the visits and users datasets, for example, the user_id field.

Besides this keyed condition, the combination may also expect some time constraints, especially when the enrichment dataset implements some form of slowly changing dimensions. In that case, you could implement a time-sensitive static joiner variation of the initial pattern.

> ## Slowly Changing Dimensions
>
> If you need to use a time-sensitive data enrichment, you can implement it as one form of *slowly changing dimensions* (SCD), which is a data modeling strategy for slowly changing datasets that may support an entity's evolution over time.

In our solution, the enrichment dataset should implement SCD type 2 or 4. These types track row evolution over time, and the only difference between them is the technical implementation.

SCD type 2 manages tracking with validity dates, and each current value has the end date empty. SCD type 4 relies on two tables. The first table stores the current value for each entity, while the second table stores all historical values, including the current one. Figure 5-1 shows how both SCD types can be used to record the history of user email changes.

SCD Type 2

User emails history				
User_id	Email	From_date	To_date	is_current
1	a@...	2024-06-01	2024-06-21	false
1	b@...	2024-06-21	2024-07-05	false
1	c@...	2024-07-05	NULL	true

SCD Type 4

User emails current		
User_id	Email	From_date
1	c@...	2024-07-05

User emails history			
User_id	Email	From_date	To_date
1	a@...	2024-06-01	2024-06-21
1	b@...	2024-06-21	2024-07-05

Figure 5-1. SCD types 2 and 4: user emails

We'll dig into a technical explanation of these SCD types in the Examples section later in this chapter.

When it comes to code implementation, the enrichment is often expressed with a SQL JOIN statement. The solution is universal as it supports modern data processing frameworks and more classical data warehouses.

Besides this declarative manner with SQL, you can enrich your dataset from a programmatic API. Here, the easiest way is to use an HTTP library to enable communication between your data processing layer and an external API.

But the fact of exposing some data behind an API doesn't mean the dataset can't be accessed from a data storage layer such as a table. If you need to, you can also materialize this API-exposed dataset as a table in a pre-processing step and use it as part of the JOIN statement. Figure 5-2 depicts both approaches.

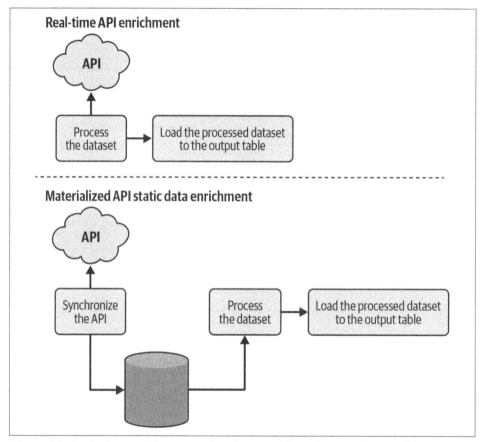

Figure 5-2. Static data enrichment with real-time and synchronized API calls

When you care about idempotency, you should opt for the solution materializing the API and leverage one of the SCD forms. That guarantees that whenever you replay the processing logic, you will always use the same dataset. By the way, this is one of the topics we develop more in the next section.

Consequences

Even though the implementation looks simple, there are some gotchas, like the afore-mentioned idempotency.

Late data and consistency.   To help you understand this point, let's take a look at the example of visits and users datasets. In an ideal scenario, users would evolve at the same pace as events are produced (i.e., if a user performs a profile change and imme-diately thereafter performs a navigation action, the processed visit should include the most recent changes). Unfortunately, as you learned in Chapter 3 and in "Late Data" on page 51, this scenario may not happen.

To mitigate the latency issue in streaming pipelines, you can use the Dynamic Joiner pattern presented next. It considers the enrichment dataset to be a dynamic one and uses adapted join conditions in that context. The mitigation is simpler for batch pipe-lines, where you can rely on the orchestration to wait for the enrichment dataset to be present (for example, by leveraging the Readiness Marker pattern discussed in Chapter 2).

Idempotency.   Besides consistency, you should also consider idempotency. If you backfill a batch pipeline, you should ask yourself whether the outcome must be idem-potent for the enrichment dataset. If that's the case and the data provider doesn't let you perform any time-based queries, you may need to bring the enrichment dataset into your data layer to control the time aspects before doing the join.

The situation is even trickier when it comes to the external datasets hidden behind an API. Here too, ideally, you should be able to issue time-based queries, but this may not be possible. The solution could be adding this temporality into your internal data store and writing all enrichment records there, as you saw in Figure 5-2.

For both cases, using SCD should be a good option.

Examples

Let's start this section by focusing on the SCDs, as they require more effort than sim-ple join conditions. The first SCD we'll analyze is type 2. We'll use the two tables in Example 5-1.

Example 5-1. Two tables demonstrating SCD type 2

```
CREATE TABLE dedp.users ( # ...
 id TEXT NOT NULL,
 login VARCHAR(45) NOT NULL,
 start_date TIMESTAMP NOT NULL DEFAULT NOW(),
 end_date TIMESTAMP NOT NULL DEFAULT '9999-12-31'::timestamp
 PRIMARY KEY(id, start_date)
);
```

```
CREATE TABLE dedp.visits ( # ...
 visit_id CHAR(36) NOT NULL,
 event_time TIMESTAMP NOT NULL,
 PRIMARY KEY(visit_id, event_time)
);
```

The users table in Example 5-1 is a slowly evolving reference dataset that enriches a more dynamic website visits dataset. The `start_date` and `end_date` columns define the validity of the attributes for each user. Therefore, to combine the visits and users, you need to use these dates as shown in Example 5-2.

Example 5-2. Example of SCD type 2 join

```
SELECT v.visit_id, v.event_time, v.page, u.id, u.login, u.email
FROM dedp.visits v JOIN dedp.users u ON u.id = v.user_id
  AND NOW() BETWEEN start_date AND end_date;
```

The condition in Example 5-2 uses the `NOW()` function as part of an ad hoc query to get the current state of the dataset. You can use any other date here that fits your needs. For example, it could be the execution time provided by your data orchestrator, which is an immutable property related to the pipeline run that helps enforce idempotency.

We're omitting SCD type 4 here as it relies on the same query as type 2. The only difference is that type 4 stores current values in a separate table while in type 2, both current and past rows are present in the same dataset. You will find this example in the GitHub repo (*https://oreil.ly/xqRcF*).

To complete this list of examples, let's see how to combine batch and streaming datasets in Apache Spark. Technically, the operation is not rocket science as it relies on the same API as for regular batch joins (see Example 5-3).

Example 5-3. Stream-to-batch join in PySpark

```
devices: DataFrame = spark.read.format('delta').load(...)
visits: DataFrame = (spark.readStream.format('kafka').load()...

(visits.join(devices_table, [visits.device_type == devices.type,
  visits.device_version == devices.version], 'left_outer'))
```

The operation in Example 5-3 combines the static devices reference dataset with the visits. It doesn't include any temporal condition because the devices table is an insert-only table, and not having the matched records is fine (the left join is used). But this relaxed condition hides a tricky point. The static dataset and the streaming job have separate lifecycles. Put differently, the streaming job doesn't wait for the static dataset

---

to update. Therefore, this might lead to not only join misses but also, in the case of a full rewriting, to joining with an empty reference table.

This could happen if the static dataset were written with a raw file format such as JSON or CSV. In our case, the devices table relies on a table file format that provides atomicity and consistency guarantees. Unless the consumer decides to read uncommitted files, there is no risk of processing empty tables because of the concurrency issue.

Finally, you can also combine the raw dataset with a dataset exposed from an API. One of our recommendations here is to leverage bulk operations, where you can ask for information on multiple items at once. This optimizes network throughput, which often is the most expensive operation in data enrichment. In Example 5-4, you can find an example of an Apache Spark writer calling a locally managed IP mapping service.

Example 5-4. PySpark writer with data enrichment

```
class KafkaWriterWithEnricher:
 BUFFER_THRESHOLD = 100
# ...
 def process(self, row):
    if len(self.buffered_to_enrich) == self.BUFFER_THRESHOLD:
      self._enrich_ips()
      self._flush_records()
    else:
      self.buffered_to_enrich.append(row)

 def _enrich_ips(self):
   ips = (','.join(set(visit.ip for visit in self.buffered_to_enrich
     if visit.ip not in self.enriched_ips)))
   fetched_ips = requests.get(f'http://localhost:8080/geolocation/fetch?ips={ips}',
               headers={'Content-Type': 'application/json','Charset': 'UTF-8'})
   if fetched_ips.status_code == 200:
     mapped_ips = json.loads(fetched_ips.content)['mapped']
     self.enriched_ips.update(mapped_ips)
```

As you can see in Example 5-4, the code buffers the records, and once the buffer size reaches the threshold, the writer makes the API call with a unique list of IPs.

Pattern: Dynamic Joiner

As you might have guessed, the Static Joiner pattern, due to its static character, isn't the best fit for combining two streaming datasets. The problem lies in the data perception. Streaming stands for a continuously moving dataset, with as-soon-as-possible processing, while static batch workloads operate on more slowly evolving data. But the good news is this section will show you an alternative which is better adapted to these dynamic environments.

Problem

Even though you've implemented the Static Joiner for the users-to-visits use case, you're still not satisfied with the final outcome. With thousands of new users coming online each week, the number of profile changes has increased. As a result, the enriched dataset is irrelevant and becomes problematic for your downstream consumers. Since each user change is registered to a streaming broker from the Change Data Capture pattern, you're looking for a better way to combine events for both sides.

Solution

As both datasets are in motion, you can't use the Static Joiner. Instead, you should consider its alternative, the Dynamic Joiner pattern, which is better suited for that kind of data.

Even though the implementation shares some points with the Static Joiner—namely, the identification of the keys and the definition of the join method—there is one extra requirement: *time boundaries*. Without this dedicated time management strategy, there's a risk that many of the joins will be empty. Why? It's simply because the two datasets may have different latencies. In other words, the enrichment dataset can be late compared with the enriched dataset or vice versa. To mitigate this issue, dynamic joins are often completed with additional time conditions.

Defining these time conditions implies having a time-bounded buffer for joined records on both streams. That way, the faster data source can align its time semantics with the slower data source. As a result, the buffer gives some extra time for joins to happen. This extra time is often an allowed latency difference between the data sources. For example, if the users from our example are one hour late compared with the visits, the buffer will store the visits for an extra hour, hoping to find a match once the user stream catches up.

Besides improving the join's outcome, the buffer involves a streaming aspect called the *garbage collection* (GC) *watermark*. Even though technically, you can always decide to keep events from both streams forever, this will require significant hardware resources and will fail sooner or later if you cannot scale your infrastructure indefinitely. A better approach is to define when events that are too old should go away from each buffer, meaning when you should use a GC watermark. This obviously means losing the join if one of the records comes really late, but that's the trade-off for having a manageable size buffer.

The component that's responsible for cleaning the buffer of the elements that are too old is the GC watermark. Figure 5-3 shows an example.

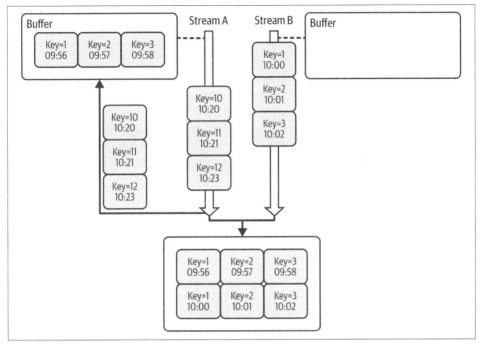

Figure 5-3. Dynamic Joiner with buffering for two streams of different latencies

Here, you can see two streams where Stream A is several minutes faster than Stream B. Due to this difference, to maximize the success rate of the joined records, Stream A buffers all unmatched keys for a period time. Then, when Stream B catches up, Stream A tries to find the corresponding rows either from the incoming data or directly from the buffer. If there is no match, the GC watermark removes records that are older than Stream B's oldest event time. (You learned about watermarks in the Late Data Detector pattern.)

Even though it sounds complicated, you won't need to deal with the entire buffering logic as it's natively implemented by data processing frameworks.

Consequences

Even though it addresses one of the Static Joiner's major issues, the Dynamic Joiner has its own drawbacks.

Space versus exactness trade-off. Due to the GC watermark and time boundaries, you may not be able to get all the joins that are possible. You can optimize efficency by increasing buffer space, but it'll cost you more hardware resources. On the other hand, reducing space optimizes storage but may reduce the likelihood of matching if the latency difference is too big.

For that reason, you will always need to balance these two factors, and unfortunately, there is no one-size-fits-all formula. Each solution will depend on your business requirements and the usual latency difference between joined datasets.

Late data. Late data is another reason for missed joins. Stream processing, due to its inherently lower latency processing semantics, has a weaker tolerance for late data integration in the pipelines. For example, our users stream could encounter temporary connectivity issues in some areas, leading to delayed delivery of a subset of events. As a result, the GC watermark will move on and invalidate the buffered state, and these late events will be ignored.

But neither of the two data enrichment patterns presented here will give you a 100% guarantee of the join results without any extra effort, due to this late data arrival issue. To overcome this limitation, you'll need to track and integrate late data, as explained in Chapter 3.

Examples

Unsurprisingly, to see this pattern in action, you'll need a streaming job. Let's begin with Apache Spark Structured Streaming. In Example 5-5, you can see a join condition used to combine visits with displayed ads.

Example 5-5. Time-based condition for Apache Spark Structured Streaming

```
visits_from_kafka: DataFrame = (visits_data_stream # ...
  .withWatermark('event_time', '10 minutes'))

ads_from_kafka: DataFrame = (ads_data_stream # ...
  .withWatermark('display_time', '10 minutes'))

visits_with_ads = visits_from_kafka.join(ads_from_kafka, F.expr('''
    page = visit_page AND
    display_time BETWEEN event_time AND event_time + INTERVAL 2 minutes
  '''), 'left_outer')
```

Currently, the join condition has business and technical meanings. It makes explicit the business rule that says an ad can be displayed at most two minutes after a user visits a page. From a technical standpoint, this also means there is room left for late data. The withWatermark expression allows late records to be up to 10 minutes late on both sides.

Even though this kind of join is also supported in Apache Flink, the framework also offers an alternative and more managed way to combine streaming data sources called *temporal table joins*. Let's take a look at Example 5-6. The code is written in Java this time due to the lack of support for temporal table joins in the Python API.

Example 5-6. Temporal table join in Apache Flink

```
tableEnv
 .createTemporaryTable("visits_tmp_table", TableDescriptor.forConnector("kafka")
 .schema(Schema.newBuilder().fromColumns(SchemaBuilders.forVisits())
   .watermark("event_time", "event_time - INTERVAL '5' MINUTES")
   .build()).option("topic", "visits")
// ...

tableEnv
 .createTemporaryTable("ads_tmp_table", TableDescriptor.forConnector("kafka")
 .schema(Schema.newBuilder().fromColumns(SchemaBuilders.forAds())
   .watermark("update_time", "update_time - INTERVAL '5' MINUTE")
   .build()).option("topic", "ads")
/// ...

TemporalTableFunction adsLookupFunction = adsTable.createTemporalTableFunction(
  $("update_time"), $("ad_page"));

tableEnv.createTemporarySystemFunction("adsLookupFunction", adsLookupFunction);

Table joinResult = visitsTable.joinLateral(call("adsLookupFunction",
 $("event_time")), $("ad_page").isEqual($("page"))).select($("*"));
```

Example 5-6 starts with the tables declaration. As you can see, besides the schema and topic configuration, the command defines the allowed watermark for each topic. Next, the code initializes a `TemporalTableFunction` used later in the `joinLateral` command. This function performs the important role of getting the most recent ad for each page. Put differently, it gets an ad whose `update_time <= event_time`.

Data Decoration

Once the dataset has gained increased value through a data enrichment pattern, the next question to ask is, is that enough? Data is a crucial asset in modern organizations, but in the enrichment scenario, where the data is still raw or unstructured, the data is rarely in its final form. Without additional preparation work, it can be hard to understand and seize. This is where data decoration patterns may help.

Pattern: Wrapper

In software engineering, *wrapping* consists of adding an extra behavior or attribute(s) to an object. This same definition is valid in the data world, where wrapping also helps separate the original parts of a record from transformed parts.

Problem

Your streaming layer processes the visits data. Visits come from different data providers, and as a consequence, they result in different output schemas.

You need to write a job that extracts the different fields and puts them into a single place so that downstream consumers can rely on it for easy processing. The requirement here is to clearly separate these computed values from the original ones to simplify processing logic but keep the original structure for debugging needs.

Solution

The requirement to keep the original record untouched reduces the transformation scope. You can't simply parse the row and generate a new structure because you'll lose the initial values. To preserve them, you should use the Wrapper pattern.

The idea is to add an extra abstraction at the record's level. The abstraction wraps the original values with a high-level envelope. In addition to these initial attributes, the envelope references computed attributes that may come from the input data itself or from the execution context (e.g., processing time or job processing version). For example, our input visit event could transform into an event composed of *raw* and *computed* fields, corresponding respectively to the two sections.

In addition to formats used in streaming, such as Apache Avro, Protobuf, or JSON, the pattern is supported in structured formats, like tables. In this context, you can implement it either as a separate table that you can join with the original one if needed or as extra columns within the same table. Figure 5-4 depicts possible implementations.

As you can see in the figure, there are four different wrapping implementations for structured data:

- Implementation 1 stores the original row in a flat structure and all computed columns as nested attributes.
- Implementation 2 does the opposite (i.e., it stores computed rows as a single flat structure).
- Implementation 3 stores all columns in a flat structure at the same level.
- Implementation 4 stores the data in two separate tables that can be joined later by a unique key.

The first two implementations use a denormalization approach that may be faster at reading. The third one uses the normalized approach, which may be slower at reading but can be a better choice if you need to logically isolate the datasets or when you simply can't change the original structure. All these approaches share the need for schema management that you will discover along with the schema consistency patterns in Chapter 9.

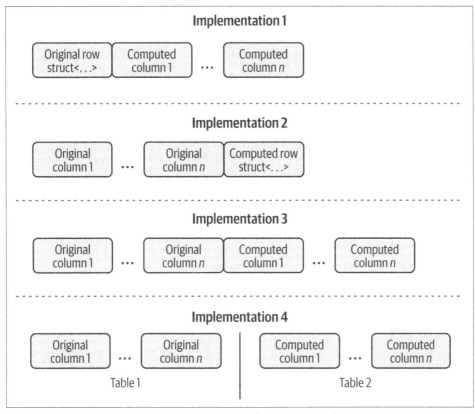

Figure 5-4. Possible Wrapper implementations for structured data

A Wrapper in a Table?

Even though the wrapper envelope is not directly visible in structured formats, it's still there. In fact, the envelope is a row of a table. Therefore, there is no need to break from the normal columnar format and, for example, put fields from multiple columns into one column with nested attributes.

Consequences

This logical and physical separation may have some serious consequences for your dataset, however, mostly related to the storage footprint.

Domain split. This is the logical implication because the pattern divides attributes for a given domain. Let's take a look at an example of a user. If you implement the Wrapper, you'll find user-related fields in two different high-level structures: raw and computed. Although this approach has some advantages, such as making a clear distinction between transformed and nontransformed values, it also makes data retrieval more complicated. Consumers must be aware that user data is in these two locations.

As a trade-off, you could consider the wrapped data to be the data belonging to the first storage layers of your system, like the Silver layer from our use case, and not the final data exposed to the users, for whom this separation may be confusing.

Size. Decorated values form an intrinsic part of the processed record, and therefore, they impact the overall size and network traffic. This differs from the behavior of the Metadata Decorator pattern, which you'll see in the next section.

When it comes to the size impact in the Wrapper pattern, you can mitigate the limitations if your data storage format supports data source projection. With this feature, you can select the columns you are interested in and ask the data source to physically access only them. This practice is very common for all solutions leveraging columnar data storage, such as data warehouses (e.g., AWS Redshift, GCP BigQuery).

Examples

The Wrapper supports both business and technical attributes. The second category includes the metadata values of the execution context, such as the job version or execution time, that may help with debugging production issues later. Let's take a look at Example 5-7 which shows how to integrate them into the row with Apache Spark.

Example 5-7. Wrapping metadata with PySpark

```
visits_w_processing_context = (visits.withColumn('processing_context', F.struct(
  F.lit(job_version).alias('job_version'), F.lit(batch_number).alias('batch_version')
)))

visits_to_save = (visits_w_processing_context.withColumn('value', F.to_json(
  F.struct(F.col('value').cast('string').alias('raw_data'),
  F.col('processing_context')))))
```

Example 5-7 defines the metadata as a new column of the input dataset. Next, it includes these extra attributes with the help of a new structure composed of the initial value (`raw_data`) and the technical context (`processing_context`). The whole is then transformed into a JSON document and written to the output database.

Although the code uses the PySpark API, it's also possible to do the wrapping in Apache Spark SQL. Example 5-8 shows a query enriching the input rows with an additional structure called `decorated`.

Example 5-8. Wrapping with an extra struct in SQL

```sql
SELECT *, NAMED_STRUCT(
  'is_connected',
  CASE WHEN context.user.connected_since IS NULL
     THEN false ELSE true END,
  'page_referral_key', CONCAT_WS('-', page, context.referral)
) AS decorated FROM input_visits
```

The difference with the query in Example 5-8 is the NAMED_STRUCT function, which provides a convenient way to alter the struct key names with values such as key1, value1, key2, value2, keyn, and valuen. Alternatively, you can consider the decorated data to be first-class table columns and all raw data to be additional context, as demonstrated in Example 5-9.

Example 5-9. Wrapping with the raw value struct in SQL

```sql
SELECT
  CASE WHEN context.user.connected_since IS NULL
    THEN false ELSE true END AS is_connected,
  CONCAT_WS('-', page, context.referral) AS page_referral_key,
  STRUCT(visit_id, event_time, user_id, page, context) AS raw
FROM input_visits
```

As you can see, Example 5-9 promotes all computed values as the table columns and relegates the raw values to a column of a struct type. Finally, you can also have a table with all computed columns at the same level as the input ones. But you must be aware that in that context, the end users may not be able to distinguish the raw values from the computed ones if the names don't clearly differentiate raw from computed values.

Pattern: Metadata Decorator

The Wrapper pattern is universal since it's always possible to wrap a record. However, when the added values shouldn't be directly exposed to end users, it can be misleading to consumers. After all, your end users won't care whether the record was generated by job version 1 or 2. To overcome this problem, you can hide the extra records in the metadata layer of your data store.

Problem

Your streaming jobs evolve quite often, and you release a new version almost once a week.

Although your deployment process is smooth, you lack some visibility into the impact of the released version on the generated data. To simplify your maintenance activity, you need to add some technical context to each generated record, such as the job version. However, you don't want to include this information in the records sent to end users.

Solution

Including the technical context in the record with the Wrapper pattern is not an option here. This information may not be relevant to your consumers since they're not interested in your internal data processing details. Instead, you can leverage the metadata layer of your data store to apply the Metadata Decorator pattern.

The implementation will depend on your data store capabilities for handling metadata, though. If it supports the metadata out of the box, you will be able to associate each written record with a dedicated metadata attribute. Since this attribute is a native part of the data producer's capabilities, the implementation is relatively straightforward. This is the case with Apache Kafka, which, besides the key and value attributes, supports a list of optional header key-value pairs for each record.

If you work with object stores and your metadata decoration applies to all rows present in a given file, you can define the metadata attributes as tags associated with the file.

If tags are unavailable, other data stores may not support metadata decoration natively. That's the case with relational or NoSQL databases. With them, you can simulate the decoration by including the metadata within the data part but without publicly exposing it to end users. To help you understand how to do this, let's take a look at an example of a data warehouse table. If you want to track the metadata individually for each record, you can write it to a dedicated column and either expose the table from a view without this technical information or use permissions to block reading of that column by nontechnical users (see "Pattern: Fine-Grained Accessor for Tables" on page 207). Table 5-1 shows an example of this type of schema.

Table 5-1. A table with a Metadata Decorator column, which consumers should access via a view or with privileges for reading all but the metadata columns

event_id	event_time	...	processing_context
1	2023-06-10T10:00:59Z		{"job_version": "v1.0.3", "processing_time":"2023-06-10T10:02:00Z"}

In addition to the row-based approach shown in Table 5-1, you can opt for an alternative approach and store the processing context in a dedicated table that will be joined with the dataset. Here, the implementation is even simpler as you can literally hide this table in a schema available only to the technical members of your team. Tables 5-2 and 5-3 show this approach.

Table 5-2. Processing context table approach, data table

event_id	event_time	...	processing_context_id
1	2023-06-10T10:00:59Z		1

Table 5-3. Processing context table approach, technical table

processing_context_id	job_version	...	processing_time
1	v1.0.3		2023-06-10T10:02:00Z

These tables present another implementation that's possible where the metadata context is normalized as a separate table; therefore, it's not duplicated for each row. Again, users shouldn't have access to the technical table or the `processing_con text_id` field from the data table, to avoid any confusion.

Wrapper and Metadata Semantics

This metadata decoration is similar to the one you saw for the Wrapper pattern. The only difference is the semantics. Metadata is not supposed to be exposed publicly to business users because by definition, it's a description of the data. That's not the case with the Wrapper because it's intended to decorate business attributes in addition to technical ones.

Consequences

The support of data stores for metadata handling will probably be your biggest limitation in implementing the pattern. But it's not the only one.

Implementation. Even the streaming brokers from the problem statement may lack native metadata support, making implementation impossible for them. For example, Amazon Kinesis Data Streams doesn't support headers.

Implementation can also be challenging for table datasets, where, as demonstrated before, you'll often need to define an extra column or table to handle the metadata information. Although this works, it requires more effort than for data stores that natively support metadata decoration.

Data. Even though there is no technical limitation on what type of information you can put into the metadata layer, you should avoid writing business-related attributes there, such as shipment addresses or invoice amounts. Otherwise, they remain hidden to consumers, most of whom will never think about querying the metadata part. By definition, metadata is data about data, and any external dataset users will primarily be interested in the data from the second part of the sentence.

Examples

For each new concept, it's always better to start with an easy example, so let's take a look at Example 5-10 to see how to add metadata to an Apache Kafka record written from an Apache Spark Structured Streaming job.

Example 5-10. Adding a metadata header for Apache Kafka in PySpark

```
visits_with_metadata = (visits_to_save.withColumn('headers', F.array(
  F.struct(F.lit('job_version').alias('key'), F.lit(job_version).alias('value')),
  F.struct(F.lit('batch_version').alias('key'),
  F.lit(str(batch_number).encode('UTF-8')).alias('value'))
)))
(visits_with_metadata.write.format('kafka')
 .option('kafka.bootstrap.servers', 'localhost:9094')
 .option('includeHeaders', True).option('topic', 'visits-decorated')
 .save())
```

Example 5-10 has two important parts. First, the metadata is an array of key-value pairs. Second, the `includeHeaders` option commands Apache Spark to include the headers column in the generated record out of the box.

Another implementation of the Metadata Decorator is an external metadata table whose schema is present in Example 5-11.

Example 5-11. Metadata table initialization

```
CREATE TABLE dedp.visits_context (
    execution_date_time TIMESTAMPTZ NOT NULL,
    loading_time TIMESTAMPTZ NOT NULL,
    code_version VARCHAR(15) NOT NULL,
    loading_attempt SMALLINT NOT NULL,
    PRIMARY KEY (execution_date_time)
)
```

The context table is later referenced as a part of the job loading input data to the user-exposed table. The loading script first inserts new execution context and later adds the primary key of the `visits_context` to the visits weekly table. As a result, you'll be able to combine the visits with the metadata. The full code is present in Example 5-12.

Example 5-12. Inserting new visits with a metadata table

```
{% set weekly_table = get_weekly_table_name(execution_date) %}
INSERT INTO dedp.visits_context
 (execution_date_time, loading_time, code_version, loading_attempt)
VALUES ('{{ execution_date }}', '{{ dag_run.start_date }}',
 '{{ params.code_version }}', {{ task_instance.try_number }});

INSERT INTO {{ weekly_table }} (SELECT tmp_devices.*,
   '{{ execution_date }}' AS visits_context_execution_date_time FROM tmp_devices);
```

Data Aggregation

So far, you have been "adding" information. But can you imagine that removing it is also a way to generate data value? If not, the two patterns from this section should prove you wrong.

Pattern: Distributed Aggregator

The first pattern leverages distributed data processing frameworks. One of their great features is the capability to combine multiple physically isolated but logically similar items.

Problem

You've written a job that cleans the raw visit events from the Bronze layer of our use case architecture and writes them to the Silver layer. From that place, many consumers implement various final business use cases.

One of the use cases requires building an *online analytical processing* (OLAP) *cube*, thereby reducing all visits to an aggregated format that's well suited to your dashboarding scenarios. The result should include basic statistics (count, average duration, etc.) across multiple axes (user geography, devices, etc.).

The dataset is stored in daily event time partitions, and the analytics cubes should represent daily and weekly views.

Solution

For datasets that fit into a single machine or container, you don't need any specific tool to perform the aggregation. The native group by function of your programming language, followed by a reduced logic, should be enough. However, in the big data era, when related records can be split across multiple physical places, this requirement doesn't hold every time. That's where the Distributed Aggregator pattern helps.

The pattern leverages multiple machines that together form a single execution unit called a *cluster*. These servers individually don't have enough capacity to process the whole input dataset, but together, they divide the work and can handle this scenario.

Despite this hardware difference, the code-based implementation may remain the same as for small, local datasets. This means you can still use a grouping function to bring the related rows together and later apply a reduce function on top of them. The first step is optional, though, as you can also combine the whole dataset as is (for example, to get a total count of rows or a global average across all rows).

But the devil is in the details. Although the API might look the same, under the hood, execution of the Distributed Aggregator involves a step to exchange records that were initially loaded into different machines, across the network. As a result, the reduce function can operate on all necessary collocated rows, as you can see in the schema in Figure 5-5.

Here, the action depicted is called a *shuffle*. Often, it is one of the first latency trouble-makers because of the network traffic cost.

Even though the example shows a raw record exchange, not all record exchanges are raw. Any aggregation that supports partial generation can be optimized by performing a partial aggregation locally, before the shuffle. As a result, the exchanged records will be smaller and the whole operation should be faster. A great example here is the count operation. Instead of shuffling all the raw records and counting them on the final reduce nodes, the compute layer can perform a partial count on each initial node for all keys that are present locally and shuffle only the numbers to sum in the end.

MapReduce

The Distributed Aggregator pattern is a typical example of the MapReduce programming model, which greatly contributed to simplifying distributed data processing back in 2004. Over the years, its implementations have evolved from disk-based Hadoop MapReduce to memory-first Apache Spark.

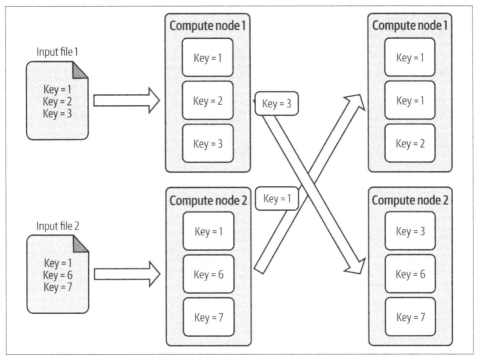

Figure 5-5. Data exchange in Distributed Aggregator

Consequences

Even though frameworks fully implement the pattern, with their high-level API and low-level cluster orchestration, there are some gotchas related to the data itself.

Additional network exchange. The pattern involves two network exchanges. The first brings input data to each node. This is difficult to avoid as nowadays, storage and compute colocation is not a common pattern. The second network exchange comes from the Distributed Aggregator pattern because it's a required step to gather related data on the same server. This is one of the possible latency issues to look at when problems arise.

Unlike the input part, this shuffle can be avoided under specific conditions, which are all explained in the next section on the Local Aggregator pattern.

Data skew. *Data skew* is a term describing unbalanced datasets in which at least one key has way more occurrences than the others. In that case, the cost of moving it across the network and processing it in a single node will be the highest. Thankfully, some techniques exist to prevent the skew, such as *salting*, which consists of adding an extra value (aka *salt*) to the grouping key and performing the first grouping operation on the salted column. Next, if you need to get the results for the original grouping key, you'll need to aggregate the outcome of the salted column's aggregation again (see Example 5-13).

Example 5-13. Salting example in PySpark for skewed column `column_a`

```
dataset.withColumn('salt', (rand()*3).cast("int"))
  .groupBy('group_key', 'salt').agg(...)
  .groupBy('group_key').agg(...)
```

Also, data processing frameworks may have some native data skew mitigation, like Apache Spark with Adaptive Query Execution.[1]

Scaling. In addition to this network traffic impact, shuffle has also another implication: scaling. If, for whatever reason, a node has completed all planned reduce operations, it may still be in use by the hardware layer for fault tolerance reasons. If the whole reduce computation fails and gets restarted, this data won't need to be reshuffled again—but when there is no failure, the node will still be there but will not be reclaimed as long as the processing is running. If you want to avoid keeping it for all that time, you can opt for a component called shuffle service.

Shuffle service is an additional compute component that is responsible for storing and serving only shuffle data. Therefore, if one node is not used anymore, the compute layer can free it at any time, even when the job is still running. Among the implementations here, you'll find Apache Spark's External Shuffle Service and GCP Dataflow's Shuffle.

Examples

The best way to understand the Distributed Aggregator and have a demo that's easily reproducible locally at the same time is to use two different data stores. In our case, we'll use PostgreSQL and a local file system with JSON files. Although the data stores are physically isolated, Apache Spark can combine them with the code in Example 5-14.

Example 5-14. Aggregation of two physically isolated data stores in PySpark

```
visits: DataFrame = spark_session.read.json(f'{base_dir}/input-visits')
devices: DataFrame = spark_session.read.jdbc(url='jdbc:postgresql:dedp',
    table='dedp.devices', properties={'user': 'dedp_test',
  'password': 'dedp_test', 'driver': 'org.postgresql.Driver'})
visits_with_devices = visits.join(devices,
  [devices.type == visits.context.technical.dev_type,
```

---

1 You can learn more about Adaptive Query Execution in the Apache Spark documentation (*https://oreil.ly/v-ln6*).

```
        devices.version == visits.context.technical.dev_version],
     'inner')
```

Apache Spark provides a convenient way to check whether the operation contains shuffle or not. To perform this verification, you need to call the `explain()` method on top of your `DataFrame` and look for the `Exchange hashpartitioning` node. Example 5-15 shows output from the `explain()` command for the join between the PostgreSQL and JSON datasets from Example 5-14. As you'll notice, the job performs local operations such as filtering before preparing the data to be exchanged across the network.

Example 5-15. The execution plan for our devices-to-users join

```
== Physical Plan ==
AdaptiveSparkPlan isFinalPlan=false
+- SortMergeJoin [ctx#8.technical.dev_type, ctx#8.technical.dev_version],..
 :- Sort [ctx#8.technical.dev_type ASC NULLS FIRST, ctx#8.technical.dev_version..
 : +- Exchange hashpartitioning(ctx#8.technical.dev_type, ...
 :    +-Filter (....))
 :       +- FileScan json [.....
 +- Sort [type#20 ASC NULLS FIRST, version#22 ASC NULLS FIRST], false, 0
   +- Exchange hashpartitioning(type#20, version#22, 200), ENSURE_REQUIREMENTS,..
       +- Scan JDBCRelation(....
```

In addition to a distributed data processing framework, the pattern works for databases, which can read datasets from a different storage location. For example, in GCP BigQuery, a serverless data warehouse offering on the public cloud, you can combine a table with files stored on the Google Cloud Storage (GCS) service. This looks similar to our example with Apache Spark, by the way.

To enable this combination, you need to declare the GCS objects to be an *external table* and later just reference them as any regular BigQuery objects in the queries. By the way, external tables are also supported in other data warehousing systems, including AWS Redshift, Azure Synapse Analytics, and Snowflake.

Pattern: Local Aggregator

Network exchange may not be necessary if the data is correctly partitioned in the input or when the dataset fits into a single machine. Both scenarios can be addressed with a new aggregation pattern.

Problem

You have a streaming job that generates windows for incoming visits stored in a partitioned streaming broker. The data volume is static, and you don't expect any sudden variations or changes in the underlying partitioning. As a result, the partitions number will never change. You're looking for a way to optimize the job and remove the grouping shuffle step that's added automatically by your data processing framework.

Solution

A costly shuffle, static data source partitioning, and related attributes stored together are three factors in favor of the alternative to the Distributed Aggregator, which is the Local Aggregator pattern.

Although on the surface, the pattern still performs some aggregations, it does so locally with the single network exchange of reading the input data. This solution works thanks to the fixed partitioning schema and correct input data distribution. All records that are relevant for a given grouping key are already present in the same input partition, so there's no need to load them from other places.

In addition to the lack of shuffle, this implementation brings another advantage. The tasks can be *fully isolated*, meaning they won't need to wait for the data on other tasks and can move forward. This is especially useful for streaming applications, where some slower processing units may delay the whole execution.

The implementation effort should focus here on the producer side. It must guarantee to write a record with a particular grouping key to the same physical partition. This can be achieved with a static per-record partitioning key and an immutable number of partitions.

On the consumer side, some of the tools provide facility methods to adapt the pre-partitioned dataset to its shuffle format. This is the case with Kafka Streams and its `groupByKey` method. Apache Spark doesn't provide any hints or methods for avoiding shuffle, but thanks to its per-partition operations, such as `mapPartitions` and `for each Partition`, you can leverage your programming language's API capability to perform local aggregations. In addition to these convenience methods, Apache Spark avoids shuffle for the datasets that are saved in buckets with the same key and the same number of buckets.

About the Buckets

Bucketing (aka *clustering*) is a way of partitioning the partitions. You'll learn more about it in the Bucket pattern in Chapter 8.

The logic we've just presented applies to the partitioned data sources whose volume is too big to be processed in a single machine. However, if you are working on a non-partitioned or partitioned but small dataset, you don't need to worry about static numbers of partitions. That's because you can load the whole dataset into your processing node and leverage the shared memory to perform any aggregations.

Consequences

The pattern requires some immutability, which may not always be possible, for the storage and grouping keys.

Scaling. Scaling is the most visible issue. The pattern depends on the static nature of the data source and consistent partitioning (i.e., a guarantee that a given key will always be available from only one processing partition). If you can't guarantee one of these conditions, the pattern won't work correctly because it'll create one or multiple groups for a given key whenever you change storage partitions.

If you needed to scale and adapt the organization, you could do it with a dedicated data storage reorganization task, which would regenerate the partition assignments for all the records. This operation may be costly as it requires processing the whole dataset. Also, it's even trickier to achieve in streaming applications since it would involve a stop-the-world event to enable processing all remaining data on the old partitions before the data producers can write records to the newly organized partitions.

As you can see, Local Aggregator avoids an extra shuffle but makes this important scaling part a lot more challenging.

Grouping keys. For partitioned data sources with static numbers of partitions, the pattern also expects one grouping key logic for all consumers. Unfortunately, this may not be easy to achieve because it would involve writing the same record in multiple places, each time with a different grouping key.

For example, if your application that reads user profile changes groups them by change type while other consumers perform some user ID–based aggregation, you'll need to opt for the Distributed Aggregator pattern for one of those customers.

Examples

Let's start the examples with Kafka Streams, which is a Java-written data processing layer that processes data from Apache Kafka. The library has a `groupByKey` method that implements the Local Aggregator pattern. Example 5-16 shows how.

Example 5-16. Local aggregation in Kafka Streams

```
KStream<String, String> visitsSource = streamsBuilder.stream("visits");
KGroupedStream<String, String> groupedVisits = visitsSource.groupByKey();
KStream<String, AggregatedVisits> aggregatedVisits = groupedVisits
  .aggregate(AggregatedVisits::new, new AggregatedVisitsAggregator(),
    Materialized.with(Serdes.String(), new JsonSerializer<>())).toStream();
```

```
aggregatedVisits.to("visits-aggregated", Produced.with(new Serdes.StringSerde(),
    new JsonSerializer<>()));
```

Example 5-16 starts by declaring the visits topic to be the KStream abstraction. In the next line, it calls the groupByKey to perform local aggregation. How is that possible? There is no mention of any key, after all. The method uses the key attribute associated with each incoming record to combine all records sharing the same key without a network exchange.

If this API capability is not explicitly provided by your library, there may be an implicit way to use it. To understand this better, let's take a look at an Apache Spark code that aggregates visit events without a network exchange. Example 5-17 shows the job logic. It sorts the visit events in each partition by the visit_id and event_time fields.

Example 5-17. Local Aggregator for visits in PySpark

```
sorted_visits: DataFrame = (visits_to_save
  .sortWithinPartitions(['visit_id', 'event_time']))
def write_records_from_spark_partition_to_kafka_topic(visits):
  kafka_writer = KafkaWriter(...)
  for visit in visits:
    kafka_writer.process(visit)
  kafka_writer.close()

sorted_visits.foreachPartition(write_records_from_spark_partition_to_kafka_topic)
```

After ordering the records, still separately for each partition, Apache Spark calls the KafkaWriter from Example 5-18. This class uses the sorted rows to generate an aggregate of the pages visited in a session. Whenever the visit_id is different from the currently buffered visit, the writer sends the aggregation result to the output Kafka topic.

Example 5-18. Local Aggregator for visits in PySpark: partition-based writer

```
class KafkaWriter:
  def __init__(self, bootstrap_server: str, output_topic: str):
    self.in_flight_visit = {'visit_id': None}

  def process(self, row):
    if row.visit_id != self.in_flight_visit['visit_id']:
      send_visit_to_kafka(self.in_flight_visit)
      self.in_flight_visit = {'visit_id': row.visit_id, 'pages': [],...}

    self.in_flight_visit['pages'].append(row.page)
    # ...
```

In addition to open source tools, cloud services provide local aggregation capability. That's the case with the AWS Redshift distribution types presented in Example 5-19. The code configures a users table with the ALL distribution. That way, Redshift copies the users table to all nodes in the cluster. As a result, any join operation with the users table will be performed locally, without shuffle. Another possible configuration is the KEY distribution applied in the example to the visits table. The KEY distribution groups all rows sharing the same DISTKEY on the same storage node. That way, any combination involving the DISTKEY column can be performed locally.

Example 5-19. Storage distribution in AWS Redshift

```
CREATE TABLE visits (
  visit_id INT,
  user_id INT, ...
) ...
DISTSTYLE KEY,
DISTKEY(visit_id);

CREATE TABLE users (
  user_id INT,  ...
) ...
DISTSTYLE ALL;
```

Sessionization

Sessions are special kinds of aggregators since they combine events related to the same activity. Sessions are also popular. You generate them in your daily life whenever you watch streaming videos, work out, or even cook. In each of those activities, you create a session composed of a starting point, session events, and an ending point. In a data engineering context, depending on the nature of your data, which may be at rest or in motion, you can choose from two available sessionization patterns that you are going to learn about in this section.

Pattern: Incremental Sessionizer

A session sounds like a real-time component. Indeed, most of the time, it results from real-time data, but the generation method also supports batch processing. The pattern you're going to see right now is adapted to batch pipelines.

Problem

The data ingestion team stores visit events from our use case architecture in an hourly partitioned location. You want to aggregate them into sessions that start with the first visit and end if there are no new visits from the given user within two hours.

The typical duration of a visit session is between several minutes and three hours. As a result, one visit can spread across at most three different partitions. Data analysts from your team are struggling to get the sessions right because each time, they need to process many consecutive partitions for a given user. They've explained to you what the problems are, and thankfully, you know about Incremental Loader design pattern and have an idea about how to leverage it for the sessionization use case.

Solution

Since records for one session may be present in multiple consecutive partitions, the problem belongs to the incremental processing family. To solve it, you can leverage the Incremental Sessionizer pattern.

The implementation requires setting up the following three storage spaces:

Input dataset storage
> This stores the raw events you need to correlate in the sessionization pipeline. There, you'll find the hourly partitioned visits from the problem statement.

Completed sessions storage
> This is the place where you'll write all finished sessions. Eventually, you could also write the ongoing sessions here as well, but ideally, you should distinguish them from the completed sessions (for example, by using an attribute like is_final set to false whenever a session is still active).

Pending sessions storage
> Here, you store all sessions spread across multiple partitions that will be closed in one of the next executions. There are two differences between this and completed sessions storage. First, it must remain private as this space will belong to you and evolve with your internal logic. End users doesn't need to be aware of the details, and if they were, you would have less evolution flexibility. Second, the data format for the sessions can be different from the format in completed sessions storage. You could include some technical or internals details here, such as execution ID, if it would be helpful in defining the processing logic (for example, in guaranteeing idempotency).

However, storage won't be enough. You also need to define the workflow logic. The logic starts by combining the input dataset with all pending sessions generated in the previous execution. The combination happens for each session entity—such as a user, product, or visit—and it can generate the following:

- A new session if there is no pending session for a given session entity.
- A restored session with new data coming from the read input.

- A restored session without new session data. This session will probably be about to expire in this or the next execution, depending on the expiration rules you've defined.

Once you complete this combination, you'll get session data to process, possibly composed of previous and new records. On top of that, you need to apply sessionization logic that defines three states:

Initialization
When a session starts. For example, it can start when a particular event type occurs such as visiting the home page of your blog.

Accumulation
When a session is live. What do you do with new incoming data? For example, you could store the visited pages in order.

Finalization
When a session stops. A session can finish when a particular event type occurs or because of a period of inactivity (for example, when a user closes the browser or goes away for three hours).

Figure 5-6 explains this in visual form.

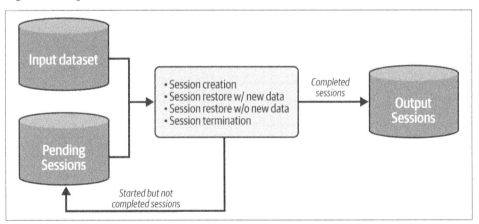

Figure 5-6. Incremental Sessionizer with three storage spaces

In the schema, you can see the execution flow with all involved storage spaces. The transformation loads pending sessions created in the previous run and new data available in the input dataset. Afterward, all completed sessions go into the publicly exposed storage while all pending sessions are written elsewhere to keep them alive and available for the next job execution.

You can define the processing logic with a WINDOW function or a GROUP BY expression, followed by a custom mapping function in the programming language of your choice.

Depending on the logic's complexity, the implementation may be easier to express with a programmatic API than with SQL.

Consequences

The implementation should be clear by now. However, that's just the bright side. The Incremental Sessionizer is no exception to the fact that you may encounter some surprises in any pattern.

Inactivity period. The inactivity period defines how long you can keep a session open. The longer it is, the more late data you can include in the session. On the other hand, you'll need more compute and storage resources to handle the late data. Again, you should find the right balance between the compute requirements and the business logic because it'll be challenging to have both. What that balance is, of course, is entirely dependent on your specific business needs.

A long inactivity period threshold will also keep the sessions in the hidden space for that amount of time. If your users can accept partial session views, you can also emit them to the output sessions storage. But there is a consistency risk your consumers must be aware of.

A partial session is not a completed session, and it may change in subsequent versions. Imagine a partial session for fraud detection in a banking system (which is better to do in real time, but it's a good example for partial sessions). After you process the first partition, the partial session will be classified as "not at risk" and only the next partition will change the status to "risky." If consumers consider partial sessions to be final, they may apply the wrong logic to the first instance.

It's therefore important to flag the ongoing sessions—for example, with an attribute like is_completed: false—to help downstream consumers ignore them if they only care about the finished state.

Data freshness. The Incremental Sessionizer works for batch pipelines, which are still the first choice of processing mode for data teams. As a result, insights often come very late compared to real time. To mitigate this issue and still be able to use batch pipelines, you can create the partial sessions introduced in the previous section.

Late data, event time partitions, and backfilling. If your sessionization logic relies on event time partitioning, late data will be a problem as you may miss sessions for already processed partitions.

Sessions are a specific data asset that is forward dependent. Yeah, that sounds weird at first, but it's true. A session generated for the partition at 09:00 directly impacts the session at 10:00, the one at 10:00 impacts the one at 11:00, and so on. Therefore, even if you manage to integrate late data for one entity, there is no guarantee that this data won't impact the next sessions!

This dependency is also visible in backfilling. If you rerun the session generation logic for one partition, you'll have to do the same for all subsequent partitions. This can become expensive very quickly.

Unfortunately, there is no silver bullet that will keep your codebase easy and your costs optimized. The simple solution of replaying all partitions after the backfilled one is easy for the code but costly. On the other hand, having a smart detection method to find entities to backfill and rerunning only them from a dedicated backfill pipeline optimizes the cost but adds extra complexity.

Examples

Incremental is the key word of the pattern since it implies using a data orchestrator to coordinate the loading work. For that reason, let's start the section with the task list for Apache Airflow presented in Example 5-20.

Example 5-20. Incremental Sessionizer steps

```
clean_previous_runs_sessions = PostgresOperator(...)
clean_previous_runs_pending_sessions = PostgresOperator(...)
generate_sessions = PostgresOperator(...)

([clean_previous_runs_sessions, clean_previous_runs_pending_sessions]
 >> generate_sessions)
```

We omitted the configuration from Example 5-20 as the task names are self-explanatory, and you will find all the missing details in the GitHub repo (*https://oreil.ly/lw-yj*). The pipeline starts with two simultaneous tasks that clean all completed and pending sessions generated in this and all subsequent executions. As you can see in Example 5-21, they use simple DELETE FROM statements applied to the Apache Airflow's immutable ds parameter.

Example 5-21. Idempotency component for the Incremental Sessionizer

```
DELETE FROM dedp.sessions WHERE execution_time_id >= '{{ ds }}';
DELETE FROM dedp.pending_sessions WHERE execution_time_id >= '{{ ds }}';
```

After this context preparation step, the pipeline runs the session generation query, which is composed of four blocks. Example 5-22 shows the first part, which loads all input data into a temporary and session-scoped visits table. That way, if the session query fails, you won't have to replay the loading step each time.

Example 5-22. Session generation: loading new data

```
CREATE TEMPORARY TABLE visits_{{ ds_nodash }} (# ...);

COPY visits_{{ ds_nodash }} FROM '/data_to_load/date={{ ds_nodash }}/dataset.csv' CSV
```

After loading the data, the session generation logic combines the input data with pending sessions. An important thing here is to use an idempotent property to identify previously generated pending sessions. Our snippet leverages Apache Airflow's execution time for that. The query also applies the WINDOW function to the new data so that the visits get formatted into the same schema as the pending sessions. On top of that, the SELECT statement uses facility methods to get the first nonnull element (COALESCE), get the first or last values (LEAST or GREATEST), or concatenate two arrays (ARRAY_CAT). Finally, it also computes the session expiration time only when the session has new data. The whole query is presented in Example 5-23.

Example 5-23. Session generation: the logic

```
CREATE TEMPORARY TABLE sessions_to_classify AS
 SELECT
  COALESCE(p.session_id, n.session_id) AS session_id,
  # ...
  LEAST(p.start_time, n.start_time) AS start_time,
  GREATEST(p.last_visit_time, n.start_time) AS last_visit_time,
  ARRAY_CAT(p.pages, n.pages) AS pages,
  CASE
   WHEN n.user_id IS NULL THEN p.expiration_batch_id
   ELSE '{{ macros.ds_add(ds, 2) }}'
  END AS expiration_batch_id
 FROM (SELECT ... FROM visits_{{ ds_nodash }}
  WINDOW visits_window AS (PARTITION BY visit_id, user_id ORDER BY event_time)
 ) AS n
 FULL OUTER JOIN (
  SELECT ... FROM dedp.pending_sessions WHERE execution_time_id = '{{ prev_ds }}')
  AS p ON n.session_id = p.session_id;
```

In the end, there are two writing steps, which are shown in Example 5-24. The first INSERT writes all pending sessions, that is, the sessions whose expiration time is different than the current run (expiration_batch_id != '{{ ds }}'). Next, it writes all finished sessions.

Example 5-24. Session generation: the writing component

```
INSERT INTO dedp.pending_sessions (...)
    SELECT ... FROM sessions_to_classify WHERE expiration_batch_id != '{{ ds }}';
INSERT INTO dedp.sessions (...)
    SELECT ... FROM sessions_to_classify WHERE expiration_batch_id = '{{ ds }}';
```

Pattern: Stateful Sessionizer

If data freshness is an issue, the Incremental Sessionizer will not help you. Instead, you should use another sessionization pattern that performs great on top of the stream processing layer, thanks to its more frequent and smaller iterations.

Problem

Stakeholders are now quite happy with the session's availability. However, more and more of them need to access the session in a lower latency. That's impossible to achieve with the Incremental Sessionizer as the partitions are hourly based and the best latency you can provide is one hour.

The good news is that the visits are also available in your streaming broker within seconds. You are looking for a way to rewrite the batch pipeline and generate sessions in near real time.

Solution

Achieving the "as soon as possible" guarantee for sessions is hard with batch pipelines, but default streaming pipelines won't help either because they are stateless. For that reason, you need to use a more advanced version and solve the problem with the Stateful Sessionizer pattern.

How is that different from stateless streaming pipelines? Stateful pipelines bring an extra component called a *state store* that you discovered when you were learning about the Windowed Deduplicator pattern. In our sessionization context, the state store plays the same role as the pending sessions storage zone in the Incremental Sessionizer (i.e., it persists all in-flight sessions and keeps them available throughout the processing).

But this storage for pending sessions is not the Stateful Sessionizer's only similarity to the Incremental Sessionizer. The Stateful Sessionizer's implementation follows the same workflow as for the Incremental Sessionizer:

- The pattern starts by creating a session, or resuming it, if it's present in the state store.

- Next, the Stateful Sessionizer combines the created or resumed session with new incoming records according to your business logic. For example, it may store visited pages in order.

- In the end, if the session is completed or the partial sessions need to be available to consumers, the pattern transforms and writes the pending session record into the final output. Additionally, if the session is not completed, this step also writes the new state to the state store.

If you implement the pattern on top of a data processing framework, you'll likely get the state store support out of the box. On the other hand, if you implement the job fully on your own, you will need to code these interactions. Figure 5-7 shows a pretty common state store interaction implementation present in Apache Spark Structured Streaming and Apache Flink.

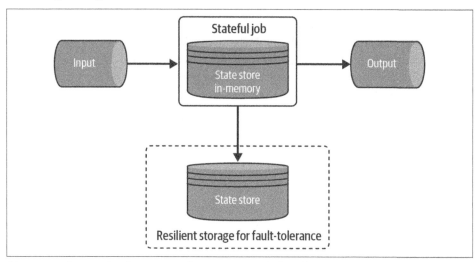

Figure 5-7. Interaction between a data processing job and its state store

The schema illustrates the interaction between a stateful data processing job and its state store. As you can see, there are two flavors of the store. The first one is for fast access. For that reason, it lives in memory, which of course involves volatility. To overcome the risk of losing the state in case of failure or restart, the job synchronizes the state regularly to a more resilient fault tolerance storage.

The data processing logic can rely on the following data processing abstractions:

Session windows

A *session window* is a window created for each session key. Its length is specified by a *gap duration*, which is the maximum allowable period of inactivity between two events with the same session key. If the amount of time between two events with the same session key is greater than the gap duration, a new session window will be created. If not, the new event will be part of the already opened session. Figure 5-8 shows a session window logic with the gap duration of 20 minutes. Two session windows are created once the difference between events is greater than this threshold.

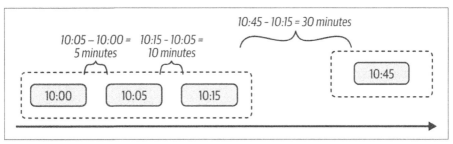

Figure 5-8. Two session windows for the same key where the gap duration is 20 minutes

Arbitrary stateful processing

This approach requires more implementation effort than for the session window, but it also provides more flexibility. It's up to you to define the gap duration logic, which can be a static timer, as in the previous example, or a dynamic operation, possibly different for each session key. Modern data engineering frameworks such as Apache Spark Structured Streaming, Apache Flink, and even GCP Dataflow provide this capability out of the box.

Consequences

Fault tolerance and the state store, despite their positive impact on the sessionization pipeline, also have some gotchas.

At-least-once processing. Saving the state on fault tolerance storage doesn't happen during every state update. Instead, the writing process, which is called *checkpointing*, occurs irregularly. As you may deduce, any stopped job restarts from the last successful checkpoint, leading to at-least-once processing. This semantic is not bad in itself, but it's better to be aware of it and avoid any side effects of operations that might impact the session's idempotency, such as relying on an attribute that changes between the runs to generate the session key. An example of that type of attribute is real time, which obviously will be different at each restart.

Scaling. Changing the compute capacity in this stateful context may involve state rebalancing. This means that the job will not be able to process the data as long as the particular state keys are not assigned to new workers. That doesn't make scaling impossible, but it makes it more costly than for stateless jobs.

Inactivity period length. As for the Incremental Sessionizer, here too you'll need to strike the right balance to keep the total cost acceptable and include as many sessions as possible. Having a longer inactivity period implies more hardware pressure and output freshness.

Inactivity period time. Besides emitting the sessions to the output storage, the solution will also need to manage the expiration of the state for all completed sessions. The cleaning relies on two different temporal aspects. The first one is the event time from incoming events, which is more reliable and should be preferred in most cases. But there is also processing time–based expiration, which is a bit dangerous, though.

Processing time–based logic relies on the current time, meaning that any unexpected latency (for example, due to writing retries) may cause sessions to expire too early. Because of this unpredictability, it is always easier to reason in terms of event time in stateful pipelines.

Examples

To help you understand the Stateful Sessionizer, we're going to implement a sessionization job with Apache Spark and arbitrary stateful processing. The key part of the implementation is the method in Example 5-25.

Example 5-25. Stateful mapping in PySpark

```
grouped_visits = (visits_from_kafka.withWatermark('event_time', '1 minute')
  .groupBy(F.col('visit_id')))

visited_pages_type = ArrayType(StructType([StructField("page", StringType()),
  StructField("event_time_as_ms", LongType())]))

sessions = grouped_visits.applyInPandasWithState(
  func=map_visits_to_session,
  outputStructType=StructType([
    StructField("visit_id", StringType()), StructField("user_id", StringType()),
    StructField("start_time", TimestampType()),
    StructField("end_time", TimestampType()),
    StructField("visited_pages", visited_pages_type),
    StructField("duration_in_milliseconds", LongType())]),
  stateStructType=StructType([StructField("visits", visited_pages_type),
    StructField("user_id", StringType())]),
  outputMode="update", timeoutConf="EventTimeTimeout"
)
```

The logic presented in Example 5-25 starts by defining the expiration column (event_time) and the grouping key (visit_id). Next, it calls a stateful mapping function composed of the following:

- The function with the stateful logic (func)
- The structure of the session written to the output location (outputStructType)
- The structure of the pending session interacting with the state store (state StructType)

- The output mode that configures the output generation to the updated rows (outputMode)

- The session expiration configuration based on the event time (timeoutConf)

As you can see, this is a purely declarative part of the code. The real generation and accumulation logic is present in the map_visits_to_session function. You can get a high-level view of it in Example 5-26. The code first detects whether the session state has timed out. If it has, the code aggregates the accumulated values into the final format. I'm omitting that part here for brevity's sake but you can retrieve it in the GitHub repo (*https://oreil.ly/Ef4ZF*). If the state is still active, the code applies the accumulation logic explained next.

Example 5-26. Session generation logic: high-level view

```
def map_visits_to_session(visit_id_tuple:Any, input_rows:Iterable[pandas.DataFrame],
    current_state:GroupState) -> Iterable[pandas.DataFrame]:
  session_expiration_time_10min_as_ms = 10 * 60 * 1000
  visit_id = visit_id_tuple[0]
  # ...
  visit_to_return = None
  if current_state.hasTimedOut:
    visits, user_id, = current_state.get
    visit_to_return = get_session_to_return(visits, user_id)
    current_state.remove()
  else:
    # ... accumulation logic

  if visit_to_return:
    yield pandas.DataFrame(visit_to_return)
```

Now comes a two-part accumulation logic. You can see the first part in Example 5-27. It's responsible for detecting the base time for the state expiration. Since the watermark will be missing in the first job iteration, the code uses either the event time or a watermark.

Example 5-27. Expiration base time detection

```
should_use_event_time_for_watermark = current_state.getCurrentWatermarkMs() == 0
base_watermark = current_state.getCurrentWatermarkMs()
new_visits = []
user_id: Optional[str] = None
for input_df_for_group in input_rows:
  input_df_for_group['event_time_as_ms'] = input_df_for_group['event_time'] \
    .apply(lambda x: int(pandas.Timestamp(x).timestamp()) * 1000)
  if should_use_event_time_for_watermark:
    base_watermark = int(input_df_for_group['event_time_as_ms'].max())
# ... visits accumulation, omitted for brevity
```

Why might using the event time every time not be the best idea, despite the fact that it greatly simplifies the code logic? Relying on a watermark is a better approach here since it's related to the job progress and thus the `.withWatermark('event_time', '1 minute')` operation. To help you understand this better, let's take a look at Table 5-4, where the watermark-based and event time–based expiration strategies are shown for a watermark of one minute.

Table 5-4. Event time and watermark expiration strategies for a job with 1-minute watermark and 10-minute state expiration

State key	Event time	Expiration times	New watermark
A	10:00	Watermark: 10:10 Event-time: 10:10	09:59
A	10:01	Watermark: 10:09 Event-time: 10:11	10:00
A	10:08	Watermark: 10:10 Event-time: 10:18	10:07
B	10:15	Watermark: 10:17 Event-time: 10:25	10:14

Table 5-4 shows state accumulation for two keys, A and B. As you can see, A is active for eight minutes, and according to the watermark expiration strategy, it could be emitted right after processing the first element of the state B (10:10 < 10:14). However, that's not the case with the event-time strategy as the expiration time is beyond the new watermark (10:18 > 10:14).

Just after this expiration section comes the second part of the logic. Example 5-28 shows the function that interacts with the state store to load the previous state and update the in-flight session with the new expiration time.

Example 5-28. State and expiration time update

```
visits_so_far = []
if current_state.exists:
  visits_so_far, user_id, = current_state.get
visits_for_state = visits_so_far + new_visits
current_state.update((visits_for_state, user_id,))

timeout_timestamp = base_watermark + session_expiration_time_10min_as_ms
current_state.setTimeoutTimestamp(timeout_timestamp)
```

The example relying on the session window is much simpler, so let's see how to define it with Apache Flink. Example 5-29 shows the transformation section that starts with the code extracting the session key. Next, the code configures the session window with the 10-minute gap duration and an allowed lateness of 15 minutes. The last parameter defines how late the events that are going to be integrated into the already emitted session windows can be. In the end, the `VisitToSessionConverter` converts all records from the window into the final output structure.

Example 5-29. Session window with Apache Flink

```
sessions: DataStream = (visits_input_data_stream
  .key_by(VisitIdSelector())
  .window(EventTimeSessionWindows.with_gap(Time.minutes(10)))
  .allowed_lateness(Time.minutes(15).to_milliseconds())
  .process(VisitToSessionConverter(), Types.STRING()).uid('sessionizer'))
```

The full snippet is available in the GitHub repo (*https://oreil.ly/4WFJW*).

Data Ordering

Data transformation resulting from data aggregation and combination is not the only valuable property with which you can enhance your dataset. Another one is order (for example, events delivered chronologically to your downstream consumers). That's why the last data value patterns you're going to see are about ordering. Even though this feature is often reduced to an `ORDER BY` clause in SQL, ordered data delivery is challenging. It provides chronology that is important for many use cases, especially those requiring real-time data insight. Imagine a car fleet tracking system that doesn't respect the order of the cars' positions on the road. You will likely see cars jumping over buildings or swimming across rivers instead of following their ordered and real positions on the roads. Depending on your data store, you will likely be providing the ordering guarantee via one of two available patterns.

Pattern: Bin Pack Orderer

One of the nightmares for ordered data delivery at scale is partial commits. Some databases provide a *bulk* API to write multiple items at once and consequently optimize network communication. However, this feature may come with partial commits. In other words, you can get a fully successful, partially successful, or fully failed request. The first and last outcomes are fine, but the second, unfortunately, may break the ordering within your dataset. Despite these challenging semantics, there is a solution.

Problem

Your blogging platform from the use case enables external websites to embed your pages. The visit events generated by these embeddings are arriving in your system, and you're processing them as your own events. Besides keeping them internally, you need to expose them from an external API to external websites for analytics purposes.

The project is reaching the last stage, and you need to write the synchronization job to feed the external API storage. To optimize the cost, the job must be common for all partners. It has to create a processing time window of 10 minutes with per-minute aggregates, and in the end, it must flush the buffer to different outputs provided by partners. The events must be delivered individually for each minute and provider, and in event time order.

Unfortunately, the API ingestion storage is a streaming broker with partial commit semantics. You need to be particularly careful while implementing the ordering logic to overcome any issues related to retries.

Partial Commits

Beware of partial commits. Unlike classical ones, where only two states (success and failure) are possible, they have one more state for partial failure. In that state, the database manages to ingest only a subset of records.

Why can this partial mode break the ordering? Let's take a look at an example of records timestamped with 10:00, 10:10, and 10:20. The database can write all, two, one, or none of them. The two scenarios in the middle are risky because there is no way to know which records have not been delivered and when they will succeed. For example, if only 10:20 has been written, you'll need to retry 10:00 and 10:10, which will leave you with writing that's out of order.

Although this issue is most visible on streaming systems, ordering semantics can also be important for data-at-rest stores, where a temporarily partially empty dataset can trigger some downstream processing on top of disordered data.

You'll find this partial commit semantic in the PutRecords API from Amazon Kinesis Data Streams, the BatchWriteItem from AWS DynamoDB, and the bulk operation from Elasticsearch.

Solution

You can solve the problem if you deliver each record individually. However, that implies significant network overhead as you'll need to initialize as many requests as there are records. You can mitigate the issue by relying on the bulk operations that together with the Bin Pack Orderer pattern can guarantee ordered delivery in the context of partial commits.

The implementation follows two important steps. The first step is responsible for grouping all related events and sorting them. Typically, you'll implement it as a sort by grouping key and event time operation.

The result will be records sorted within the same entity. Next, you need to pack those rows in bins individually (i.e., you need to group events of different entities sharing the same position together, in the same bin). That way, you create isolated subsets that you can deliver through a bulk API without worrying about completeness, duplicates, and more importantly, partial commits. The process is summarized in Figure 5-9.

The workflow follows the steps from the previous paragraph:

1. First it sorts the records by their grouping key and time.

2. Then, the algorithm places the sorted rows into delivery bins so that there is only one grouping key in each bin. The bins can be arrays or lists in your programming language.

3. Finally, the workflow emits bins sequentially. If there is any retry within the delivery bin, it remains local to the group. Put differently, it doesn't interfere with the ordering for the retried grouping key because there is only a single occurrence per bin. The next bin isn't delivered as long as the current one is not fully written to the output.

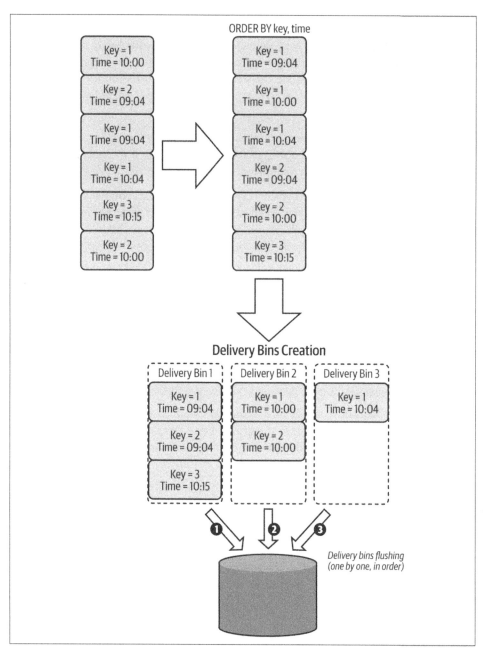

Figure 5-9. Bin packer records delivered with three bulk requests

Consequences

As you might have guessed, the pattern looks great for the ordering guarantee, but if your compute runtime is not adapted, some items may still be out of order. Let us explain.

Retries. The pattern guarantees ordering inside the same execution. If your whole pipeline fails, then the retry will involve already emitted results. Consequently, the overall ordering will be broken despite the fact that you're using the pattern.

Complexity. The bin packer is definitely more difficult to implement than a classical sort. It requires a custom sorting and bin creation logic, whereas performing classical sorting is just a matter of calling an appropriate sorting function.

Examples

Let's see how to implement the pattern with Apache Spark and Amazon Kinesis Data Streams. First, the preparation step uses a local sorting mechanism. The locality consists of partitioning the dataset in each task individually, without involving the network exchange (see Example 5-30).

Example 5-30. Bin packer preparation step

```
(events.sortWithinPartitions([F.col('visit_id'), F.col('event_time')])
  .foreachPartition(lambda rows: write_records_to_kinesis(...))
```

The Bin Pack Orderer pattern sorts the input rows by visit_id and later, inside each group, by event_time. Therefore, prepared rows are later processed via the write_records_to_kinesis method demonstrated in Example 5-31.

Example 5-31. Bin Pack Orderer for Amazon Kinesis Data Streams

```
def write_records_to_kinesis(output_stream, visits_rows):
  producer = boto3.client('kinesis')
  delivery_groups = []
  groups_index = 0
  last_visit_id: Optional[str] = None
  for visit in visits_rows:
    if visit.visit_id != last_visit_id:
      last_visit_id = visit.visit_id
      groups_index = 0
    if len(delivery_groups) <= groups_index:
      delivery_groups.append([])
    delivery_groups[groups_index].append(visit)
    groups_index += 1
```

As you can see, the code in Example 5-31 iterates all input rows and puts each of them into a dedicated bin, as long as the `visit_id` doesn't change. If it does, the bin's position is reset to 0. After this preparation step comes the delivery, group by group, to the Kinesis output stream. I'm omitting the code for brevity's sake because it's a simple iteration over the groups. Instead, you can view it in the GitHub repo (*https://oreil.ly/Uoo76*).

Pattern: FIFO Orderer

The Bin Pack Orderer is a pattern that keeps data stores in proper order with partial commit semantics and optimizes throughput thanks to bulk operations. However, there is a simpler alternative that can be good for use cases that don't require low latency or a large volume of data.

Problem

One of your streaming jobs runs on top of the visits dataset. It needs to detect a subset of particular events and forward them in processing order to a different stream. The requirement is to deliver each record as soon as possible, so any buffering to optimize the network traffic is not an option.

Solution

Buffering and bulk requests help reduce network overhead in data transmission. However, in environments with more relaxed delivery constraints, you may want to consider a simpler alternative, like the FIFO Orderer pattern.

The implementation is more straightforward than the one for the Bin Pack Orderer. It doesn't require any specific sorting algorithm since the requirement is to send data in the *first in, first out* (FIFO) manner. Instead, it only detects the records and issues the delivery request. An important thing is to get the delivery acknowledgment for each record before proceeding to the next one. Otherwise, it may lead to issues of data being out of order or lost.

The pattern can be implemented with either an API delivering one record at a time or a bulk API with its concurrency level set to 1. In the first implementation, you'll find AWS Kinesis Data Streams' PutRecord API or Apache Kafka's `send(...)` function followed by a synchronous `flush(...)` invocation.

Also, though it may sound surprising at first, you can use the pattern with a bulk API, but only for data stores that support full commit semantics. Here, the only requirement is to avoid too many bulk requests being sent at once, which may lead to data being out of order if the data store fails to write one of them. If you use Apache Kafka, you can achieve this by setting the `max.in.flight.requests.per.connection` to one or by using the idempotent producer feature that accepts up to five concurrent requests and still guarantees correct ordering.

In-Flight Requests

Using in-flight requests is a great way to optimize throughput. With them, the producer can issue the delivery request for the first bulk API and then, without waiting for the server's response, create and deliver the next one. However, this can also break the ordering. For example, if only the second of two in-flight requests succeeds and the first is retried, the ordering between them will be broken.

Consequences

The pattern's simplicity is appealing, but you shouldn't consider it for all use cases involving FIFO delivery.

I/O overhead and latency. The biggest drawback of this simple implementation, despite the possibility of using bulk API under some conditions in some data stores, is the I/O overhead and resulting increased latency. Instead of sending one network request for many records, the FIFO Orderer pattern sends one request for each input row.

This overhead leads to increased latency as the data store and data producer must handle requests individually. The problem will be particularly visible if you have a lot of data to deliver and a monitoring dashboard to observe the number of delivered records and records to deliver per minute.

You can slightly reduce this impact by leveraging multithreading, meaning by issuing the individual requests from multiple processes of your producer. The only problem is guaranteeing the ordering between these processes because remember, they're isolated and not aware of each other. A good strategy here is to create scopes of ordered records. Put differently, if you need to guarantee the ordering for an entity such as a user or product, you can allocate all records of that entity to the same process. This looks similar to bins, except that each container stores all the records of the same entity and delivers each of them individually from the asynchronous process.

FIFO is not exactly once. Don't get this wrong: FIFO stands only for delivering the oldest records first, and it doesn't guarantee the exactly-once delivery by itself. Let's see why in Example 5-32.

Example 5-32. Snippet showing challenges with exactly-once delivery

```
fifo_messages_to_deliver = ....
for message in fifo_messages_to_deliver:
  producer.send(message)
  consumer.ack(message)
```

Example 5-32 shows what a naive implementation of exactly-once delivery with the FIFO Orderer might look like. First, the producer sends the message, and soon after, the consumer acknowledges it so that the event is not processed again. However, even after a successful send(...), the subsequent ack(...) call can fail. As a result, the exactly-once guarantee will be broken after the code restarts because the producer will try to send already delivered records.

To mitigate this issue, you'll need to rely on one of the idempotency patterns from Chapter 4.

Examples

How do you implement the FIFO Orderer with Apache Kafka? Example 5-33 shows the most basic implementation, in which a producer delivers each record individually.

Example 5-33. FIFO Orderer with individual records delivery

```
producer.produce(...)
producer.flush()
```

It's pretty easy, isn't it? You produce a record, flush the buffer immediately, and wait for the broker to perform the write. But as you know already, it'll be costly in terms of network traffic because you will send one record at a time. Can you do better, then? Yes, there is an alternative with bulk requests, shown in Example 5-34.

Example 5-34. FIFO Orderer with bulk requests

```
producer = Producer({
  'max.in.flight.requests.per.connection': 1,
  'queue.buffering.max.ms': 1000
})
producer.produce(...)
```

Example 5-34 shows an approach that's different from the one in the previous example. It doesn't perform the flush(...). Instead, it delegates the bulk request generation to the producer, who is asked to buffer the records for at most one second. Also, to avoid the issue of concurrent writes, the concurrency flag is set to 1. This approach is indeed more efficient than individual delivery, but the single concurrency flag may still be a slowness factor. To optimize that part, you can use the idempotent producer configuration from Example 5-35.

Example 5-35. FIFO Orderer with idempotent producer

```
producer = Producer({
  'max.in.flight.requests.per.connection': 5,
  'enable.idempotence': True,
  'queue.buffering.max.ms': 2000
})
producer.produce(...)
```

Example 5-35 uses Apache Kafka's idempotent producer,[2] which accepts up to five concurrent requests and still guarantees ordering. The configuration also increases the buffering time so that there is a greater chance to fill the buffer and issue more bulk requests to the broker.

Unfortunately, you may not always have a chance to leverage the bulk API for the FIFO delivery. It won't be possible on data stores with partial commit semantics, where you'll have to rely on individual requests. That's the case with AWS Kinesis Data Streams, where, to guarantee correct ordering, you have to use the PutRecord API and set the SequenceNumberForOrdering as does the code in Example 5-36.

Example 5-36. Using SequenceNumberForOrdering in AWS Kinesis Data Streams

```
records_to_deliver = [...]
previous_sequence_number = None
for record in records_to_deliver:
  put_result = client.put_record(StreamName=..., Data=...,
    SequenceNumberForOrdering=previous_sequence_number)
  kinesis_client.put_record(record)
  previous_sequence_number = put_result.sequence_number
```

---

2 The idempontent producer was introduced as a part of KIP-98 (*https://oreil.ly/4cyCw*).

Without this `SequenceNumberForOrdering` property, Kinesis may put the records in rough order. Another cloud streaming service, GCP Pub/Sub, also has a built-in ordering guarantee mechanism, but it works only within the same producer writing to the single region. Besides, the feature requires setting an `ordering_key` attribute (see Example 5-37).

Example 5-37. Using `ordering_key` for GCP Pub/Sub

```
records_to_deliver = [Record(data=..., ordering_key="a"),
  Record(data=..., ordering_key="b"), Record(data=..., ordering_key="c"),
  Record(data=..., ordering_key="a")]
previous_sequence_number = None
for record in records_to_deliver:
  publisher.publish(..., data=..., ordering_key=record.ordering_key)
```

Example 5-37 shows the `ordering_key` attribute. As you can see, unlike the `Sequence NumberForOrdering`, it's more of a grouping key used by Pub/Sub's publisher to ensure all records sharing it are delivered in the FIFO manner.

Summary

In this chapter, you discovered common ways to increase the value of your dataset. Generally, two improvement scenarios are possible:

- When you add information to the input data
- When you reduce the information to make it more understandable

In the first scenario, you can use the data enrichment and data decoration patterns. Data enrichment patterns are a great candidate for combining datasets. You saw that this is possible not only for homogeneous pipelines but also for heterogeneous ones, where streaming meets the batch world. When it comes to data decoration patterns, you learned about two approaches to annotating raw records. The first approach wraps the input data and computes extra attributes separately, which is a great way to introduce data consistency in terms of data representation. Additionally, in the second approach, you can hide these extra attributes with the hidden metadata layer if they are not relevant to end users.

In the second scenario, information is reduced with the goal of making the data more understandable. Here, the data aggregation patterns work in a distributed or local environment. In addition, this is the place where you'll be able to summarize your users' experience with Sessionization patterns that are adapted to incremental batch workloads or real-time streaming pipelines.

Finally, you learned about two solutions to preserve correct order in data ordering patterns. The Bin Pack Orderer shows how to address this requirement in the context of data stores with partial commit semantics. The second pattern, FIFO Orderer, is an alternative that sacrifices network exchange for simplicity.

But your journey doesn't stop here. You've already learned how to ingest data and generate value with data value patterns supported by error management and idempotency patterns. However, there is still one point missing: how do you connect them all? The good news is that the next chapter is all about that topic!

## CHAPTER 6

Data Flow Design Patterns

Generating business value from raw data enables a fact-based decision process, and the data value design patterns from Chapter 5 will help you create this smart process. However, at this stage of our exploration of data engineering design patterns, the generated data insight remains local to you. It is indeed beneficial, but what if I tell you that you can create even more benefits by opening it up to a much wider scale than just local?

For example, you might expose one of your valuable datasets to other teams within the organization to enable them to enrich their local use cases and consequently increase their data value assets. It works the opposite way too, as other teams could share their valuable datasets that would increase the value of your data! Although this sounds like a data value patterns family, there's a different set of rules to apply. That's why you'll retrieve them as data flow design patterns.

The goal of data flow design patterns is to design and coordinate all steps required to generate a dataset. This involves actions like chaining various tasks in a pipeline, creating parallel or exclusive execution branches, or even managing the dependency of physically separated pipelines.

Data flow design patterns operate at two different levels. The first level is data orchestration, where they work in one or many data pipelines. This is particularly useful when you want to address the cross-teams collaboration issue. The second level is the data processing layer, which is the environment of your job. Here, data flow design patterns help to better organize business logic to make it more obvious and easier to maintain over time.

How can you achieve all that with data flow design patterns? First, with sequence patterns, you can coordinate tasks or pipelines within a single pipeline or across many pipelines. In the next section, you'll see how to enhance pipelines with two other types of patterns. The first of them, fan-in, handles the merge situation where one step depends on many others. The second category does the opposite, meaning it creates two or more branches from the same task. Finally, you will discover orchestration patterns that you can leverage to manage the concurrency of your pipelines.

Curious to see the patterns? Let's get started!

Sequence

The first category of patterns that you'll inevitably encounter while designing data flows concerns the sequence of steps. This is an important factor that will impact the complexity, performance, and maintenance of the pipelines. An example here is a data processing job writing the processed dataset to multiple places. If you represent it as a single unit in your workflow, whenever you need to replay only the loading part for one of the databases, you'll have to restart the whole execution. The patterns from this section will show you how to address this issue.

Pattern: Local Sequencer

The first design pattern from this section is probably the easiest one as it orchestrates tasks locally (i.e., within the same pipeline or data processing job).

Problem

You're in charge of one of the oldest jobs in your data analytics department. Over the years, the codebase has grown from dozens to hundreds of lines, and the number of transformations has increased three times. The job itself fails very often, and each time, it must start again from the beginning, leading to long debugging journeys.

You were tasked with simplifying the code and improving daily maintenance. Unfortunately, you can't remove any business logic.

Solution

A good software engineering practice to simplify complex logic consists of decomposing it into smaller and therefore more approachable steps. This is also valid for data engineering, where reorganization improves readability and also highlights the separation of concerns. That's where the Local Sequencer pattern shines.

The end goal is to decouple one big component into multiple smaller but connected items that will be run sequentially (i.e., one after another). The dependency between tasks should be organized according to the dataset dependencies. For example, if task B needs the data generated by task A, then the sequence should be defined as B executing after A completes. To help you understand this better, let's think about a full data ingestion and the patterns covered in Chapter 2.

To implement the ingestion, you'll need to create two tasks: one implementing the Readiness Marker pattern to determine whether the data is there and another using the Full Loader pattern to physically load the data. (We discussed both patterns in Chapter 2.) As you can see in Figure 6-1, you can implement them either as dependent tasks (with data orchestration layer dependency) or as a single task (with data processing layer dependency).

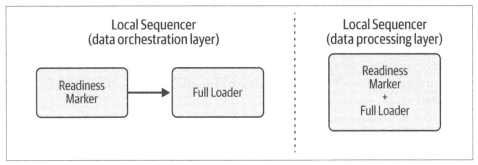

Figure 6-1. Local Sequencer versus single task

The following three criteria should help you decide whether the sequence should be based on the data orchestration layer or the data processing layer:

Separation of concerns

Putting all operations in the same item can make things harder to understand. A good indicator here is naming difficulty. If you struggle to find the name or if the name is too long in your opinion, this may be an indicator that you put too many operations into the single task on the data processing layer.

Maintainability

Relying on data processing sequentiality is also challenging for maintenance. In cases of backfilling or automatic retries, you will recompute all successful tasks prior to the failed one. For example, if your readiness check involves calling 10 paid APIs and you need to restart a job that failed three times, you'll quickly see the cost increase if you include the API call to your job.

Implementation effort

The data orchestrator may provide different abstractions to perform common tasks out of the box, such as running a SQL query or executing an API call. If you combine all tasks into a single unit, you won't be able to leverage this facility and you'll probably need to reinvent the wheel.

Consequences

Even though the tips we've presented thus far can be helpful, they may not guarantee a perfect organization from day one. For that reason, defining boundaries remains a challenge, among many others presented in the following sections.

Boundaries. If you define boundaries incorrectly, execution time may grow too much or even impact other pipelines if you can't scale the scheduler in your data orchestration logic. It's therefore important to find a good balance between the scope and the number of tasks.

A good rule of thumb that applies to both the data processing layer and the data orchestration layer is to think about restart boundaries (i.e., what are the tasks that should be able to restart individually?). In our data ingestion example, the Readiness Marker and Full Loader tasks should fail individually and shouldn't impact each other. Put differently, the Readiness Marker shouldn't run if the loading step fails.[1] The loading execution already implies the presence of data.

Regarding the data processing job, you'll often put the boundary between the most compute-expensive operations. For example, if generating an intermediary dataset before transforming it into the final one is costly, you might put the separation line there in your job. Thanks to this, whenever your final transformation fails, you won't need to execute this costly intermediate dataset generation at each retry.

Besides the restart boundaries, you can also reason for the logic separation in terms of transactions. If two or more operations must be performed as a single unit, it makes sense to keep them together. An example of thisis the data processing job implementing the Dynamic Late Data Integrator pattern (code available on GitHub (*https://oreil.ly/dl9y3*)), which, besides processing the data, also updates the last processed version in the state table. The processing logic and the processed version storage depend on each other, so it makes sense to execute them as a single unit.

Examples

Giving an example of the Local Sequencer is relatively easy. Both the libraries for data orchestration and the data processing layers used in this book provide native abstraction to chain tasks. Let's start with Apache Airflow, meaning the orchestration part. Combining tasks consists of using the >> sign to express the dependency because the left side must run before the right one. The code in Example 6-1 shows this.

---

1 This assumes immutable data at the source. If the producer can remove the dataset, you should of course run the Readiness Marker step again.

Example 6-1. Local Sequencer in Apache Airflow

```
input_data_sensor >> load_data_to_table >> expose_new_table
```

If you needed to translate the snippet from Example 6-1 into a human language, you could say, "The pipeline starts by waiting for the data to be available. Once this condition is met, the next task loads the input data into an internal table. Later, the last task exposes the internal table to the end users." But I hope you agree with me that Airflow's language is more concise!

The same concise implementation is available in other orchestrators, including the cloud ones. If you use AWS EMR to run your data procesisng jobs, you can use the Step API to add tasks to run one after another. Example 6-2 shows the last two tasks from Example 6-1 implemented as sequential steps of the cluster.

Example 6-2. Local Sequencer with AWS EMR

```
aws emr add-steps --cluster-id j=cluster_id --steps Type=Spark,Name="Spark Program",
  ActionOnFailure=TERMINATE_CLUSTER,Args=[--class com.waitingforcode.DataLoader]
aws emr add-steps --cluster-id j=cluster_id --steps Type=Spark,Name="Spark Program",
  ActionOnFailure=TERMINATE_CLUSTER,Args=[--class com.waitingforcode.DataPublisher]
```

An important thing here is the dependency configuration on failure. As you can see, the code asks to terminate the cluster in case of any task failure. Otherwise, you could introduce some inconsistency by exposing partial data and considering the job to be successful. Such configuration is not required for Apache Airflow, which by default enables sequential processing based on the success of the upstream job (i.e., one task can't advance as long as its parent didn't succeed).

Besides the data orchestration, the pattern also works at the data processing level. You can express it in SQL or a programmatic API, like Python for PySpark. The idea here is to consider each previously defined variable as an input for the next step, until you reach the data writing stage. Example 6-3 shows that while there is no explicit chaining argument, the usage remains intuitive.

Example 6-3. Local Sequencer with PySpark and programmatic API

```
input_dataset: DataFrame = spark_session.read...
valid_and_enriched_dataset_to_write: DataFrame = input_dataset..
valid_and_enriched_dataset_to_write.write...
```

> **More Than CRON**
>
> The Local Sequencer pattern shows the power a data orchestrator has compared to a simple CRON expression when it comes to building advanced processing logic. However, a CRON expression can still be a valid solution if you have an isolated use case that doesn't require any dependencies.

Pattern: Isolated Sequencer

Often, the pipelines implementing the Local Sequencer are not the final steps. Instead, they are part of a more complex workflow where multiple isolated workflows must collaborate to generate the final insight. Here, although the rules may sound similar, there are completely different triggering conditions and constraints.

Problem

Your team is responsible for cleaning and enriching raw datasets to expose them as various views used in a data visualization tool. After the technical meeting with the data visualization team, you agreed that it's not a good idea to include the dashboards dataset transformation directly in your data preparation pipeline, as your team won't be responsible for that part. Instead, the data visualization team asked you to provide the cleansed and enriched dataset only. The data visualization team will handle the transformation on its own.

Solution

The problem statement introduces two pipelines where one provides data to another. However, due to organizational separation, it's not possible to merge them into a single process. That's the perfect scenario in which to use the Isolated Sequencer pattern.

The objective here is to find a way to combine physically isolated pipelines. As with the Local Sequencer, the most important concern is the identification of boundaries. The easiest solution consists of dividing the pipeline in terms of consumers and providers, or teams. If your team provides the dataset to a different team, then naturally, you can draw a boundary to create two isolated pipelines.

On the other hand, you may also face a situation in which you are the provider and a consumer at the same time. This may happen when the processed dataset is used by other pipelines within your team's scope to generate other datasets. To define boundaries in that context, you can analyze the complexity of the pipeline. If combining all producer and consumer logic in a single place makes things unreadable, you should consider splitting it into multiple pipelines following the producer and consumer approach. Otherwise, you might prefer to keep them together and thus use the Local Sequencer pattern.

Defining boundaries is only the first step, though. The second step consists of finding the triggering mechanism. There are two strategies here: data based and task based.

The data-based strategy is based on the Readiness Marker pattern from Chapter 2. In other words, the data producer generates the dataset and a marker file to indicate it's ready for processing. The consumer listens for this marker file and starts the work as soon as it detects the creation.

In the task-based strategy, the data producer doesn't create a marker file. Instead, it directly triggers the pipeline responsible for consuming the generated dataset. As you can see, the two approaches have different couplings and shared responsibilities:

- Pipelines from the data-based solution are loosely coupled, meaning there is more room for evolution. The only requirement is to respect the marker file. On the other hand, the pipelines that form the task-based solution are tightly coupled. This means that, albeit physically separated, they can't live alone. This is particularly visible on the data producer side because a simple task or pipeline renaming operation on the consumer side will make the whole dependency chain fail, since the producer will try to trigger a task that doesn't exist anymore.

- This brings up another topic: which side can change? In the data-based approach, the dataset consumer has more freedom. It can even decide to use a different dataset without notifying the data provider. On the other hand, in the task-based strategy, the consumer can't simply decide to skip the dataset as the producer has the direct trigger mechanism. If the dataset is removed, the producer's pipeline can fail.

Figure 6-2 summarizes both approaches.

As you'll notice, the data-based dependency approach relies on the presence of the dataset generated by the data provider pipeline. The consumer leverages the Readiness Marker pattern to start its pipeline as soon as the data is there. On the other hand, the task-based dependency approach shown on the bottom considers the dataset to be a local asset of the data provider. In that case, the provider directly triggers processing on the data consumer side with a dedicated task. That can be a good approach if there is no shared dataset (for example, when the consumer must send some notification to the users instead of working on the provider's data).

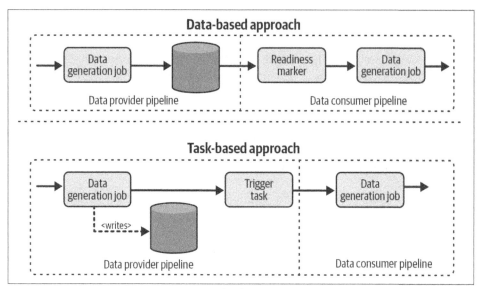

Figure 6-2. Two strategies to implement the dependencies between two pipelines

Consequences

As you've already learned in the Solution section, the biggest challenge is to keep all the pipelines in sync. Plus, the biggest drawback of the pattern is that by adding some logical isolation, it also adds an extra operational constraint.

Scheduling. The task-based solution doesn't impact just the evolution part. It also involves something important, which is the scheduling frequency. Ideally, the two pipelines should share the same schedule so that the producer can directly trigger the consumer. If that's not the case, one of them will need to introduce more complexity.

If it's the producer, it will need to add a condition to skip the triggering part for some of the planned execution schedules. If it's the consumer, it'll have to do the same but by adapting its schedule to the producer and running the physical data processing only when needed.

Communication. The Isolated Sequencer addresses pipelines managed by different teams, among other things. That may be a problem if the organization doesn't have a good communication culture.

And it's not easy to overcome this issue. Either as a producer or as a consumer, you can add a mechanism that checks if the condition on the other side didn't change. That requires a lot of effort and may even be impossible to implement if the other side doesn't accept any incoming connections for security reasons!

A more resilient approach requires more effort and time. It involves an organizational change to make communication efficient. Each isolated team must be aware of its inputs and outputs, so that it can effectively communicate with all dependent parties planning work, particularly the one introducing any breaking changes. You may be the catalyst of this evolution, but the implementation goes far beyond the technical aspect of your work.

Examples

But let's remain in the code and see now how to implement the data-based and trigger-based solutions with Apache Airflow. The data-based approach relies on the same waiter components (sensors) as the Readiness Marker pattern. The first example from this section shows two dataset-dependent pipelines.

Example 6-4 demonstrates an implicit dependency between the `devices_loader` and `devices_aggregator` pipelines. The `input_data_sensor` from the `devices_aggregator` is a kind of dependency enforcer. If it fails, this means the data provider couldn't deliver the data as agreed before. However, there is no way to know whether the two pipelines are interdependent.

Example 6-4. Dataset dependency for the Isolated Sequencer

```
# devices_loader
@task
def load_new_devices_to_internal_storage():
  ctx = get_current_context()
  partitioned_dir = f'{devices_file_location}/{ctx["ds_nodash"]}'
  internal_file_location = f'{partitioned_dir}/dataset.csv'
  shutil.copyfile(input_devices_file, internal_file_location)

input_data_sensor >> load_new_devices_to_internal_storage()

# devices_aggregator
input_data_sensor = FileSensor(
 task_id='input_data_sensor',
 filepath=devices_file_location + '/{{ ds_nodash }}/dataset.csv',
)
input_data_sensor >> load_data_to_table >> refresh_aggregates
```

Data Lineage

An important component in complex data system is the data lineage tool you use to represent dependencies between datasets. In our example, you could use it to see what datasets or pipelines are consuming the `devices_loader`'s output. Chapter 10 covers two data lineage design patterns. You can also learn more about the lineage from OpenLineage,[2] which is an open source standard supporting major data tools used nowadays.

Implicitness is not the case for the next, trigger-based example. Example 6-5 shows two dependent pipelines that use `ExternalTaskMarker` and `ExternalTaskSensor` operators, respectively, instead of data dependencies. The sensor is there to represent the consumer pipeline waiting for the data provider's task execution. The marker automates backfilling, and the marker task detects any backfilling made on the `devices_loader` pipeline and automatically runs it locally.

Example 6-5. Trigger-based dependency for the Isolated Sequencer

```
# devices_loader
success_execution_marker = ExternalTaskMarker(
 task_id='trigger_downstream_consumers',
 external_dag_id='devices_aggregator',
 external_task_id='downstream_trigger_sensor',
)
(input_data_sensor >> load_new_devices_to_internal_storage()
  >> success_execution_marker)

# devices_aggregator
parent_dag_sensor = ExternalTaskSensor(
 task_id='downstream_trigger_sensor',
 external_dag_id='devices_loader',
 external_task_id='trigger_downstream_consumers',
 allowed_states=['success'],
 failed_states=['failed', 'skipped']
)
parent_dag_sensor >> load_data_to_table >> refresh_aggregates
```

Fan-In

The two previous patterns involve a sequence, meaning steps that follow each other in a particular order. But data pipelines are not that simple every time. Often, they create branches that eventually merge again at some point. This point is where the fan-in patterns family gets involved.

---

2 To get started with OpenLineage, visit the official website (*https://openlineage.io*).

Pattern: Aligned Fan-In

The easiest fan-in pattern to explain is the Aligned Fan-In. It simply assumes that all direct parent tasks must succeed before continuing.

Problem

Your pipeline generates a daily aggregate of your blog visits from raw visit events. However, the dataset is partitioned by the hour as that organizational logic fits most of the use cases within your organization.

It doesn't make sense to process the pipeline daily on your own as the consumers of your dataset are interested in the full view only. However, you would like to leverage the hourly partitioning to avoid too much data being processed in a single job.

Solution

The use case introduced previously involves a dependency between multiple parent tasks and one task that runs after them. To solve this dependency at either the data orchestration layer or the data processing layer, you can use the Aligned Fan-In pattern.

The implementation is rather straightforward for the data orchestration. It involves defining separate branches that merge into a common task. In our example, these branches represent data processing jobs generating partial aggregates for each hour of the day. Once all are completed, the merge task takes these hourly results to compute the final output for each day. As a result, your orchestration layer generates a flow like the one presented in Figure 6-3.

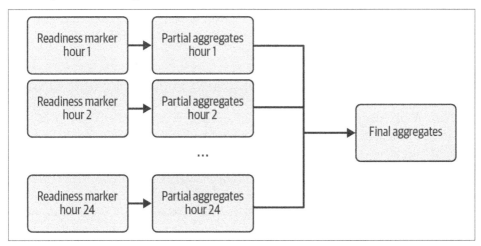

Figure 6-3. Aligned Fan-In in the example of partial aggregates

However, things are not that simple when it comes to the data processing layer. Here, you still have to define the branches, but additionally, you must define how they interact with each other. The best way to understand this is to use SQL operations.

The first interaction outcome will be a single data processing abstraction produced by multiple outputs. In this context, you will use the UNION operator and get a dataset with more rows but the same number of columns. An alternative is the JOIN operation, which will combine the datasets row-wise, thus adding extra columns. The JOIN approach will always store fewer rows than the UNION-based solution. You can think of them as vertical (UNION) and horizontal (JOIN) alignments.

A big advantage of the Aligned Fan-In pattern is the feedback loop optimization. Let's take a look at our partial aggregates schema from Figure 6-3 to understand this better. If you don't leverage the pattern and there is an issue in the processing for the last hour, the pipeline will return an error, probably by the end of the run since it's processing one day of data. On the other hand, with decoupled logic, you might have 24 smaller jobs that would work on smaller volumes of data simultaneously and as a result return the issue faster.

Besides this feedback loop, there is another advantage related to failure. If only the last of the 24 hours fails, as is the case in our example, you only need to fix and replay this hour. Therefore, without the Aligned Fan-In pattern and with a single big data processing task for the 24 hours, you would need to process the other 23 hours too. Also, as you've probably noticed, in this pattern, you'll use the separation logic based on the ease of backfilling, as was the case with the Local Sequencer pattern.

Consequences

By now, we've probably convinced you that decoupling can be beneficial for your pipelines. However, despite this positive impact, the Aligned Fan-In pattern has some gotchas.

Infrastructure spikes. One drawback of the Aligned Fan-In pattern is the infrastructure load. As you can see in the problem statement, our daily aggregation job will run 24 jobs simultaneously. That shouldn't be an issue if you have elastic provisioning capacity. If you don't, you'll need to find a good balance and reduce the allowed concurrent runs to some smaller number.

An alternative approach to reducing the concurrency is to run branches as soon as possible, in a fully incremental way. For our 24 hourly branches, this would mean running each branch hourly and aggregating the results only in the last run of the day.

Scheduling skew. Since the child tasks require all parents to be successfully executed, having unbalanced execution time for the parents will lead to a scheduling skew.

When that happens, all the successful tasks will wait for the slowest one. As a result, the child task's triggering time depends on the longest parent tasks.

Scheduling overhead. Longer parent tasks aren't the only things that can be problematic. You must also be aware that pipelines that are too granular also involve scheduling overhead. The data orchestrator will need to allocate most of their resources to schedule and coordinate tasks. However, that's the price you must pay if you want to decouple and improve readability.

Complexity. The more you decouple, the longer the pipeline you will create. This may lead to some negative effects like reduced readability and understanding. Unfortunately, there is no one-size-fits-all solution, so you must identify correct boundaries for each pipeline individually.

Questions this chapter raises that may help you are "What tasks belong to a single unit of execution?" and "What operations should be backfilled individually?"

Examples

What about examples? First, let's see how to implement the Aligned Fan-In with Apache Airflow, meaning at the data orchestration layer. The implementation leverages the dynamic character of pipeline creation. As you can see, Example 6-6 defines the pipeline sequence only once. However, the definition is inside a for loop. Apache Airflow will interpret this declaration, create a dedicated task for each iteration, and connect them to the common clear_context parent task.

Example 6-6. Aligned Fan-In in Apache Airflow

```
clear_context = PostgresOperator(...)
generate_trends = PostgresOperator(...)

for hour_to_load in [f"{hour:02d}" for hour in range(24)]:
 file_sensor = FileSensor(
  task_id=f'wait_for_{hour_to_load}',
  filepath=input_dir +'/date={{ ds_nodash }}/hour=' + hour_to_load+'/dataset.csv'
)
 visits_loader = PostgresOperator(
  task_id=f'load_hourly_visits_{hour_to_load}',
  params={'hour': hour_to_load}
 )

 clear_context >> file_sensor >> visits_loader >> generate_trends
```

If you have a static list of tasks, you can also declare all tasks located at the same level with "[...]," (for example, [load_data_1, load_data_2] >> process_data). This is more verbose but also more readable as the connection between branches and the common child task is explicit.

In addition to the data orchestration level, you can implement the pattern at the data processing level. A great operation representing the Aligned Fan-In is UNION. As its name indicates, it combines two separate datasets into a single one so that you can apply one transformation on top of it. Example 6-7 shows an example for PySpark.

Example 6-7. UNION in PySpark

```
input_dataset_1: DataFrame = ...
input_dataset_2: DataFrame = ...
output_dataset = input_dataset_1.unionByName(input_dataset_2)
```

PySpark has an interesting solution for dealing with one of the trickiest parts of the UNION operation. By default, UNION is position based, meaning that you can combine incompatible fields, though this will result in an error (see Example 6-8).

Example 6-8. Position-based error

```
SELECT a, b, c FROM abc
UNION
SELECT c, b, a FROM cba
```

The operation in Example 6-8 will result in an incompatible dataset with a + c, b + b, and c + a combined. To mitigate this issue, Apache Spark provides a unionByName method that combines the datasets by column name rather than by position. It's not that popular, though, so be aware of it when you use the default UNION implementation in SQL or other data processing tools.

Pattern: Unaligned Fan-In

Sometimes, having a condition that all the parents must succeed can not only add some latency but can also be semantically wrong. Therefore, you may need a variation on the Aligned Fan-In pattern.

Problem

Your hourly-based processing of visits aggregates with the Aligned Fan-In pattern has been working great for several weeks. However, the implementation lacks a proper method for managing failed tasks.

A few times, an hour hasn't been correctly processed, and you therefore haven't produced the aggregated views for your downstream consumers. After a meeting, you agreed that it would be better to release even a partial dataset and fill the gaps later.

You're looking now for a solution that will help you evolve the pipeline based on the Aligned Fan-In pattern.

Solution

The solution consists of relaxing the dependency on the parents' outcome and transforming the Aligned Fan-In pattern into the Unaligned Fan-In pattern.

With this pattern, a child task can run even when when some of the parents don't succeed. This enables different scenarios:

- If some parents succeed and the remaining failures are acceptable, you can trigger the child task anyway. Consequently, you may be working on a partial input that will lead to the partial dataset problem, as in the problem statement.

- If all the parents fail, instead of running the task based on the success criteria, you can schedule a task based on the failures criteria. For example, the task could be a fallback or error management task.

To implement the pattern, you'll need to configure the trigger conditions that are available in your data orchestration tool. In Apache Airflow, you'll rely on the `trig ger_condition` attribute and set it to one of the available states. In less declarative environments, you may need to explicitly evaluate the parent tasks' outcomes.

Consequences

Although the Unaligned Fan-In pattern shares the drawbacks of the Aligned Fan-In, it also adds new ones.

Readability. The Unaligned Fan-In pattern may decrease the readability and general understanding of the data flow. This is particularly visible when you add two types of downstream tasks, one executed when all parents succeed and another to execute when there are some failures. Your pipeline will be confusing as you will not be able to easily determine the execution flow without going into code (see Figure 6-4).

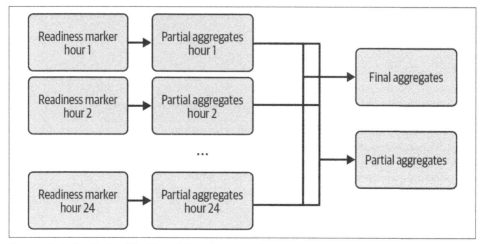

Figure 6-4. Confusing Unaligned Fan-In example

To mitigate this issue it is always better to check if the data orchestration tool provides custom functions to handle the "other" scenario. When it comes to dealing with errors, Apache Airflow has an `on_failure_callback` function to manage any failed invocation, while AWS Step Functions supports this with a `Catch` field type where you can trigger a failure handler directly.

Partial data.   If you decide to generate the dataset from partially successful parents, it's important to share this fact with the consumers of the dataset. Otherwise, they may make incorrect assumptions about the completeness status.

There are different ways to achieve this. The simplest way is to store the completeness metric in a completeness table that's a companion to the generated dataset and then do some math. For example, if only 12 of 24 parents succeed, then data will be complete at 50%; if only 6 succeed, it'll be 25%, etc. Another way is to add this information to the metadata layer (e.g., as tags for objects written in cloud object storage). You can also complete this static information with a notification shared with downstream consumers (for example, via an email).

You can also decide not to share the partial dataset but instead keep it private. In that case, you will need to determine the completeness first and write the results to an internal table or folder if the completeness status is not 100%.

Examples

If your data orchestration solution lets you define outcome dependencies between tasks, the Unaligned Fan-In implementation should be easy. After all, it's just a matter of using the correct trigger configuration. Example 6-9 shows how to do this for Apache Airflow.

Example 6-9. Triggering condition for the Unaligned Fan-In in Apache Airflow

```
clear_context = PostgresOperator(...)
generate_cube = PostgresOperator(
 # ...
 trigger_rule=TriggerRule.ALL_DONE
)

for hour_to_load in [f"{hour:02d}" for hour in range(24)]:
file_sensor = FileSensor(
  task_id=f'wait_for_{hour_to_load}',
  filepath=input_dir +'/date={{ ds_nodash }}/hour=' + hour_to_load+'/dataset.csv'
)
visits_loader = PostgresOperator(
  task_id=f'load_hourly_visits_{hour_to_load}',
  params={'hour': hour_to_load}
)

 clear_context >> file_sensor >> visits_loader >> generate_cube
```

Example 6-9 is identical to Example 6-6, except for one little detail: the `trig ger_rule`. By default, Apache Airflow starts a task only if all its parents succeed. Here, the pipeline uses a different condition. It simply expects all parent tasks to complete, regardless of the outcome. That's a pretty easy way to express the dependencies, isn't it? The only problem is that the rule remains hidden in the code, and you won't see it if you analyze the pipeline graph visually.

In addition to this purely orchestration-related change, the pipeline == includes a new flag for the output table. The flag marks a given row as approximate if the number of processed hours for the day is different from 24 (see Example 6-10).

Example 6-10. Approximate flag computation in SQL

```
INSERT INTO dedp.visits_cube (...,is_approximate)
SELECT ...,
 (SELECT CASE WHEN hours_subquery.all_hours = 24 THEN false ELSE true END FROM
  (SELECT COUNT(DISTINCT execution_time_hour_id) AS all_hours FROM dedp.visits_raw
    WHERE execution_time_id = '{{ ds }}')
 AS hours_subquery)
FROM dedp.visits_raw GROUP BY CUBE(...);
```

The code in Example 6-10 uses a subquery to determine whether the table is based on complete or incomplete input data.

AWS Step Functions is a serverless data orchestration offering on the public cloud and also an example of a less declarative implementation of the Unaligned Fan-In pattern. To demonstrate this, we're going to use three `lambda` functions (see Example 6-11).

Example 6-11. Returned elements of lambda functions

```
# lambda-partitions-detector
def lambda_handler(event, context):
 # ...
 partitions_to_process = []
 return partitions_to_process

# lambda-partitions-processor
def lambda_handler(event, context):
  # ...
 processing_result: bool
 return processing_result

# lambda-table-creator
def lambda_handler(event, context):
 table_metadata = {}
 if False in event['ProcessorResults']:
  table_metadata['is_partial'] = True
 # ...
 return True
```

Example 6-11 shows the three functions used in the Step Functions workflow. The first one detects new partitions to process, and it has only one occurrence. The second one is defined as a `Map` task in the workflow. It runs individually for each of the items returned by the `lambda-partitions-detector` and generates a boolean flag to mark the processing as successful or failed. The last function, `lambda-table-creator`, takes all the `processing_result` flags and detects whether there were any errors in processing. If there were, it annotates the table with an `is_partial` attribute. The full code of the workflow is available in the GitHub repo (*https://oreil.ly/KJeUt*), and I'm omitting it here to stay focused on the less declarative part of the implementation.

Fan-Out

So far, you have seen pipelines that always merge into a common task. But we're still missing the last type, in which one task is the input for others. This approach can be useful when one dataset is used by multiple teams for different purposes, such as data analytics or data science.

Pattern: Parallel Split

In the first fan-out pattern, one parent task is a requirement for at least two child tasks. They can run in parallel because their logic is isolated and the single common point is the same parent requirement.

Problem

You're about to replace a legacy data processing framework written in the C# programming language, which nobody in your organization knows anymore. All the maintainers left the company without leaving any useful documentation. You've performed a reverse-engineering step, and now, you are rewriting the logic with a modern open source Python library. At this point, you need to migrate the pipelines, but since your reverse-engineering approach may not be perfect, you prefer to keep the old pipelines running until their consumers have to switch to the new solution. Therefore, during the migration, you'll need to write the processed dataset in two different places.

Solution

The problem states that two different operations depend on a common parent task. That's the type of situation in which you should use fan-out patterns. The first of them is the Parallel Split pattern, and as the name indicates, it breaks the work into parallel parts.

The implementation on top of the data orchestration layer is straightforward. It relies on the data flow definition API that can use a dedicated domain-specific language (DSL) or high-level programming abstractions, like functions.

The Parallel Split also applies to the data processing world, but the implementation is not that simple as it involves several points to keep in mind. First, the split processing shouldn't trigger separate data reading operations. Instead, all common computations should run only once. You can achieve this by materializing the intermediary dataset with either a temporary table in SQL or a .persist() method in Apache Spark.

Next, you need to ensure that the parallel branches don't interfere with each other. Therefore, if your codebase uses any global and shared variables, they should either be read-only or have modifications that are compatible across all writing processes.

Finally, if your computation is execution time sensitive, you should allocate dedicated compute resources or define the auto-scaling to accommodate the split workload in parallel.

Consequences

The hardware problems from the Solution section are valid concerns, but there are even worse things that might happen. Let's see which ones.

Blocked execution. This drawback is valid for the data orchestration layer and time-dependent pipelines, where each execution runs only if the previous one succeeded. As you may have already guessed, in the case of a Parallel Split, the triggering condition will be based on the slowest branch created in the Parallel Split pattern. Put differently, each pipeline will have to wait for the slowest branch to complete. If there are failures, the consequences will be even worse as the subsequent executions will not run at all.

If there is such a risk, you might consider exporting the slow branch to a dedicated pipeline whose execution will be conditioned on one of the trigger rules presented in the Isolated Sequencer pattern, namely, the dataset- or task-based dependency.

Hardware. Let's return to the data processing layer. If the main job needs to generate an intermediary dataset for two other jobs, then they should have the same hardware expectations. For example, if one of them is CPU heavy and another is memory heavy, you won't be able to use the adapted infrastructure.

To mitigate the issue, you'll need to divide this job as you did when solving the problem stated in the Local Sequencer pattern, by generating the intermediary dataset and later starting the parallel jobs on their dedicated hardware. Figure 6-5 shows this operation in a schema.

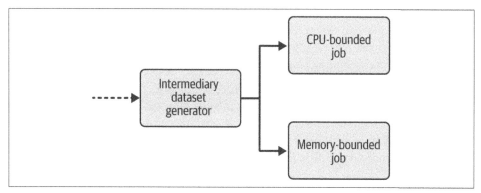

Figure 6-5. Splitting a job working on the same base dataset but requiring different compute capacity (dashed arrow indicates previous tasks in the pipeline not relevant to this example)

Examples

How should you implement the Parallel Split pattern? In the examples you've seen up until now, you can leverage the DSL capabilities. First, let's take a look at Apache Airflow (see Example 6-12).

Example 6-12. Parallel Split in Apache Airflow

```
file_sensor = FileSensor(#...
 task_id='input_dataset_waiter')

for output_format in ['delta', 'csv']:
 load_job_trigger = SparkKubernetesOperator(# ...
```

```
  task_id=f'load_job_trigger_{output_format}',
  params={'output_format': output_format}
)
load_job_sensor = SparkKubernetesSensor(#...
  task_id=f'load_job_sensor_{output_format}')

file_sensor >> load_job_trigger >> load_job_sensor
```

Example 6-12 uses the same model as the examples of the fan-in patterns. However, there is a subtle difference in the end of the sequence that doesn't end with a common task. Instead, the single common point is the first sensor operation (file_sensor).

The data processing layer also supports the Parallel Split. Even though the implementation is also straightforward, you must keep in mind one thing. You're going to apply a different processing logic on top of the same input dataset, so it's enough to read it only once! To achieve this in Apache Spark, you must call the persist() function for the read dataset (see Example 6-13).

Example 6-13. Caching the input dataset in PySpark

```
input_dataset = (spark_session.read
  .schema('type STRING, full_name STRING, version STRING').format('json')
  .load(DemoConfiguration.INPUT_PATH))
input_dataset.persist(StorageLevel.MEMORY_ONLY)
input_dataset.write...
input_dataset.write...
```

This code memorizes the read dataset in memory. If you're worried about not having enough capacity in RAM, you can also configure the function to store the dataset in memory and eventually on disk, if all available space is taken.

Besides this caching aspect, you may also want to avoid writing the data twice in case of retries. Multiple executions will increase the dataset volume but also may introduce data quality issues, such as duplicates. But the good news is that some data formats have protections against the retried writes. That's the case with Delta Lake, in which you can leverage the txnVersion and txnAppId options (see Example 6-14).

Example 6-14. txnVersion and txnAppId with Delta Lake

```
batch_id = 1
app_id = 'devices-loader-v1'

input_dataset.write.mode('append').format('delta')
 .option('txnVersion', batch_id).option('txnAppId', app_id)
 .save(DemoConfiguration.DEVICES_TABLE))

(input_dataset.withColumn('loading_time', functions.current_timestamp())
  .withColumn('full_name',
```

```
    functions.concat_ws(' ', input_dataset.full_name, input_dataset.version))
  .write.mode('append').format('delta')
  .option('txnVersion', batch_id).option('txnAppId', app_id)
  .save(DemoConfiguration.DEVICES_TABLE_ENRICHED))
```

If, for whatever reason, you need to replay the code from Example 6-14 multiple times, it'll physically write the data for the first run only. Since the values for the `txnVersion` and `txnAppId` properties don't change, all subsequent runs will be ignored. If this write deduplication feature is not natively available in your tool, you can still leverage one of the data idempotency design patterns from Chapter 4.

Pattern: Exclusive Choice

The second fan-out pattern also relies on a common parent, but instead of running parallel downstream tasks, it chooses only one.

Problem

The migration you performed with the Parallel Split pattern works perfectly. Now, you need to evolve the pipeline and start executing the new job version on January 1, 2024, only. In case of backfilling, prior days should still run the previous job. You want to make this evolution without creating a new pipeline to keep the full execution history.

Solution

As you can see from the problem statement, there are still two child tasks, but this time, only one should run at a time. These are great conditions in which to use the Exclusive Choice pattern.

The implementation is pretty similar to the Parallel Split as it consists of declaring at least two downstream processes. For their definition, you can still rely on the DSL of the data orchestrator or the functions of your programming language.

Things then change one step before branching. Instead of declaring downstream tasks directly after the last common point, you should add a condition evaluator task to decide which path to follow next.

All modern data orchestration frameworks, such as Apache Airflow (which is open source) and serverless cloud offerings (AWS Step Functions and Azure Data Factory) come with built-in support for condition evaluations with branching. Apache Airflow does it with a dedicated task type, which is a *branch operator*. When it comes to the cloud offerings, Azure Data Factory, for example, implements the Exclusive Choice pattern with an *if condition activity*.

Figure 6-6 shows the pipeline from the problem statement adapted to the Exclusive Choice pattern.

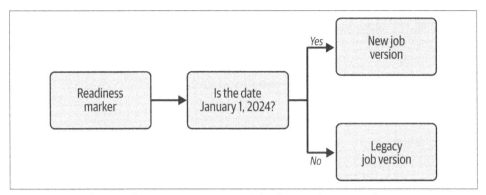

Figure 6-6. Exclusive Choice pattern on top of the data orchestration layer

In addition to the data orchestration layer, it's possible to use the Exclusive Choice pattern in the data processing layer. The implementation is even simpler since you'll inevitably use the `if-else` or `switch` statements from the programming language of your compute layer.

Consequences

The greatest danger posed by the pattern comes from its flexibility. You can add as many branches as you want, and having a large number of branches will pretty quickly degrade understanding of the pipeline.

Complexity factory. Since it's not uncommon to see applications with multiple if-else statements, it may be tempting to repeat this practice in the data orchestration layer. However , in that context, multiple conditions mean multiple execution branches that eventually merge together or split even more. Your components will then become barely readable.

There is no single accepted threshold for if-else conditions, though. To find out if there is something wrong, you can try to explain the pipeline to an imaginary friend who has joined your project recently. If the explanation is not concise and leads to lots of questions and answers, the pipeline may be too complex.

Rubber Duck Debugging

The method of explaining things to an imaginary friend is also known as *rubber duck debugging*. Even though it's often presented as a debugging method, you can use a similar approach to analyze complexity.

Hidden logic. This applies to the data processing implementation. If your job includes conditional statements and branches, possibly generating different datasets or interacting with different output data stores, this can become problematic in the future.

Often, you'll remember and understand the code for a few days or weeks after you write it. Then, over time, you'll write more code, solve other problems, and probably forget that this particular job has many possible outcomes.

For that reason, it can be better to apply the Exclusive Choice pattern on top of the data orchestration layer too for a given pipeline. That probably sounds confusing, so let's take a look at Example 6-15.

Example 6-15. Conditional execution in the data processing layer

```
if condition_a:
  process_condition_a()
else:
  process_default()
```

If your code does what the code in the example does, then you have two choices. Either you can trigger the job directly and delegate condition evaluation to the processing layer, or you can evaluate the condition in the data orchestration layer and, depending on the outcome, invoke a different entry point, as in Example 6-16.

Example 6-16. Conditional execution in the data orchestration layer

```
if condition_a:
  python job_for_condition_a.py
else:
  python job_for_default.py
```

Heavy conditions. If you implement the pattern in the data processing layer and your condition needs to process the data, be aware that this will impact the execution time of the job. For that reason, it's always better to prefer metadata-based conditions, which are faster to run as they don't interact with the dataset.

When you can't avoid processing the data, optimize this step as best you can. Ensure that you don't process it many times and that there is a way to implement an incremental processing that doesn't read the whole dataset each time.

Examples

First, let's see how to implement the Exclusive Choice pattern on top of the data orchestration layer, in our case, with Apache Airflow. Previously, you have seen how to parallelize the work just by declaring the pipeline's sequence multiple times. Unfortunately, this technique won't work for the Parallel Split. Instead, you need to rely on a `BranchPythonOperator` that will route the execution to the correct branch (see Example 6-17).

Example 6-17. Conditional router for the Exclusive Choice pattern in Apache Airflow

```
def get_output_format_route(**context):
 migration_date = pendulum.datetime(2024, 2, 3)
 execution_date = context['execution_date']
 if execution_date >= migration_date:
  return 'load_job_trigger_delta'
 else:
  return 'load_job_trigger_csv'

format_router = BranchPythonOperator(
 task_id='format_router',
 python_callable=get_output_format_route,
 provide_context=True
)
```

Example 6-17 shows a router implementation based on the execution date. As you can see, it generates CSV files or a Delta Lake table, depending on the execution date. Although the example includes two routes, you can always add more. However, keep in mind that more is not always better because it might make your pipeline less readable. For that reason, instead of branching, you could simply create another pipeline with the `start_date` and `end_date` parameters to control the time validity.

Additionally, the pattern also works in the data processing layer. It may come in one of two flavors. The first one comes from an external configuration, and you can see it in Example 6-18.

Example 6-18. The Exclusive Choice implemented as job parameters in PySpark

```
class OutputType(str, Enum):
 delta_lake = 'delta'
 csv = 'csv'

parser = argparse.ArgumentParser(prog='...')
parser.add_argument('--output_type', required=True, type=OutputType)
args = parser.parse_args()

output_generation_factory = OutputGenerationFactory(args.output_type)

spark_session = output_generation_factory.get_spark_session()
raw_data = (spark_session.read...)

output_generation_factory.write_devices_data(raw_data, args.output_dir)
```

Example 6-18 shows a batch job that, depending on the output_type input parameter, generates a Delta Lake table or a set of CSV files. But wait, where is this logic? Here, we're leveraging software engineering (SWE) design patterns and, more specifically, the Factory pattern.[3] In a nutshell, this specific design pattern hides the creation logic behind an interface, which is the single element exposed to the user. In our case, the OutputGenerationFactory is such an interface and, at the same time, the class responsible for generating correct objects to the expected input (see Example 6-19).

Example 6-19. SWE Factory design pattern supporting the Exclusive Choice in PySpark

```
class OutputGenerationFactory:

  def __init__(self, output_type: OutputType):
   self.type = output_type

  def get_spark_session(self) -> SparkSession:
   if self.type == OutputType.delta_lake:
    return (configure_spark_with_delta_pip(SparkSession....)
   else:
    return SparkSession.builder...getOrCreate()

  def write_devices_data(self, devices_data: DataFrame, output_location: str):
   if self.type == OutputType.delta_lake:
    devices_data.write.format('delta')...
   else:
    devices_data.coalesce(1).write...format('csv')...
```

As you can see in Example 6-19, the client code receives a different SparkSession and the write action is selected automatically, based on the output type argument. The only drawbacks here are the conditions repeated in each method. That's fine for our simple example, but it might not be for your use case. The good news is that you can avoid them with dedicated classes for Delta Lake and CSV writers returned by the factory, instead of particular functions.

In addition to the external parameters, you can rely on the dataset characteristics to control the execution flow (see Example 6-20).

Example 6-20. The Exclusive Choice pattern driven by a schema change

```
input_dataset = ...
input_schema = detect_schema(input_dataset)
output_location = DemoConfiguration.DEVICES_TABLE_LEGACY
```

---

3 You can learn more about this and other patterns from the Refactoring Guru website (*https://oreil.ly/PW-j8*) and *Design Patterns: Elements of Reusable Object-Oriented Software*.

```
if len(input_schema.fields) >= 3:
 output_location = DemoConfiguration.DEVICES_TABLE_SCHEMA_CHANGED
```

This example adapts the job to the input schema of the file. If it has at least three fields, the job writes it to a new location. If not, it's considered as a legacy table. Here, we're relying on the metadata layer to get this information, and as you already know from Chapter 4, metadata operations are often much faster than data operations. However, since you can use anything as the conditions, including the data, you should be aware that it may be more costly.

Orchestration

So far, you have only been organizing individual flows alongside their internal and external dependencies. At this stage, they are simple static resources sitting on top of your data orchestration layer. With the last family of patterns, they will become dynamic components running data processing tasks.

Pattern: Single Runner

The data orchestrator must run each of the declared pipelines. The question is, how? The first pattern is the most universal one, but this universality comes with some runtime costs. Let's see which ones.

Problem

In your most recent project, you implemented the sessionization pipeline with the Incremental Sessionizer pattern from Chapter 5. Since it was a proof of concept (POC), the orchestration was not in the scope. To validate the sessions with your business owners, you have been running the job manually, on demand. As the project is about to enter into the release cycle, you need to work on the data orchestration.

You already have the pipeline graph but are still looking for a way to execute it.

Solution

The solution is simple: you need a runner! The sessionization problem involves incremental, thus sequential, execution. As a result, you cannot run more than one pipeline at a time.

The Single Runner pattern ensures there is always a single execution of a given pipeline. The implementation consists of configuring the concurrency level of the data flow, and this can be easily achieved with Apache Airflow and Azure Data Factory, thanks to their configuration-driven approach. Both orchestrators support a concurrency attribute that can be set to 1 if you want to always run at most one occurrence at a time.

If the native capability is not supported, you might need to implement a Readiness Marker pattern that will be waiting for the previous execution to complete. A small gotcha here is that the solution doesn't prevent the triggering of future runs that will all be waiting for their predecessors to complete before processing the data.

Consequences

The limited concurrency does make sense from a logic standpoint. However, it may have some important implications in the daily life of the pipeline.

Backfilling. The limited concurrency probably will not be problematic as long as you don't need to backfill. However, if you do, then reprocessing will be very slow because of the sequential character of the pipeline. Unfortunately, there is not a lot you can do since the single concurrency is a business requirement that cannot be relaxed. In other words, if you run multiple pipelines in parallel, the results will be wrong.

The only thing you can do is to see whether you really need to backfill the whole pipeline each time. For example, if your data flow is composed of data processing and data loading steps, and if you only need to insert a generated dataset into a different location after changing your configuration, then you can avoid the data processing part.

Latency. Backfilling is the worst-case scenario for the Single Runner pattern. A less serious case is one with stragglers, in which some pipelines run slower than others. Let's take a look at an example of an hourly scheduled data flow. Usually, the execution of all tasks takes 30 minutes, but recently, it increased to 1.5 hours. As you can see, data will be increasingly delayed. And the consequences can be very serious. Not only will your pipeline get slower and slower, but all your downstream consumers will also suffer from this extra latency.

This shouldn't be the most common scenario, though. You can always mitigate it, assuming that you're running your workloads on scalable infrastructure, by adding more compute power or improving the processing logic.

Examples

Now, let's take a look at some examples. The first one is an Apache Airflow pipeline that compares the current day's data with the previous day's data. You can already see the sequential dependency between the steps, which would be broken if you ran multiple simultaneous executions in case of backfilling. How should you enforce this order? As with many other things, you do it with the configuration (see Example 6-21).

Example 6-21. Concurrency limits in Apache Airflow

```
with DAG('visits_trend_generator', max_active_runs=1, default_args={
  'depends_on_past': True,
  # ...
```

Example 6-21 configures the concurrency with the `max_active_runs` and `depends_on_past` properties. The first attribute determines how many concurrent pipelines are allowed. Here, as the logic relies on the sequential execution, the value must be 1. The `depends_on_past` attribute applies to each task and enforces execution upon success of the previous run. Put differently, if task A from the previous run fails, the same task for the current run won't start.

You can also control the concurrency cluster-wise. The aforementioned AWS EMR service not only provides steps to control the execution order but also provides the `StepConcurrencyLevel` parameter to determine how many jobs can run in parallel on a cluster.

The concurrency limits are present in data orchestration services on the cloud too. For example, if you create an Azure Data Factory pipeline, you can configure the concurrent executions with the `Concurrency` setting. However, the feature has some gotchas. While Apache Airflow won't schedule a new run if there is one active, Data Factory will create them and store them in a bounded queue that supports up to 100 concurrent runs. The service will still schedule other runs, but if the queue is full, the scheduling action will return a 429 error, which stands for "Too many requests."

Pattern: Concurrent Runner

The backfilling and latency issues of the Single Runner pattern can be easily addressed with the next pattern. All you need to do is relax the concurrency constraint.

Problem

You're on the data ingestion team, and your goal is to bring data from external at-rest sources to your internal database as soon as possible. Usually, the ingestion frequency goes from 30 minutes to 1 hour, but sometimes the whole process takes longer. Since it's running with the Single Runner pattern, all subsequent deliveries are delayed. You're wondering whether sequential execution is required, because the loaded datasets are not dependent on each other.

Solution

The datasets ingested by your team are independent. That means you can ingest in any and therefore with a relaxed concurrency constraint. This is where you can use the Concurrent Runner pattern.

The implementation is rather simple. It consists of defining a concurrency that's higher than 1. However, with great power comes great responsibility. You need to strike a proper balance that will take other pipelines into account in the context of your infrastructure.

Once this concurrency step is defined, the data orchestrator will pick the next pipeline execution available for scheduling as long as the currently running instances don't reach the allowed maximum concurrency level.

Consequences

Running multiple pipelines at the same time may have some important impacts, especially if your concurrency level is too restrictive.

Resource starvation. This is particularly true if you work in a multitenant environment (i.e., if when your orchestrator is used by many different teams). If a bunch of pipelines have a pretty high concurrency level and they run backfilling at the same time, the scheduler may not have enough capacity to start other pipelines.

The best way to handle this is with concurrency control of the pipelines with the *workload management feature.* This consists of allocating a specific compute capacity to a group of users running their pipelines. That way, even if a team sets the allowed concurrency to a very high level, it won't be able to use more capacity than the threshold assigned in the workload.

Resource starvation may not be an issue for serverless orchestrators, which often offer a pretty high concurrency level. For example, as of this writing, AWS Step Functions allows up to 10,000 parallel child workflow executions.

Shared state. The shared state is a pretty common gotcha for everything that allows concurrent execution. If the pipeline works on a shared component, concurrent and therefore nondeterministic execution can be a source of many problems due to unexpected side effects. One example could be the Dynamic Late Data Integrator pattern from Chapter 4, in which concurrent runs could at best trigger backfilling multiple times or, at worst, not trigger it at all for some execution dates.

Examples

The concurrent execution example is straightforward. You simply need to configure allowed concurrency to a value of more than 1 (see Example 6-22).

Example 6-22. Concurrent orchestration in Apache Airflow

```
with DAG('devices_loader', max_active_runs=5,
  default_args={
```

```
 'depends_on_past': False,
# ...
```

Although the example defines `depends_on_past` as `False`, you can change this value if particular tasks should depend on their prior executions. That won't affect the concurrency configuration, but it might prevent the pipeline from moving when it encounters a task with failed past execution.

This flexibility level doesn't exist in all data orchestrators, though. In Azure Data Factory, which we introduced in the previous section, you can define the concurrency and also trigger-based dependency but not task-based dependency.

Summary

In this chapter, you learned different ways to organize data flow dependencies. First, we discussed sequences. There, you saw two patterns you can use to coordinate a workflow, either at a local level with the Local Sequencer or globally with the Isolated Sequencer. Using a good approach here will help you define the pipeline boundaries to keep them readable and maintainable.

In the next section, you discovered fan-in patterns. Their purpose is to merge isolated execution branches, and using them is a great way to parallelize the work of isolated parts of a pipeline. Depending on your business constraints, you can use the aligned or unaligned versions. The former requires all parallel branches to succeed, whereas the latter relaxes this constraint and is a good candidate for generating partial results.

At the opposite end of the spectrum from fan-in patterns are fan-out patterns that create the branches. They also come in two flavors. The Parallel Split pattern starts two or more branches from a single task. Put differently, the output of one task is the input for many other tasks that can be isolated on purpose due to hardware or business reasons. An alternative to this simultaneous execution is the Exclusive Choice pattern that follows only one of the many declared branches, a little bit like the code you write for if-else statements.

In the last section, you saw two different orchestration patterns. The first of them was the Single Runner, whose goal is to always run one instance of the pipeline at a time. That's crucial for incremental data processing, in which the current instance's logic depends on the previous instance's output. On the other hand, you have the Concurrent Runner. As the name implies, it allows multiple instances to run in parallel. It's a good candidate for accelerating isolated executions (for example, during backfilling).

But your responsibilities as a data engineer don't stop there, at defining data flow. There is another, maybe even more important aspect: data security. The next chapter will show you data engineering design patterns that should help you approach this essential area.

## CHAPTER 7

Data Security Design Patterns

Undoubtedly, the easily accessible and valuable datasets we've created so far with the data value and data flow design patterns are important business assets. They are also objects of envy for other market actors, including malicious ones.

Consequently, data engineering can't stop at writing data processing jobs. Nowadays, data engineers also need to think about the security aspects. One aspect that has received enormous traction over the last few years is compliance. Data privacy laws, such as the General Data Protection Regulation (GDPR) in Europe or the California Consumer Privacy Act (CCPA) in the US, define precisely the boundaries between you (the data provider) and a customer (the data consumer).

Another important aspect is access control. Imagine that your dataset is open within your organization and a different team accidentally overwrites it. The consequences for you and downstream consumers can be huge.

Data protection is another important security aspect. Even if you accidentally give access to a dataset location, such as a table or a path in the file system, it doesn't mean the user will be able to read the data. If you used an extra protection layer, such as encryption, the consumer would also need the decryption key to access the dataset.

Finally, data security also concerns connections. You, as either a human or an application user, will need to connect to a data store to read and write your work's outcome. Clearly, storing credentials in your Git repository increases the data leak risk and is therefore not the best idea. Instead, you should store them in an external and safer place.

It all may sound scary, but no worries. The design patterns presented in this chapter will address the introduced issues and give you some real-world application use cases. This chapter starts with the data removal patterns that show how to comply with users' right to be forgotten in your datasets. Next, you're going to discover fine-grained access patterns for tables and cloud resources. After that comes the data protection patterns that secure datasets with encryption and anonymization techniques. Finally, you're going to see two approaches that address the connectivity issue. One will use references instead of real credentials, while another will rely on identity-based access.

Hopefully, you now feel ready to start exploring the first category, data removal!

Data Removal

Privacy regulations, such as the CCPA and the GDPR, define several important compliance requirements. One of these important requirements focuses on personal data removal requests, in which you must delete a user's data upon receiving a removal request from the user. In this first section, you're going to see two possible implementation approaches that address this issue.

Pattern: Vertical Partitioner

Smart data organization or workflow isolation can often solve even the most challenging problems. This rule applies to the first data removal pattern.

Problem

You recently presented the first design doc for a new personal data removal pipeline. Your peers were very enthusiastic, but some of them pointed out an important storage overhead. Several of the columns of your dataset are immutable. Put differently, they never change, but at the same time, they're present in each record. Examples of these attributes are the birthday or personal ID number.

In their feedback, your peers asked you to store each immutable property only once. As a result, you'll have less data to delete in case of a data removal request.

Solution

The announced problem implies dividing the dataset into two parts, a mutable one and an immutable one. This is where the Vertical Partitioner pattern helps.

In data engineering, you can partition a dataset horizontally or vertically. Horizontal partitioning puts all the records with related attributes together. Some of the most frequent examples of this are date-based partitions, which are often used in batch jobs for incremental data processing. You're going to discover this storage approach in Chapter 8.

Vertical Works with Horizontal

You can combine vertical partitioning with horizontal partitioning and group related but split parts of a record in the same storage zone.

An alternative to horizontal partitioning is vertical partitioning. This approach splits each row and writes the parts into different places. The attribute-based division can help you implement an efficient personal data removal pipeline.

The first step consists of identifying the columns to split and an attribute that you will use to merge the split rows again. After this preparation step, you need to adapt your data ingestion job by adding the attribute-based split logic. This logic will divide a row into two parts and write each of them into a separate storage space. Figure 7-1 shows this logic, in which event attributes with values that are different with each new record are delivered to a separate storage, while the unchanging ones and those related to the personal data scope are written to a different place.

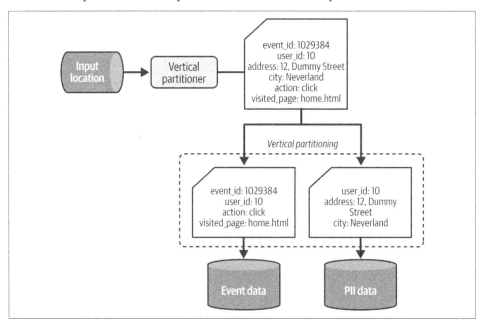

Figure 7-1. Vertical Partitioner extracting and writing PII and immutable attributes to a dedicated storage (note that user_id is the field a consumer can later use to merge the split rows)

The easiest way to implement the split is to use the SELECT statement or an equivalent attribute projection method in a data processing framework. That way, you issue multiple queries, each of which targets a different set of columns and writes the result to a dedicated data store. Eventually, each query can have some business rules, such as deduplication.

When it comes to the personal data removal request, the solution considerably reduces the amount of data to remove. The private attributes being repeated in each record are now written only once. Consequently, the removal process has less data to process. It should be less expensive from both the computational perspective and the financial perspective than a removal from nonpartitioned storage. Finally, thanks to this fully separated storage layer, you can apply different data access or data retention rules.

Consequences

Unfortunately, despite being a good performance optimization technique for the data removal use case, the Vertical Partitioner pattern has some drawbacks for consumers.

Query performance. Vertical partitioning introduces a kind of data normalization in which immutable properties live apart from mutable ones. This optimizes write performance by reducing volume, but it also reduces read performance as each reader will need to join split rows. Any reading operation will then involve network traffic, while normally, for the nonpartitioned version, at the row level, the reading would remain local.

Querying complexity. Data separation also brings some extra complexity to queries. Consumers will be aware that some properties may be located in a different place. Thankfully, it's pretty easy to mitigate this issue by exposing the dataset from a single entry point (such as a view) by providing data documentation (for example, with data catalogs), or by clearly exposing the data lineage (cf. "Pattern: Dataset Tracker" on page 321).

Complexity in a polyglot world. Another challenge affects the polyglot persistence world, where one dataset lives in different kinds of storage (such as NoSQL databases and relational databases) at the same time. Polyglot persistence is great for readers, as it exposes a given record in technology that's adapted to the consumers. For example, a search engine feature would like to leverage a search-optimized database, while a low-latency microservice might need to get the same record but very quickly from a key-value store. As a consequence, you may need to apply this vertical partitioning across different storage systems, including multiple data removal pipelines.

A solution for that is depicted in Figure 7-2, where a job splits each row, and later, dedicated consumers process the split result according to their expected storage layer.

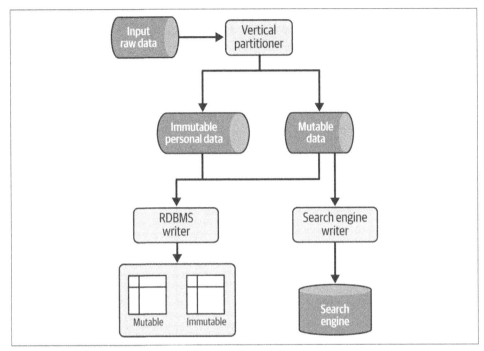

Figure 7-2. Polyglot persistence with vertical partitioning

Raw data. If you need to keep the raw (not divided) data for some time, you'll need a complementary solution to deal with data removal. The Vertical Partitioner pattern applies only from the first data transformation step.

An easy solution would be to use a short retention period for the unsplit data if it complies with the data removal request delay. However, that can reduce data availability for backfilling purposes.

Examples

Now, let's see how to implement the Vertical Partitioner with Apache Kafka, Apache Spark, and Delta Lake. The first part consists of the job that splits the incoming records. As shown in Example 7-1, it leverages the `foreachBatch` output operation to create two datasets, each of which is written to a different Apache Kafka topic.

Example 7-1. Vertical partitioning with Apache Spark's `foreachBatch`

```
def split_visit_attributes(visits_to_save: DataFrame, batch_number: int):
  visits_to_save.persist()

  visits_without_user_context = (visits_to_save
    .filter('user_id IS NOT NULL AND context.user.login IS NOT NULL')
```

```
    .withColumn('context', F.col('context').dropFields('user'))
    .select(F.col('visit_id').alias('key'), F.to_json(F.struct('*')).alias('value')))
  # save to visits_without_user_context

  user_context_to_save = (visits_to_save.selectExpr('context.user.*', 'user_id')
    .select(F.col('user_id').alias('key'), F.to_json(F.struct('*')).alias('value')))
  # save to user_context_to_save

  visits_to_save.unpersist()
```

The split method uses simple column-based transformations to remove user information from the visits dataset and to transform only the user attributes for the user context dataset. The partitioned user context topic can be later converted into a Delta Lake table, with another job using the MERGE operation to deduplicate the entries (see Example 7-2).

Example 7-2. Converting input rows into a Delta Lake table

```
def save_most_recent_user_context(context_to_save: DataFrame, batch_number: int):
  deduplicated_context = context_to_save.dropDuplicates(['user_id']).alias('new')

  current_table = DeltaTable.forPath(spark_session, get_delta_users_table_dir())
  (current_table.alias('current')
    .merge(deduplicated_context, 'current.user_id = new.user_id')
    .whenMatchedUpdateAll().whenNotMatchedInsertAll()
    .execute()
  )
```

After these preparation steps, it's time to talk about data removal. In the Delta Lake table, it relies on the delete action (see Example 7-3).

Example 7-3. Data removal from a Delta Lake table

```
user_id_to_delete = '140665101097856_0316986e-9e7c-448f-9aac-5727dde96537'
users_table = DeltaTable.forPath(spark_session, get_delta_users_table_dir())
users_table.delete(f'user_id = "{user_id_to_delete}"')
```

This action requires running an additional VACUUM operation to remove the files from the deleted user that exceeded the retention period. Otherwise, you will still be able to retrieve the user's data by reading an older version of the table.

When it comes to Apache Kafka, the cleaning part is a bit different as it relies on a so-called *tombstone message*, which is a special marker record for a deleted row. A tombstone message is composed of a key of the removed record and a null value. If you send it to a topic with a compaction cleanup policy (cleanup.policy), Apache Kafka will run a background compaction process that will delete all tombstone messages.

One way to generate a tombstone message is by using the console producer (see Example 7-4).

Example 7-4. Deletion marker (aka tombstone) message

```
docker exec -ti ... kafka-console-producer.sh --bootstrap-server .... \
--topic ... --property parse.key=true --property key.separator=, \
--property null.marker=NULL

140665101097856_0316986e-9e7c-448f-9aac-5727dde96537,NULL
```

After you execute the compaction process, user 140665101097856_0316986e-9e7c-448f-9aac-5727dde96537 shouldn't be in the topic anymore. As you can see, this approach works for our vertically partitioned user_context topic, as there is always one occurrence per key. But it will not work for other types of records, such as user visits, where multiple events share the same visit ID key. Having a compaction process running on that topic would mean eventually exposing only the last visit entry to consumers.

Pattern: In-Place Overwriter

The Vertical Partitioner pattern is great if you start a new project or have enough time and compute resources allocated to migrate existing workloads. However, if you are not in one of these comfortable positions, you may have no other choice than to rely on the tried and true overwriting strategy.

Problem

You inherited a legacy system in which terabytes of data are stored in time-based horizontal partitions. There is no personal data management strategy defined. Despite this legacy character, the project is still widely used within your organization, and because of that, it needs to comply with new privacy regulations from your government. One of them requires personal data removal upon user request.

Solution

The current architecture and lack of resources for refactoring leave you with no choice but to apply the In-Place Overwriter pattern.

The implementation heavily depends on the data storage technology. If your data store natively supports in-place operations, the implementation consists of running a DELETE statement that targets entities to remove via a WHERE condition.

Eventually, you may need to complete this deletion query with a data cleaning operation. This applies especially to open-table file formats such as Apache Iceberg and Delta Lake, which often provide a time travel feature to restore the dataset to a prior version in case of an erroneous action. If you delete personal data but don't reclaim the data blocks storing the removed rows, the personal data will still be there.

Deletion Vectors

There are two approaches to managing deletes in table file formats. The first simply identifies removed rows and writes them to a smaller *side file* to reduce the writing footprint; this is commonly known as a *deletion vector*. With that approach, the consumer has to remove deleted rows at reading time. An opposite approach is more writer heavy as it writes all but removed entries to the files so that the consumer can directly use them.

If your storage doesn't provide this native deletion capacity—for example, when you use raw file formats (JSON and CSV)—you have to simulate it. The simulation job will process the whole dataset and filter out all records representing the removed users. It's a compute-intensive operation that replaces the existing data with the filtered dataset.

To avoid any side effects, you shouldn't replace the dataset directly, as the job can retry or even fail, causing data loss. But that doesn't mean you should overwrite each file individually, as this will be both time- and compute-intensive. As an alternative, you can rely on a job writing data to an internal storage area, also known as a *staging area*, where the results are kept private as long as the job doesn't complete. Only once the data removal succeeds can you run a data promotion job that will overwrite the existing public dataset. Figure 7-3 shows this workflow.

Figure 7-3. Data removal with an intermediary (aka staging) storage

Although this implementation adds some extra complexity with intermediary storage, it avoids the data quality issues that might be introduced by a retried data removal job. Of course, the data promotion job can still fail, but the failure will not lead to data loss since the dataset is already fully computed in the staging area.

Finally, overwriting can also work for compactable data stores, such as an Apache Kafka topic with the compaction strategy enabled and written key-based records. This implementation follows these steps:

1. Read the records stored in the topic.
2. If a record belongs to the removed entity, use the record key and send it with a null payload to the topic.

That way, the compaction process, since it always keeps the most recent entry for each key, will remove previous records with personal data and store empty delete markers, exactly like you saw in the Examples section of "Pattern: Vertical Partitioner" on page 198. However, the implementation requires key-based records and a compaction strategy defined in the topic.

Retention Period

If your data retention period is shorter than the delay for taking data removal action, you might consider it as a data removal compaction strategy. After all, the data will be automatically removed within the legal delay period. However, this is just an implementation suggestion, and before considering it as a final solution, please double-check with your Chief Data Officer (CDO) and legal department.

Consequences

At this point, you can probably already see the issue: the pattern performs a lot of read and write operations. Both have consequences for the system.

I/O overhead.   Reading and overwriting files incurs serious I/O overhead. Over time, the storage space can nearly double in size and lead to increased throughput.

This overhead will be smaller if your data storage layer can avoid reading irrelevant files for the filter condition. That's the case with Apache Parquet and the table file formats that rely on it, such as Delta Lake and Apache Iceberg. Apache Parquet, besides storing the records in data blocks, has a metadata layer where it saves statistics about the rows from each data block. If the query engine analyzes these statistics and sees there are no rows matching the removed user or users, it can skip the more costly data block reading operation.

Cost.   As the pattern requires reading all the data, it's a more costly solution than the Vertical Partitioner pattern. Let's take a look at an example. If you have 2,000 records for one removed entity, with the Vertical Partitioner, you will need to read and drop only one entry, while with the In-Place Overwriter pattern, 2,000 records will be impacted.

To mitigate this impact, you might try to group data removal requests and instead of running one pipeline for each demand, execute one for all the requests.

Examples

To help us analyze the complexity of the In-Place Overwriter pattern, let's see how to delete a row in the Delta Lake and JSON file formats with Apache Spark. In fact, the Delta Lake example is just a formality as it uses the same code as in Example 7-3, so instead of repeating it, I'll show you why overwriting data in flat file formats like JSON is more challenging. Let's take a look at the Apache Spark job that removes a user, shown in Example 7-5.

Example 7-5. Removing rows in a flat file format with PySpark

```
input_raw_data = spark_session.read.text(get_input_table_dir())
df_w_user_column = input_raw_data.withColumn(
  'user', F.from_json('value', 'user_id STRING')
)

user_id = '139621130423168_029fba78-15dc-4944-9f65-00636566f75b'
to_save = df_w_user_column.filter(f'user.user_id != "{user_id}"').select('value')
to_save.write.mode('overwrite').format('text').save(get_staging_table_dir())
```

There are two important things to keep in mind here. First, we don't want to alter the dataset, hence our use of the simplest writing API possible, which is the text one. Second, to save some space, we don't extract all attributes but only the one(s) used in the filter (`user_id` in our case).

There is one remaining detail: the writer generates a new filtered dataset in a staging location. This is a temporary storage area where you can keep your data private before exposing it to end users. As Apache Spark is a distributed and transactionless processing layer, we can't simply overwrite the files in the final location as this may leave a partially valid result in cases of failure. For that reason, the writer first generates a dataset in this staging location and only later promotes it to the final output with the rename-like[1] command that's adapted to your storage layer. Example 7-6 demonstrates this for moving files on S3.

Example 7-6. Dataset promotion from staging area to final location with AWS CLI

```
aws s3 rm ${BUCKET}/output --recursive
aws s3 mv ${BUCKET}/staging ${BUCKET}/output --recursive
```

Of course, the copy can also fail, but in that case, you still have the new dataset ready to be copied in the staging location.

---

[1] Renames in the cloud object stores don't follow the same transactional semantic as in the local file system. They're often implemented as copy-and-remove operations, which in cases of failure can leave empty valid states.

Impossible Rollback

The staging-based approach works for our scenario, but it's not perfect either. Let's imagine that your data removal job has some bugs and you need to replay it. Unfortunately, you won't be able to use the original dataset because it was overwritten. To mitigate this issue, you can rely on the Proxy pattern or enable data versioning at your infrastructure level.[2]

Access Control

However, even the most efficient data removal pattern will not be enough to provide the basic security that should come with access control. Indeed, besides being compliant, you also want to let only authorized users access the most critical sections of your data. Keeping personal data private is crucial, but the data itself can be the biggest competitive asset in your possession.

Pattern: Fine-Grained Accessor for Tables

The first pattern fits perfectly into the classical analytical world, where you create users or groups and assign them permissions to access particular tables. As it turns out, it's possible to have finer access control than that.

Problem

After migrating your previous HDFS/Hive workloads to a cloud data warehouse, you need to implement a secure access policy. The first part of the requirement is relatively easy to fulfill as the new data warehouse supports classical users and the creation of groups to manage access to the tables. However, there is an extra demand from your stakeholders. Users, despite their authorization to access a given table, may not have the permissions to read all column and rows. You need to implement an authorization mechanism for these low-level resources as well.

Solution

The Fine-Grained Accessor for Tables pattern solves the low-level data access issue.

When it comes to column-based access, the easiest implementation relies on the GRANT operator, which lets you define the columns within the authorized action scope. It's supported in Amazon Redshift and PostgreSQL. Example 7-7 shows an authorization policy to read only two columns (col_A and col_B).

---

2 All major object stores that are most often used for storing nontransactional file systems support versioning. These include S3 (*https://oreil.ly/iPRfh*), Azure Storage (*https://oreil.ly/_RT62*), and GCS (*https://oreil.ly/HUM3A*).

Example 7-7. Granting access on two columns with the GRANT operator

```
GRANT SELECT(col_A, col_B) ON my_table TO some_user;
```

The second implementation for column-level access relies on a data catalog and its tags set to the columns. That's how the pattern works for GCP BigQuery. The implementation starts by creating policy tags in Data Catalog and assigning them to the protected columns in a BigQuery table. The next step is to authorize users to access protected tables by assigning them a Fine-Grained Reader role for each policy tag.

Finally, there is a third implementation based on the data masking feature. Here, users can see protected columns, but their content will be hidden if users don't have access to it. That's how Databricks with Unity Catalog and Snowflake implement column-level access policies. Example 7-8 shows how to achieve this with a column-masking function that shows the column content only if the user is part of a group of engineers.

Example 7-8. Example of a column-masking function in Databricks where only members of a group of engineers can see the ip column

```
CREATE FUNCTION ip_mask(ip STRING)
  RETURN CASE WHEN is_member('engineers') THEN ip ELSE '.' END;

CREATE TABLE visits (
  visit_id STRING,
  ip STRING MASK ip_mask);
```

Column-level security does not provide complete fine-level access protection, but you can make it complete with row-level security. The row-level approach often relies on somewhat dynamic functions that add a WHERE condition to the executed query on the fly. They may have a different name, though. Databricks calls them ROW FILTER, Amazon Redshift calls them Row-Level Security, while GCP BigQuery and Snowflake classify them as row access policies. This implementation consists of defining a separate database object that will add some dynamic condition to all select requests made on a protected table.

On the other hand, if the database doesn't provide native support for row-level access authorization, you can simulate it by exposing a table from a view with an access guard condition (see Example 7-9).

Example 7-9. Row-level access with a view

```
CREATE VIEW users_blogs AS
SELECT ... FROM blogs WHERE table.blog_author = current_user
```

The created view returns the blogs owned by the user issuing the query. The condition will then be different for each user, and consequently, each user will have a dedicated version of the view.

Consequences

This feature is natively supported in databases, so its number of drawbacks is relatively small compared to those of the other patterns you've seen so far.

Row-level security limits. Most of the row-level security implementations have a limited scope of applications that consist of the attributes that you can get directly from the connection session, such as user name, user group, and IP.

Data type. If your column is of a complex type, such as a nested structure, you may not be able to apply the simple column-based access strategy. Column-based permissions, as the name indicates, refer to column, so to apply them to initially nested attributes, you'll need to unnest them first and expose them from another table or use the Dataset Materializer pattern if the latter supports fine-grained permissions.

Query overhead. As you saw in the Solution section, row-level and column-level security protections may be expressed as SQL functions dynamically added to the queries executed against the secured table. If this overhead causes unexpected latency, you can try to mitigate it by creating a dedicated table or view with the Dataset Materializer pattern, only with the data the user or group is allowed to read. Of course, this mitigation also has some limitations, such as data duplication or governance for many access groups.

Examples

PostgreSQL is a great open source implementation supporting both column- and row-level access policies. Let's begin with column-based access, which relies on the GRANT statement that's used to define the scope of access of a user or group. Example 7-10 demonstrates this.

Example 7-10. GRANT access to a subset of columns in PostgreSQL

```
GRANT SELECT(id, login, registered_datetime) ON dedp.users TO user_a;
```

After that, whenever user_a issues a query that includes the unlisted columns, such as SELECT *, the database will return an error like "ERROR: permission denied for table users."

When it comes to row-level controls, PostgreSQL uses policies that add conditions whenever someone queries a protected table. Example 7-11 shows a policy that adds the login = current_user condition to the reading query.

Example 7-11. Row-level access policy in PostgreSQL

```
ALTER TABLE dedp.users ENABLE ROW LEVEL SECURITY;

CREATE POLICY user_row_access ON dedp.users USING (login = current_user);
```

Besides PostgreSQL, other data stores, including managed cloud services, also support row-level access. That's the case with AWS DynamoDB, which is a NoSQL database with key-based access. If you want to simulate the row access policy based on the user login, you can do this with an identity and access management (IAM) policy (see Example 7-12).

Example 7-12. Fine-grained access policy in AWS DynamoDB

```
{
 "Statement":[{
  "Sid": ...,
  "Effect":"Allow",
  "Action":[...],
  "Resource":["arn:aws:dynamodb:us-west-1:123456789012:table/users"],
  "Condition":{
   "ForAllValues:StringEquals":{
    "dynamodb:LeadingKeys":["${www.amazon.com:user_id}"]
   }
  }
 }]
}
```

The condition in DynamoDB relies on the dynamodb:LeadingKeys attribute, which allows each user to read only the rows starting with their user_id value (${www.amazon.com:user_id}).

Pattern: Fine-Grained Accessor for Resources

The access-based pattern is great when it comes to table-based datasets. However, databases are not the only data stores used by data engineers. A lot of data engineers, probably including you, also work with other data stores that are often fully managed by their cloud provider. The next pattern applies to these cloud-based resources.

Problem

A security audit detected overly broad permissions in your cloud account. One of the spotted dangers is the possibility that one data processing job could overwrite all datasets that are available in your object store. The auditor presented you with a security best practice called *at-least privilege*, which assigns the least required permissions for each component of your system, so that a data processing job can only manipulate the dataset it's really working on.

You're now looking for a technical solution to implement the at-least privilege on your cloud provider.

Solution

The good news for you is that all major cloud providers—including AWS, Azure, and GCP—come with an implementation for the at-least privilege principle, which is the backbone of the Fine-Grained Accessor for Resources pattern.

Cloud providers have two different strategies when it comes to limiting access to resources. The first approach is resource based because it defines the access scope at the resource level directly. For example, to control access to a GCS bucket on GCP, you'll need to assign the IAM policy from Example 7-13.

Example 7-13. IAM policy for GCS in Terraform

```
data "google_iam_policy" "admin_access" {
  binding {
    role = "roles/storage.admin"
    members = [
      "user:admingcs@waitingforcode.com",
    ]
  }
}

resource "google_storage_bucket_iam_policy" "policy" {
  bucket = google_storage_bucket.default.name
  policy_data = data.google_iam_policy.admin_access.policy_data
}
```

The second approach uses identities instead of resources. Here, the access permissions are defined directly at the identity level (for example, a human or an application user). AWS supports this mode with IAM roles that are assumed by the services. Example 7-14 shows how an Apache Spark EMR job on AWS gives read and write permissions to Kinesis Data Streams.

Example 7-14. Read and write access to AWS Kinesis Data Streams with Terraform

```
data "aws_iam_policy_document" "emr_assume_role" {
  statement {
    effect = "Allow"
    principals {
      type        = "Service"
      identifiers = ["elasticmapreduce.amazonaws.com"]
    }
    actions = ["sts:AssumeRole"]
  }
}
resource "aws_iam_role" "job_role" {
  name               = "visits-processor-role"
  assume_role_policy = data.aws_iam_policy_document.emr_assume_role.json
}
resource "aws_iam_policy" "visits_read_writer_policy" {
  name   = "visits_rw"
  policy = jsonencode({
    Version = "2012-10-17"
    Statement = [{
    Action = ["kinesis:Get*", "kinesis:Describe*", "kinesis:List*",
             "kinesis:Put*"]
    Effect  = "Allow"
    Resource = ["arn:aws:kinesis:us-east-1:1234567890:streams/visits"]}]
  })
}
resource "aws_iam_role_policy_attachment" "policy_attachment" {
  role       = aws_iam_role.job_role.name
  policy_arn = aws_iam_policy.visits_read_writer_policy.arn
}
```

Figure 7-4 summarizes both approaches. As you can see, for the resource-based approach, the access controls are directly attached to each resource, while for the identity-based approach, they're located at the user level.

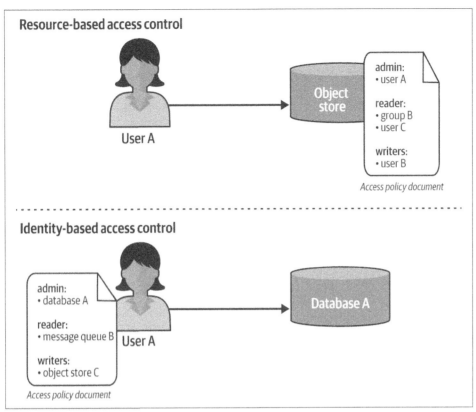

Figure 7-4. Simplified illustration of resource-based and identity-based access controls

Fine-grained permissions are often flexible. They can target a specific resource, a set of resources starting with the same prefix, or even a resource based on runtime conditions (as you saw with user ID in Example 7-12). The last implementation looks like the row-level access from the previous pattern because it controls access at the lowest levels of the infrastructure. Example 7-15 shows an example of a tag-based access control for AWS S3 where you rely on custom metadata attributes (tags) that are associated with each resource individually.

Example 7-15. Tag-based access policy for AWS S3

```
"Statement": [{
 "Effect": "Allow", "Action": "s3:PutObject",
 "Resource": "*", "Condition": {
  "ForAllValues:StringEquals": {"aws:TagKeys": ["${www.amazon.com:user_id}"]}}}
}]
```

Consequences

Defining access policies shouldn't be difficult from a technical standpoint as you can rely on an infrastructure as code (IaC) tool or a custom script. That doesn't mean there are no consequences, though.

Security by the book trade-off.   A security rule of thumb is the at-least privilege principle, which holds that a user or group should have access only to the resources it needs at the moment. Although this is a great principle, it can lead to the creation of many small access policy definitions that will be difficult to maintain in complex environments.

To mitigate this issue and keep resources down to a manageable size, you might use wildcard-based access, so instead of defining each of your cloud resources individually, you could use a prefix like *visits**. As a result, the access policy would apply to all resources starting with "visits." However, this may violate the at-least privilege principle because you can't guarantee that the user should have access to all visits-prefixed resources created in the future. For that reason, you should discuss this simplification strategy with your security department.

Complexity.   If you use both resource- and identity-based approaches in the same project, you may be inadvertently increasing the complexity of your system. Whenever possible, it's better to prefer one solution, preferably the one that covers more of your use cases.

Quotas.   As for any other cloud resource, even access policies have limitations. For example, the AWS IAM service allows 1,500 custom policies by default, and GCP IAM has a limit on custom roles within a project (300). Some limits are flexible, though, so that you can ask your cloud provider to increase them.

Examples

To help you understand the Fine-Grained Accessor for Resources pattern, let's see how it behaves in the context of reading data from an S3 bucket. Assuming you don't have access to the tested bucket, you should get the permission error from Example 7-16.

Example 7-16. Exception from a reading operation without permissions

```
$ aws s3 ls s3://dedp-visits-301JQN/

An error occurred (AccessDenied) when calling the
ListObjectsV2 operation: Access Denied
```

As you can see, the error message explicitly says what the issue is. To start, let's fix it with the identity-based approach. To do so, we need to create a role with the S3 reading actions scoped to our bucket (see Example 7-17).

Example 7-17. Permissions required to read an S3 bucket

```
{"Version": "2012-10-17", "Statement": [{"Sid": "VisitsS3Reader",
 "Effect": "Allow", "Action": ["s3:Get*", "s3:List*"],
 "Resource": ["arn:aws:s3:::dedp-visits-301JQN/*",
    "arn:aws:s3:::dedp-visits-301JQN"]
}]}
```

After creating this role and assigning it to your user, you should see the listing operation succeed.

As an alternative, you can use the resource-based approach. Example 7-18 shows a command that authorizes a `visits-s3-reader` user to read data from our S3 bucket.

Example 7-18. A command to authorize an AWS role to read objects from an S3 bucket

```
$ aws s3api put-bucket-policy --bucket dedp-visits-301JQN --policy file://policy.json

# policy.json
{"Statement": [{"Effect": "Allow",
   "Principal": {"AWS": "arn:aws:iam::123456789012:user/visits-s3-reader"},
   "Action": ["s3:Get*", "s3:List*"],
   "Resource": "arn:aws:s3:::dedp-visits-301JQN/*"
}]}
```

Data Protection

You might be thinking that controlling data access at the logical level, meaning either the database or the cloud services scope, is enough to build a fully secure system. Unfortunately, it's only part of the solution. A missing part concerns securing data itself, hence protecting it against unexpected usage.

Pattern: Encryptor

Even though you run your infrastructure on the cloud, the data is still physically stored somewhere, and unauthorized people may try to read it. If you need to reduce the access risk, you can first implement the access policies from the previous section, and then make sure the data will be unusable if access controls get compromised.

Problem

After you implement fine-grained access policies for both your tables and your cloud resources, you're tasked with enforcing the security of your data at rest and in transit.

Your stakeholders are worried that an unauthorized person could intercept the data transferred between your streaming brokers and jobs, or that the same person could physically steal your data from the servers.

Solution

One way to reduce this data intrusion risk is with the Encryptor pattern. As there are two protection levels required, the pattern has two implementations.

The first implementation is for the data at rest. It encrypts the stored data with a client-side or server-side approach, and the difference between the two approaches boils down to encryption key management. In the client-side implementation, the data producer is responsible for encrypting the data prior to sending it to storage. Naturally, it's also responsible for managing the encryption key.

When it comes to server-side encryption, all the encryption and decryption work is done on the server side. A consumer or producer only issues a request, and the server does the rest, including encryption key management.

Server-side encryption, while it looks challenging, is widely supported by public cloud providers. Each of the major providers has its own encryption keys store that you can freely apply to all offered services supporting server-side encryption. On AWS and GCP, you'll use the *Key Management Service* (KMS), while on Azure you'll use the *Key Vault* service.

Figure 7-5 depicts the encryption workflow based on these services.

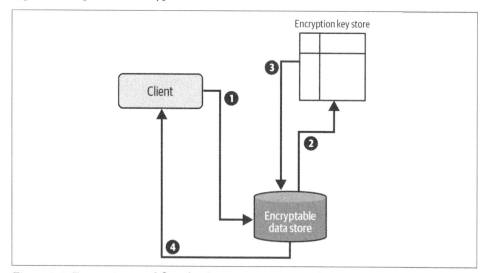

Figure 7-5. Encryption workflow for data-at-rest server-side encryption with an encryption store service

The interaction with an encrypted data store is based on the four main steps that are numbered in the diagram:

1. The request first reaches the encrypted data store. However, it doesn't return directly.

2. Instead of returning the data, the store identifies the encryption key and asks the encryption key store for the decryption key. If the client is not authorized to decrypt the data, the request will fail. Otherwise, it continues.

3. Next, the data store decrypts the data with the retrieved decryption key.

4. Finally, the decrypted records are sent back to the client.

If you are a cloud user, this complex exchange is fully abstracted to you by the cloud provider. Your only responsibility is to configure an appropriate encryption strategy for the data store and manage access to the data store and encryption key store for all reading and writing clients.

But data at rest is not the only encryption layer. Another layer is data in transit, meaning the place where clients and data stores exchange data across the network. The implementation on the cloud is relatively easy as it's limited to enabling secure communication at the SDK level on the client side and configuring the required protocol version on the service. That way, the exchanged data will remain encrypted.

Consequences

Encryption is a data access security strategy applied to the physical data storage level. Like other security protections, you can't get it for free.

Encryption/decryption overhead. CPU overhead is probably the first consequence that comes to mind. As you've seen, the data is not stored in plain text but in a somehow altered, unreadable version. Without an encryption and decryption action, it's unusable. For that reason, each writing and reading request puts some extra pressure on the CPU.

Data loss risk. Even though the Encryptor pattern tends to protect data at rest against unauthorized access, it can also, as a side effect, block access for authorized users. That said, this can happen only if you either lose the encryption key or simply lose access to it.

To mitigate the issue, cloud providers often implement *soft deletes* on the encryption stores. That means any delete request you send will not take immediate effect. Instead, it will benefit from a grace period during which you can restore the key in case of an accidental deletion.

Protocol updates.   Encryption in transit is much easier to set up than encryption at rest. However, it's still an extra component in your system that must be kept up-to-date. That's the case with the Transport Layer Security (TLS) protocol, which is a possible encryption channel in HTTPS. Over the years, there have been various security issues detected that led to the deprecation of the 1.0 and 1.1 versions of TLS.[3] For that reason, any services using these old releases must be upgraded.

This operation looks like a difficult extra maintenance task, but with cloud offerings, it is very often simplified and reduced to upgrading the new encryption protocol version at the service level.

Examples

Now, let's see encryption at rest in action for the AWS S3 object store with some Terraform code. The encryption configuration has two main implementation steps, and the first one is in Example 7-19. It defines the encryption key in the AWS KMS service and grants an AWS Lambda user decryption and encryption permissions.

Example 7-19. A Terraform definition for AWS KMS encryption

```
module "kms" {
  source   = "terraform-aws-modules/kms/aws"
  key_usage = "ENCRYPT_DECRYPT"
  deletion_window_in_days = 14
  aliases = ["visits-bucket-encryption-key"]
  grants = {
    lambda_doc_convert = {
      grantee_principal = aws_iam_role.iam_key_reader.arn
      operations        = ["Encrypt", "Decrypt", "GenerateDataKey"]
    }
  }
}
```

An AWS KMS key declaration is pretty self-explanatory. The only mysterious but essential parameter is the `deletion_window_in_days`. Do you remember when I mentioned the data loss drawback? Currently, this property is there to ensure an encryption key restore window in case of an erroneous removal. Also, the declaration assigns some `grants` to other services. In our example, the grant applies to an IAM role that you can later associate with a compute or a querying service.

After defining the encryption key, the next step is to combine it with an S3 bucket (see Example 7-20).

---

3 You can learn more about the deprecation in RFC 8996 (*https://oreil.ly/t97Xv*).

Example 7-20. An S3 bucket encryption at-rest configuration

```
resource "aws_s3_bucket_server_side_encryption_configuration" "visits" {
  bucket = aws_s3_bucket.visits.id
  rule {
    apply_server_side_encryption_by_default {
      kms_master_key_id = module.kms.key_arn
      sse_algorithm     = "aws:kms"
    }
  }
}
```

To sum up the two previous snippets, we could say that the encryption is just a matter of associating the key with the encrypted resource and all authorized identities.

Additionally, you can enforce the encryption in motion for some data stores and ensure that any client applications using older versions will be ignored. For the Azure Event Hubs streaming broker, you can define a minimum TLS version (see the last line of Example 7-21).

Example 7-21. Minimal TLS encryption version for Azure Event Hubs

```
resource "azurerm_eventhub_namespace" "visits" {
  name                = "visits-namespace"
  location            = azurerm_resource_group.dedp.location
  resource_group_name = azurerm_resource_group.dedp.name
  sku                 = "Standard"
  capacity            = 2
  minimum_tls_version = "1.2"
}
```

Pattern: Anonymizer

As you saw in Chapter 6, you can improve the value of a dataset if you share it with other pipelines. However, it's not always that simple. If your dataset contains PII attributes and the user hasn't agreed to share those details with your partners, you will need to perform a special preparation step before sharing the dataset.

Problem

Your organization contracted an external data analytics company to analyze your customers' behavior and optimize your communication strategy. Since the dataset contains a lot of PII attributes and some of your users didn't agree to share them with third parties, your data engineering team was tasked to write a pipeline to make the shared dataset compliant with the privacy regulations.

Not Only PII

The examples refer to PII data as it's probably the most commonly discussed use case, but it's not the only data type requiring protection. Other examples are protected health information (PHI) and intellectual property (IP) data. In the following pages, we're going to stick to PII for the sake of simplicity.

Solution

The problem states that some parts of your dataset cannot be shared. Put differently, you need to remove or transform them. That's the perfect task for the Anonymizer pattern.

The goal of this pattern is to remove the sensitive data from the dataset, thereby transforming each row into anonymous information. Thanks to this process, the data consumer won't be able to identify the user.

The Anonymizer pattern supports various implementations:

1. Data removal
2. Data perturbation
3. Sythentic data replacement

All of them consist of removing or altering the initial sensitive attribute. How? Let's quickly look at each of the methods:

1. Data removal is the easiest one to implement as it takes the selected columns out of the input dataset.
2. Data perturbation is more complex. It adds some noise to the input value so that the value has a different meaning. For example, in an IP column, you could add extra attributes in random positions, so that "123.456.789.012" becomes "1823.456.7809.012".
3. Synthetic data replacement substitutes the original values with the values coming from the synthetic data generator. What does that mean? It means that there is a smart model (probably a machine learning model) that is capable of interpreting the type of input column and generating a corresponding replacement. The replacement looks the same as the original attribute but has a different value. For example, in a country column, "Portugal" could be synthetically replaced with "Croatia."

The easiest methods to implement are the first two. You can use either a mapping function or a column transformation to remove the value or to perturb it. The synthetic data method may involve some work with the data science team to build a model capable of analyzing and generating replacement values. In a less ideal version, you could eventually implement the solution on your own by creating a replacement function for each column that generates some random values.

Consequences

The Anonymizer pattern does indeed protect your sensitive data, but it greatly impacts the data's usability.

Information loss.   It's clear that when you remove or replace information, your dataset becomes something new. This means your end users, including technical users like data analysts and data scientists, won't be able to rely on these sensitive columns in their work. That can lead to many issues, including false data prediction models and incorrect data insights.

Examples

Let's see how to anonymize a dataset by removing a birthday column and replacing an email address with a lower-quality version of the synthetic data. The pipeline leverages the Apache Spark API for the former task and the Faker Python library for the latter.

To start, you can remove a column two different ways. First, you can omit it from the list of columns to read in the SELECT statement. This approach is good if you don't have a lot of columns to read. If that's not the case, you can take the opposite approach and remove the columns with the drop function.

Next, to replace a value, you can use a column-based function such as withColumn or a row-based function like mapInPandas. Since our example only involves replacing one column, we're going to use the former approach. Example 7-22 shows both the removal approach and the replacement approach. The replacement scenario uses the Faker library,[4] which can, among other things, generate random email addresses.

Example 7-22. Dropping a column and replacing its value with an anonymization example in PySpark

```
@pandas_udf(StringType())
def replace_email(emails: pandas.Series) -> pandas.Series:
  faker_generator = Faker()
  return emails.apply(lambda email: faker_generator.email())

users.drop('birthday').withColumn('email', replace_email(users.email))
```

---

4 You can learn more about Faker from the official repository (*https://oreil.ly/RDqZH*).

As a result, the output dataset doesn't contain the birthday column and has the email value replaced by a randomly generated email address.

Pattern: Pseudo-Anonymizer

The "Pattern: Anonymizer" on page 219 offers strong data protection. However, the pattern's impact on data science and data analytics pipelines can be very bad because of missing or altered values. The Pseudo-Anonymizer pattern reduces this impact.

Problem

An anonymized dataset you shared with the external data analysts' company doesn't contain all the columns. You chose to remove them because that was the simplest data anonymization strategy. However, because of that, the team can't answer most of the business queries. The team members asked you to provide them with a new dataset that still hides real PII values but replaces them with a more usable form.

Solution

Data sharing, PII data, and the requirement to keep some business meaning are perfect conditions in which to apply the Pseudo-Anonymizer pattern. Depending on your context, you can use one of its four implementations:

1. Data masking

2. Data tokenization

3. Hashing

4. Encryption

All of them consist of replacing the initial data with a different value that is more or less related to the original. How? Let's quickly look at each of the methods:

1. Data masking replaces sensitive data with meaningless characters or more realistic substitution values. For example, a Social Security number (SSN) like 999-55-1040 could be masked as XXX-XX-1040 or 9XX-5X-1XXX. As you can see, if you apply this masking strategy, several different users may share the same masked SSN.

2. Data tokenization substitutes initial values with fictive ones. However, it stores the mapping between the original values and their substitutes in a token vault store. The key here is to secure access to the vault to avoid compromising the protected attributes. If the vault access security is compromised, an unauthorized person could access and thus reverse the tokenized values.

3. Hashing fully and irreversibly replaces the sensitive values. For example, an email like *contact@waitingforcode.com* could become a string like *gD0B+pUp-*

XYVZ9nqhgLRuban0CilZRKVp4dcmvmocsYE=, if it was hashed with an SHA-256 algorithm and encoded with a Base64 scheme.

4. Encryption relies on the encryption keys that are applied to columns or rows, a little bit like the keys for the datasets in the Encryptor pattern. Here, a user with access to the encryption key should be able to restore the original value.

Once you've identified the method that fits best with the data types of your dataset, you can proceed to implement the anonymization functions. Some of them, such as data masking, can be represented as easy column transformation functions. The others, such as tokenization that requires an extra mapping table, might need additional implementation effort.

Anonymization Versus Pseudo-Anonymization

The pseudo-anonymization techniques included in the currently described pattern are sometimes presented as part of the anonymization process. However, there is an important difference between them. Pseudo-anonymized PII data can become identifiable if it's combined with other datasets. That's not the case with anonymized datasets, where even in cases of combinations, the data will remain unidentifiable.

Consequences

The Pseudo-Anonymizer pattern, despite the fact that it protects personal data, doesn't provide as strong a protection guarantee as the Anonymizer pattern.

False sense of security. The Pseudo-Anonymizer, even though it blurs personal data, provides a weaker security guarantee than the pattern described in the Anonymizer pattern. One of the biggest issues comes from the combination of datasets, in which a pseudo-anonymized column can become a PII column identifying a person.

Let's take a look at an example of an imaginary but very popular data processing framework called Cheetach Processor, which was invented by a data engineer named John Doe who lived in San Marino, a small country in Europe. Your database has two pseudo-anonymized tables. The first, Table 7-1, stores user food preferences, and the second, Table 7-2, persists user registration information.

Table 7-1. Food preferences table

User ID	Liked foods	Disliked foods
1000	carrot, broccoli, potato	chips, chocolate bar

Table 7-2. User registration table

User ID	Country	Role
1000	S*n M****o	C******h P*******r i******r

As you can see, Table 7-1 perfectly protects the identity of the user. However, if you combine it with Table 7-2, you'll get something like "C******h P*******r i******r living in S*n M****o likes carrot, broccoli, and potato." There are not a lot of countries whose names match the one in the masked country column. Once you get to San Marino here, you may also discover the "inventor" part and identify that the user ID number 1000 refers to our famous John Doe. I know, this example is pretty abstract, but its obviousness is there to clearly demonstrate the false sense of security pseudo-anonymization gives when combining datasets.

Identification wouldn't be possible with full anonymization because the Country and Role columns would both be removed or altered to, for example, "Europe" and "Software engineer." You can see now that even after combining both tables, it wouldn't be clear who this software engineer is.

Information loss. The best example illustrating this is the data masking strategy. As you saw in our previous example with the SSN, some of the numbers are preserved. Because of that, two different SSNs can now point to the same user. For example, numbers like 999-55-1040 and 999-13-1040 can both be masked in the same format, which is XXX-XX-1040.

Besides this loss, there is also a data type loss. A great example of this is the generalization method, in which a numeric value can be replaced by a numeric range represented by a text type.

Examples

Implementing the Pseudo-Anonymizer pattern relies on using the mapping function. In our example, let's see how to do this with PySpark's `mapInPandas` and column transformations that will work on the table in Example 7-23.

Example 7-23. Table to pseudo-anonymize

```
+-------+-------+---------------+------+
|user_id|country|            ssn|salary|
+-------+-------+---------------+------+
|      1| Poland|0940-0000-1000| 50000|
|      2| France|0469-0930-1000| 60000|
|      3|the USA|1230-0000-3940| 80000|
|      4|  Spain|8502-1095-9303| 52000|
+-------+-------+---------------+------+
```

All but the first column should be pseudo-anonymized, and we're going to use two different methods. The first one is the `mapInPandas` function shown in Example 7-24 that replaces the country value with a geographical area and masks the SSN.

Example 7-24. Pseudo-anonymization with generalization and data masking

```
def pseudo_anonymize_users(input_pandas: pandas.DataFrame) -> pandas.DataFrame:
  def pseudo_anonymize_country(country: str) -> str:
    countries_area_mapping = {
    'Poland': 'eu', 'France': 'eu', 'Spain': 'eu', 'the USA': 'na'
    }
    return countries_area_mapping[country]

  def pseudo_anonymize_ssn(ssn: str) -> str:
    return f'{ssn[0]}***-{ssn[5]}***-{ssn[10]}***'
  for rows in input_pandas:
    rows['country'] = rows['country'].apply(lambda c: pseudo_anonymize_country(c))
    rows['ssn'] = rows['ssn'].apply(lambda ssn: pseudo_anonymize_ssn(ssn))
    yield rows
```

The `mapInPandas` mapping doesn't include the range transformation for the salary column because of the type change. The salary is defined as an integer in the input dataset, while the range is of the string type. As you can see, it's a types-incompatible conversion, and to handle it, we need a simple column-based mapping (see Example 7-25).

Example 7-25. Column-based pseudo-anonymization with type conversion

```
pseud_anonymized_users = (users.mapInPandas(pseudo_anonymize_users, users.schema)
  .withColumn('salary', functions.expr('''
    CASE WHEN salary BETWEEN 0 AND 50000 THEN "0-50000"
        WHEN salary BETWEEN 50000 AND 60000 THEN "50000-60000"
        ELSE "60000+" END''')))
```

After we apply both types of transformations, the input dataset changes to the table in Example 7-26.

Example 7-26. User table after pseudo-anonymization

```
+-------+-------+---------------+-----------+
|user_id|country|            ssn|     salary|
+-------+-------+---------------+-----------+
|      1|     eu|0***-0***-1***|    0-50000|
|      2|     eu|0***-0***-1***|50000-60000|
|      3|     na|1***-0***-3***|     60000+|
|      4|     eu|8***-1***-9***|50000-60000|
+-------+-------+---------------+-----------+
```

Connectivity

So far, you have learned how to protect your data. Although this is the core part of data security, it might not be enough. Do you remember the data flow patterns from the previous chapter? Data is continuously flowing within the same system or across different systems, and you will need to access it. In this section, you'll learn about secure access strategies.

Pattern: Secrets Pointer

The login/password authentication method is still probably the most commonly used to access databases. It's simple but also dangerous if used without precautions, and the pattern presented next is one of the precautions you can apply.

Problem

The visits real-time processing pipeline from our use case leverages an external API to enrich each event with geolocation information. This API is provided to you by an external company, and the only authentication method is a login/password pair.

In the past, your team accidentally shared the login/password used for a different API. As the API was request billed, the leak led to increased billing. You want to reduce this risk right now and avoid storing the login/password for the code interacting with the new data enrichment API.

Solution

Credentials are sensitive parameters. One of the best ways to secure them is to...avoid storing them anywhere. Instead, you can use a reference (aka a *pointer*). That's what the Secrets Pointer pattern does.

The idea here is to leverage a secrets manager service (such as Google Cloud Secret Manager or AWS Secrets Manager) where you store all sensitive values, such as logins, passwords, and API keys. This approach has several advantages. First, it's a central place where you manage this sensitive data. Thanks to this centralization, access monitoring is easier. Second, the component also facilitates management. You can simply set a new set of credentials without having to update all the consumers.

Regarding the consumers, they won't reference the sensitive parameter values anymore. Instead, they'll use their names from the secrets manager service. Consequently, each consumer will retrieve the secret's value by issuing a query to the service at runtime. Additionally, to save some communication costs, consumers can store the credentials in their local cache for some time.

With the Secrets Pointer pattern, access is protected on two levels. At the first level, the consumer must have access to the secrets manager. Otherwise, it won't be able to retrieve the key. To secure this step, you can use one of the fine-grained access patterns. The second level of protection is natively guaranteed by the credentials themselves. If they're not valid, a consumer will simply not have access to the underlying API or database.

Consequences

A popular proverb in our engineering world came from Phil Karlton, who said, "There are only two hard things in computer science: cache invalidation and naming things."[5] The cache part applies to the Secrets Pointer too.

Cache invalidation and streaming jobs. If you cache the credentials, you'll never know whether you're using the most up-to-date ones, which may lead to connection issues. On the other hand, you may potentially avoid many credentials retrieval requests and hence optimize execution time if they're costly. That's a good thing, but if you implement the cache, you must also be able to refresh the credentials.

The simplest approach here, if you don't want to send a credentials refresh request, is to simply allow the job to fail. Normally, once restarted, the new execution version should reload the credentials from the secrets manager. That being said, this might not be optimal if the credentials change very often, as it would increase the number of failures. Also, remember to use one of the idempotency design patterns as they should keep your data correct even with retries.

You can also try to write an asynchronous refresh process, but here too, you may encounter some writing issues if the credentials change after you've started sending data to the output data store and before you refresh the connection parameters.

Logs. The Secrets Pointer pattern gives you a false sense of security that the credentials won't leak. Indeed, they're now stored in a secured place that only authorized entities can access. Even though this part doesn't get compromised, you can still leak the secrets if you inadvertently include them in the logs.

A secret remains secret. Even though consumers don't need to deal with credentials, it doesn't mean there are no credentials at all. In fact, to enable consumers to use references instead of secret values, there is a secrets producer that needs to securely generate secret values to the secrets storage.

In practice, this is either a human administrator who puts the secret values in storage or the IaC stack that defines random secret values while creating a database.

---

5 Philip Lewis Karlton (1947–1997) was a software developer and one of the people who was responsible for the architecture of Netscape products.

Examples

To see how to integrate the Secrets Pointer pattern into a pipeline, let's take a look at a simple Apache Spark job reading a PostgreSQL table and converting it to JSON files. Normally, the input dataset definition requires several parameters, including the login/password pair. However, as we're going to use the pattern, instead of the clear values, we're going to define the references. Example 7-27 shows this definition.

Example 7-27. A database connection from Apache Spark to PostgreSQL without plain text credentials

```
secretsmanager_client = boto3.client('secretsmanager')
db_user = secretsmanager_client.get_secret_value(SecretId='user')['SecretString']
db_password = secretsmanager_client.get_secret_value(SecretId='pwd')['SecretString']
spark_session.read.option('driver', 'org.postgresql.Driver').jdbc(
  url='jdbc:postgresql:dedp', table='dedp.devices',
  properties={'user': db_user, 'password': db_password})
```

Although the connection configuration still references the user and password, the code doesn't know about the values. Well, technically, it knows them, but only thanks to the secrets manager data store. Put differently, the credentials aren't tied to the codebase but are managed as a separate asset.

Besides keeping the secrets secret, the Secrets Pointer pattern simplifies the work on multiple environments. If you create the database with its connection attributes from a scripted project, like the IaC with Terraform, you can keep the same secret names for all environments and let the IaC automate their generation. That way, your code doesn't need to deal with any per-environment configuration files that would store different connection parameters for each environment.

Pattern: Secretless Connector

The Secrets Pointer pattern shows how to secure credentials, but what if I told you that it's even better to not have any credentials to manage? That is what the next pattern makes possible.

Problem

One of the teams in your organization has started integrating a new data processing service. All the code examples it found use API keys to interact with the cloud-managed resources available from the service.

The team is small and would like to avoid managing these APIs. It called you for the second time to see if you have an alternative solution, ideally guaranteeing access to resources without any kind of credentials to reference in the code.

Solution

If you work with cloud services and don't want to manage the credentials, you can implement the Secretless Connector pattern. How? There are two main approaches.

The first implementation uses the IAM service that's available on your cloud provider. Here, a user or administrator assigns reading and writing actions to each user, group, or role, via document access policy. This IAM-based policy approach applies to application users, such as data processing jobs. They may work on the same cloud resources as you, a human user, but their interaction is automated. For example, their job may be scheduled to run at specific times of day. Therefore, they don't log in but must somehow be authorized to access cloud resources.

Generally, the workflow for IAM-based access for both physical and application users can be summarized as the schema shown in Figure 7-6.

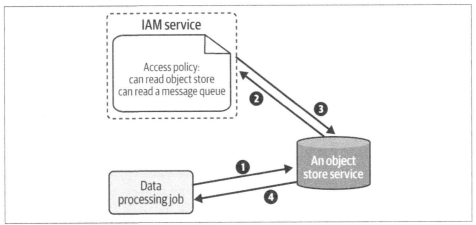

Figure 7-6. A generalized credentialless access workflow with a cloud service

The workflow is based on four main steps:

1. An application user issues a request to interact with a cloud service. In our example, it's an object store and the user wants to read one object.

2. The service doesn't return the object directly. Instead, it connects to the IAM service to validate that the user has all required permissions to fulfill the request.

3. The IAM responds to the service with the list of permissions' scope.

4. The service returns a response to the user. If the user has all required permissions, the response satisfies the request. Otherwise, the service returns an error.

The second implementation of the Secretless Connector uses certificates and is also known as *certificate-based authentication*. The workflow is similar to the one you saw in Figure 7-6, but instead of the IAM service, there is a certificate authority (CA) component. This authority validates the certificates used in the connection process before authorizing the workflow to move on.

Consequences

Despite the -less suffix that might indicate a lack of effort, the Secretless Connector pattern does require some work.

Workless impression. Although there are no credentials involved, there is still some work to do. You have to configure the entity to leverage the credentialless access. For example, on AWS, this requires setting an assume role permission that lets an entity use temporary credentials returned by the Security Token Service (STS) to interact with other services.

Rotation. This point is essentially valid certifcate-based authentication. Rotating access keys on a regular basis is often considered a security best practice to reduce the risk of leaks. However, with certificates, logins, and passwords, it adds extra management overhead.

To rotate them without impacting your consumers, you have to first generate and share new credentials with consumers. Meanwhile, you need to support both old and new credentials on your side, so that consumers who may not migrate at the same time can still use your data store. Only once the consumers confirm that they're using the new credentials can you drop the old ones.

Examples

Let's begin this section with a certificate-based connection to PostgreSQL from an Apache Spark job. As shown in Example 7-28, the connection attributes don't require any password. Instead, they rely on the certificate shared with the server.

Example 7-28. Certificate-based connection to PostgreSQL from Apache Spark

```
input_data = spark.read.option('driver', 'org.postgresql.Driver').jdbc(
  url='jdbc:postgresql:dedp', table='dedp.devices',
  properties={'ssl': 'true', 'sslmode': 'verify-full',
   'user': 'dedp_test', 'sslrootcert': 'dataset/certs/ssl-cert-snakeoil.pem',
})
```

The connection parameters use the verify-full SSL mode that ensures the server host name matches the name stored in the server certificate.

To help you understand the cloud component better, let's change the cloud provider and see what a GCP Dataflow job needs to process objects from a GCS object store. First, we need to create a *Service Account* resource, which is a GCP term for the application user. The setup requires a name and a GCP project where it should apply. Example 7-29 shows this.

Example 7-29. Service Account creation in GCP

```
resource "google_service_account" "visits_job_sa" {
  account_id = "dedp"
  display_name = "Dataflow SA for processing visits from GCS"
}
```

The next step consists of linking this Service Account to the GCS bucket the Dataflow job should process and the job itself. Example 7-30 shows how to create this link with read-only permissions in the role attribute and with the Dataflow job.

Example 7-30. Reading permissions in the visits bucket

```
resource "google_storage_bucket_iam_binding" "visits_access" {
  bucket = "visits"
  role   = "roles/storage.objectViewer"
  members = [
    "serviceAccount:${google_service_account.visits_job_sa.email}",
  ]
}

resource "google_dataflow_job" "visits_aggregator" {# ...
  service_account_email = google_service_account.visits_job_sa.email
}
```

This way, the `visits_aggregator` job gets an identity, and consequently, it doesn't need any credentials provided at runtime to read the visits bucket.

Summary

In this chapter, you learned about various aspects of identity security. In the first section, you learned how to comply with a data removal request, which is one of the important parts of data regulation policies such as the GDPR and the CPPA. There are two possible solutions. The first one is the Vertical Partitioner, which leverages data layout to perform cheaper delete operations on a reduced number of occurrences. An alternative is the In-Place Overwriter pattern, which changes the data in place for data stores without any prior data organization strategy. It's more expensive, but at the same time, it's more universal than the Vertical Partitioner.

Next, you learned about fine-grained access. In the Fine-Grained Accessor for Tables pattern, you saw how to implement column- and row-level access controls in table-oriented environments, such as data warehouses and lakehouses. However, nowadays, data engineers are not exclusively working on these storage layers. They also interact with cloud services, such as serverless NoSQL data stores. For them, you'll use the Fine-Grained Accessor for Resources pattern.

In the third part came data protection. First, you learned how to protect your data at rest and in motion with the Encryptor pattern. It's a great additional security protection against malicious users who access your encrypted data but can't use it as they don't have the encryption keys. Then, you learned about the Anonymizer and Pseudo-Anonymizer patterns that are great ways to secure the dataset in data sharing scenarios.

Finally, you learned about two connectivity patterns that can help you better secure your data applications. The Secrets Pointer pattern will help you use credentials such as passwords and authorization keys, without keeping them directly in your Git repository. But since the best strategy is to not have any credentials to manage, even outside the repository, there is also the Secretless Connector pattern that you can leverage for interactions without logins and passwords.

Even though, with the data security design patterns we're approaching the end of our journey, three important topics still remain. The first of them is data storage, which, besides helping with data removal requests, also optimizes data access. It'll be the topic of the next chapter.

## CHAPTER 8

Data Storage Design Patterns

Have you ever waited for a query or job results longer than two minutes while working in a big data environment? Many of you will probably answer yes, and some of you may have even waited more than 10 minutes. This time factor is an important aspect in our data engineering work. The faster a query or job runs, the earlier we'll get the response and hopefully, the cheaper it will cost to get it.

You can optimize this time factor in two ways. First, you can add more compute resources, which is a relatively quick and easy method without any extra organizational steps. However, it's also a retroactive step that you might need to perform under pressure, for example, after users start to complain about reading latency.

The second way to optimize is by taking preemptive action that relies on a wise data organization with the data storage design patterns covered in this chapter. This well-thought-out organization should improve execution time and provide feedback earlier.

In this chapter, you'll first discover two partitioning strategies that help reduce the volume of data to process and also enable the implementation of some of the idempotency design patterns presented in Chapter 4, such as the Fast Metadata Cleaner pattern. Unfortunately, partitioning only works well for low-cardinality values (i.e., when you don't have a lot of different occurrences for a given attribute). For high-cardinality values, you may need more local optimization strategies, such as bucketing and sorting, which are presented as the second family of data storage patterns.

Besides organizing the data, there are other approaches to improving the user experience that you will see next in this chapter. They include the following:

- Leveraging the metadata layer to avoid unnecessary data-related operations

- Running costly operations only once, hence materializing them for subsequent readers

- Simplifying the data preparation step by avoiding costly listing operations

Finally, you'll also see two data representation approaches. The Normalizer approach favors data consistency, and the Denormalizer approach trades consistency for better execution time.

If you are impatient to see how to put data storage strategies into action, let's move on to the partitioning patterns!

Partitioning

When you define your storage layer's layout, the first question you'll need to answer is, what are the best ways to divide the dataset to make it easily accessible? The answer consists of two patterns that are responsible for horizontal and vertical organization.

Pattern: Horizontal Partitioner

Among these approaches to data organization, horizontal organization is probably the most commonly used due to the simplicity of its implementation and its long-term popularity since the early days of data engineering.

Problem

You created a batch job that computes rolling aggregates for the previous four days. It ran fine for a few months, but when more data began arriving in your storage layer, the job's performance declined. The biggest issue you spotted is increased execution time for the filtering operation to ignore records older than four days.

To mitigate the problem temporarily, you added more compute power to the job's cluster. However, that increased your costs. You have to find a better approach that will keep the cost as low as it was in the beginning and reduce the execution time despite new ingested data.

Solution

The rolling aggregation from the problem statement is an example of incremental data processing that uses only a portion of the whole dataset. It's a perfect condition in which to use the Horizontal Partitioner pattern and balance execution time with costs.

The solution requires identifying a partitioning attribute, which is also known as a *distribution key*. The data ingestion process or the data store will later use this attribute to save the dataset to a physically isolated storage space for each partitioning value.

Time-based partitions are popular and illustrate the horizontal parameter. As in our problem statement, they define time boundaries for the data processing step, letting you query the relevant information in a fast and cheap manner. In that context, the time attribute can come from either of the following:

The job execution context
> In this situation, the partitioning relies on the job's execution time, and the partition value will be the same for all records. For example, for a job executed on 2024-12-31, all records will land in the same partition corresponding to the run date.

The dataset
> In this case, the partitioning logic reasons in terms of event time. Due to the late data phenomena described in "Late Data" on page 51, the partitioned dataset may contain values for different partitions.

Despite their popularity, time properties are not the only possibilities for partitioning keys. You can also use business keys, such as customer ID, partner ID, or the customer's geographical region. You can go even further and create nested partitioning schemas, for example, by combining time- and business-based attributes. Example 8-1 shows a nested partitioning based on event time partitions and the user country attribute on top of a file system storage

Example 8-1. Dataset partitioned by event time and country attributes

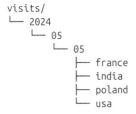

```
visits/
└── 2024
    └── 05
        └── 05
            ├── france
            ├── india
            ├── poland
            └── usa
```

You can set partitions in a declarative way (i.e., while you create a table). That's the case with Databricks' or GCP BigQuery's `CREATE TABLE ... PARTITIONED BY` statement. In this approach, the data producer doesn't need to know anything about the underlying partitioning, and it could skip defining the partition value during the data ingestion. This flexibility doesn't exist in the opposite mode, where the partitioning logic comes from the data producer. An example here is Apache Spark with the `partitionBy` method, which creates partitions from an existing column that itself can be the result of a more or less complex computation. You can use the same dynamic logic in Apache Kafka, where you can customize the partitioning logic by creating your own partitioner class.

In addition to creating the partitions, some data stores also manage partition metadata, including the last update time, the number of rows, and even the creation time. This kind of information is available on GCP BigQuery from the `INFORMA TION_SCHEMA.PARTITIONS` view, on Databricks as part of the output for the `DESCRIBE TABLE EXTENDED` command, and even on Apache Iceberg with the partitions view (`SELECT * FROM a_catalog.a_namespace.a_table.partitions`).

In addition to optimizing data retrieval, horizontal partitioning acts as an important component of idempotency. The Fast Metadata Cleaner pattern is one example of how to leverage partitioning to enable idempotent pipelines.

Consequences

Paradoxically, the biggest drawback of the Horizontal Partitioner is...horizontal partitions and, more specifically, their static character.

Granularity and metadata overhead. A partition is a physical location storing similar entities sharing the same value for one attribute. Consequently, having too many partitions will have a negative impact on the database.

To help you understand this better, let's take a look at an example of a visits dataset from our case study. If our website is visited by one million unique users daily and we partition the dataset by username, the Horizontal Partitioner will create one million partitions. This will result in slow partitions listing operations and many small files to read (cf. the small files problem described in "Pattern: Compactor" on page 27).

For this reason, a good rule of thumb is to use low-cardinality attributes, which are attributes with few distinct values. Using the event time rounded to the nearest hour or day is a great example of this because typically, you get one day or one hour, and thus one partition, for a bunch of records. On the other hand, using the ID number for IoT devices will result in thousands of small partitions. For them, a better choice is to rely on the Bucket design pattern described later in this chapter.

Skew. You may be thinking that horizontal partitioning guarantees even data distribution, but that's not always true.

Skewed partitions can often be a source of latency issues. A good example here is the microbatch stream processing model, which incrementally processes small batches of records. It processes these small batches in a blocking manner (i.e., the next microbatch can't run as long as the previous batch isn't completed).

If one partition in the microbatch is unbalanced, the unbalanced partition will determine the duration of the microbatch. Put differently, it'll block shorter partitions from being processed early as they will have to wait for the unbalanced partition to complete before moving on. To mitigate this issue, you can apply a backpressure mechanism that will store all extraneous records from the skewed partition in a separate buffer and process them only in the next microbatch. Figure 8-1 shows this mechanism with an extra backpressure buffer considered as an optional data source.

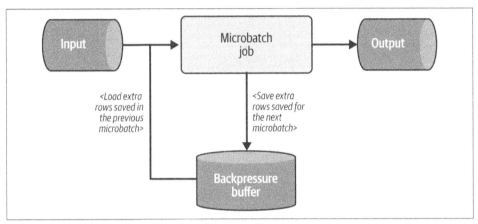

Figure 8-1. Data skew handling for a horizontally partitioned streaming broker

The backpressure buffer will increase overall data delivery latency to the skewed partition as the task will deliver buffered input later. However, this approach guarantees the other tasks can run in close to real time.

Mutability. Changing a partition key is difficult. It requires moving all already written data to a different location, which is costly and time-consuming.

Thankfully, some data stores may handle this mutability problem a bit better than others. For example, Apache Iceberg supports changing the partitioning schema at any moment. However, this operation works only at the metadata layer (i.e., it doesn't move the files to the new partition). Consequently, the partitioning storage remains unchanged for the old records, and the new organization applies only to the records created after the partition evolution.

Horizontal Partitioning Versus Sharding

Sharding consists of splitting a dataset into multiple machines, and it involves physical data division. Horizontal partitioning, although it also divides a dataset into multiple locations, doesn't require data movement across machines. Therefore, sharding is a special type of horizontal partitioning based on the physical (i.e., hardware) layer.

Examples

Let's first discover the Horizontal Partitioner pattern with Apache Spark. This data processing framework has a built-in method called `partitionBy` that natively splits the written dataset into partitions. Example 8-2 shows an example of this applied to the `change_date` column.

Example 8-2. Horizontal partitioning with Apache Spark creating granular partitioning columns

```
partitioned_users = (input_users
 .withColumn('year', functions.year('change_date'))
 .withColumn('month', functions.month('change_date'))
 .withColumn('day', functions.day('change_date'))
 .withColumn('hour', functions.hour('change_date')))

(partitioned_users.write.mode('overwrite').format('delta')
 .partitionBy('year', 'month', 'day', 'hour').save(output_dir))
```

After executing this code, the job will create a dataset partitioned by year/month/day/hour, making possible many access patterns that combine the values present in the partitioning path.

The solution is slightly different for Apache Kafka, where you can implement a custom partitioning logic with a custom partitioner. Example 8-3, which is written in Java due to partitioner implementation constraints, shows an example of a custom partitioning logic writing the records to partition 0 or 1, depending on the record's key.

Example 8-3. Custom Apache Kafka partitioner

```java
public class RangePartitioner implements Partitioner {

  private static final int DEFAULT_PARTITION = 1;
  private final static Map<String, Integer> RANGES_PER_PARTITIONS = new HashMap<>();
  static {
   RANGES_PER_PARTITIONS.put("A", 0);
   RANGES_PER_PARTITIONS.put("B", 0);
  }

  @Override
  public int partition(String topic, Object key, byte[] keyBytes,
   Object value, byte[] valueBytes, Cluster cluster) {
    String keyAsString = key.toString();
    return RANGES_PER_PARTITIONS.getOrDefault(keyAsString, DEFAULT_PARTITION);
  }
// ...
```

To declare your custom partitioner, you need to reference the created class in the `par titioner.class` property (see Example 8-4).

Example 8-4. Customizing horizontal partitioning at the producer level

```
Properties props = new Properties();
// ...
props.put("partitioner.class", "com.waitingforcode.RangePartitioner");
```

Keep It Simple!

Keep in mind that any code increases complexity. That's why it's always good to favor simplicity and add code (and thus complexity) only when necessary. As a result, most of the time, you will stick to the default partitioners in Apache Kafka.

In addition to Apache Spark and Apache Kafka, Horizontal Partitioner is present in relational databases. Example 8-5 shows an example of a PostgreSQL table storing website visits. Each partition is responsible for keeping visits from a different day.

Example 8-5. Range partitioning logic for date times in PostgreSQL

```
CREATE TABLE visits_all (
  visit_id CHAR(36) NOT NULL,
  event_time TIMESTAMP NOT NULL,
  user_id  TEXT NOT NULL,
  page VARCHAR(20) NULL,
  PRIMARY KEY(visit_id, event_time)
) PARTITION BY RANGE(event_time);

CREATE TABLE visits_all_20231124 PARTITION OF visits_all
FOR VALUES FROM('2023-11-24 00:00:00') TO ('2023-11-24 23:59:59')

CREATE TABLE visits_all_20231125 PARTITION OF visits_all
FOR VALUES FROM('2023-11-25 00:00:00') TO ('2023-11-25 23:59:59')
```

Pattern: Vertical Partitioner

As you've seen, the Horizontal Partitioner pattern processes whole rows each time. The next partitioning pattern is its alternative because it divides each row and writes the separate parts to different places, such as tables or files.

For Storage and Security

The Vertical Partitioner pattern presented in Chapter 7 is a specialization of vertical partitioning applied to security. The Vertical Partitioner presented in this chapter is a specialization dedicated to data storage.

Problem

In one of your pipelines, you track user visits to your website. The visits dataset has two categories of attributes: mutable ones that change at each visit (such as visit time or visited page) and immutable ones that remain the same throughout the visit (like IP address). You're looking for a way to avoid duplicating the immutable information and store it only once for each visit.

Solution

Having two types of attributes like in our problem statement is the perfect condition to use the Vertical Partitioner pattern.

The implementation begins with data classification, where you need to put related attributes together. For the announced problem statement, you would divide the attributes into the mutable and immutable groups. In addition to those groups, you need to identify an attribute that you're going to use to combine them if needed. In our example, it'll be the visit ID.

Once this specification step is completed, your data processing job will write the grouped attributes for each row into dedicated locations, such as tables in a data store or directories in a file system.

In addition to optimizing storage costs, the Vertical Partitioner pattern brings flexibility. Because a row is now divided, you can easily apply different data retention or data access policies to it. That would be more challenging to put in place if the row were kept undivided.

To sum up, the difference with the Horizontal Partitioner pattern comes from the partitioning heuristic. As demonstrated in Figure 8-2, the horizontal approach applies the partitioning rule to a whole row by moving it fully to a different location. On the other hand, the vertical logic splits a row and writes it to different locations.

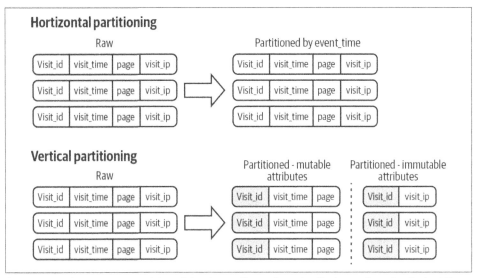

Figure 8-2. A visit row partitioned horizontally and vertically (note that the dashed line separates two partitioning locations, and the filled boxes represent unique IDs used to recombine the divided row)

Consequences

However, the Vertical Partitioner pattern has some logical implications in the following areas.

Domain split. Since each row is split apart, there may be logically related attributes that are stored in two separate places. It may not be easy to find them, and good documentation support for your end user will be key.

Querying. This drawback results from the domain split. As each row is separated, it gets harder to get the full picture than in a horizontally partitioned dataset. To mitigate this issue, you can expose the data from a view combining all tables for the vertically partitioned entity (for example, with the Dataset Materializer pattern).

Data producer. In addition to the consumers, the Vertical Partitioner impacts the producers, who from now on can't simply take a row and write it elsewhere. Instead, producers need to implement the row division logic and consequently perform multiple writes at a potentially higher network communication cost.

Examples

Let's begin this section with an Apache Spark example that extracts the user and technical visit context into two different tables. Although this task sounds easy, you must remember to call the `persist()` function so that the input dataset doesn't get read twice. Later, you need to build both tables by using `drop()` and `select()` functions to, respectively, remove and select columns. Example 8-6 shows this logic implemented.

Example 8-6. Vertical Partitioner in Apache Spark

```
visits = spark_session.read.schema(visit_schema).json(input_location)
visits.persist()

visits_without_user_technical_context = (visits.drop('user_id')
 .withColumn('context', F.col('context').dropFields('user'))
 .withColumn('context', F.col('context').dropFields('technical')))
visits_without_user_technical_context.write.format('delta').save(output_dir)

(visits.selectExpr('visit_id', 'context.user.*', 'user_id').dropDuplicates()
.write.format('delta').save(get_delta_users_table_dir()))

(visits.selectExpr('visit_id', 'context.technical.*').dropDuplicates()
.write.format('delta').save(get_delta_technical_table_dir()))

visits.unpersist()
```

When it comes to a SQL-based implementation, let's see what commands can help you implement the pattern in PostgreSQL. The first command uses the INSERT INTO...SELECT FROM operation. Here, instead of declaring each row to insert explicitly, you delegate this declaration task to the dynamic SELECT query. Example 8-7 shows this in action.

Example 8-7. Inserting technical visit context with INSERT INTO...SELECT FROM

```
INSERT INTO dedp.technical (visit_id, browser, browser_version, ...)
 (SELECT DISTINCT visit_id, context->'technical'->>'browser',
    context->'technical'->>'browser_version', ...
  FROM dedp.visits_all);
```

Also, you can use a different approach that creates the vertically partitioned table from a SELECT statement. This is commonly known as a CREATE TABLE AS SELECT (CTAS) construction, an example of which is presented in Example 8-8.

Example 8-8. CTAS construction for the technical context of a vertically partitioned visit

```
CREATE TABLE dedp.technical_select AS (SELECT DISTINCT
  visit_id, context->'technical'->>'browser' AS browser,
  context->'technical'->>'browser_version' AS browser_version, ...
  FROM dedp.visits_all;
```

Records Organization

Partitioning is often the first step in organizing data. But as you've seen, it's rather rudimentary as it moves either full or partial records to different locations. Moreover, you can't use it on all attributes. For example, you've seen that high-cardinality values are not well suited to horizontal partitioning. The next category of patterns goes one step further because it applies some smart optimizations for records colocation, addressing, among other things, the cardinality issues of the Horizontal Partitioner pattern.

Pattern: Bucket

If, for whatever reason, you need to improve access to a column with high cardinality, such as a unique user ID, there is hope. Instead of colocating rows in the same storage space with partitioning, you can colocate groups of rows. That's an oversimplified definition of what the next pattern does.

Problem

The dataset you're modeling has a business attribute that is frequently used in queries as part of the predicate. Initially, you wanted to use this attribute as a partitioning column, but its cardinality is too high. It would result in too many partitions that at some point could reach your data store metadata limits. As 80% of operations rely on this high-cardinality attribute, you still want to optimize storage, but at the moment, you don't know how.

Solution

The fact that you've got a high-cardinality column that is often involved in queries is a good reason to use the Bucket pattern. Although on the surface it also stores records in a dedicated location, unlike Horizontal Partitioner, it colocates different values in the same storage area.

As for the two partitioning patterns, the Bucket pattern's implementation starts with the data analysis step that defines the column(s) to use for bucketing. If a dataset is already partitioned with the horizontal or vertical approach, you can consider these attributes as a kind of secondary set of grouping keys (the partition key being the primary key), which are more commonly known as bucket columns.

Next, you might also need to set the number of buckets you want to create. The number depends on your bucket key's cardinality. If the cardinality is really high, it means you have a lot of unique values. A higher number would mean more smaller buckets, while a lower number would create fewer bigger buckets. This dependency comes from the grouping formula that applies a modular hashing so that the bucket number for each key is computed as `hash(key) % buckets number`.

Grouping records enables two optimization techniques for consumers:

Bucket pruning
> Whenever a bucket column is used as a predicate in the query, the query execution engine can directly use the bucketing algorithm and eliminate all buckets without the required keys. This may cause a significant performance boost for all filtering operations.

Network exchange (shuffle) elimination
> This applies to JOIN operations using the identical bucketing configuration on both sides of the join. That way, the query runner can leverage the buckets to directly load correlated records from each dataset to the same join process, thus combining them without the network exchange you discovered while you were reading about the Distributed Aggregator pattern. Figure 8-3 illustrates this optimization strategy.

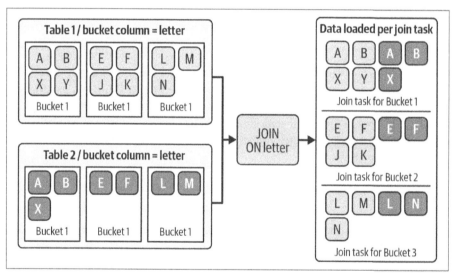

Figure 8-3. Distributed join without shuffle on top of identically bucketed tables

Historically, the bucketing feature was made popular by Apache Hive, but since then, it has been integrated into modern data solutions, including Apache Spark and AWS Athena.

Consequences

Yet again, the data is static, and that's one of the biggest issues with the Bucket pattern.

Mutability. The bucketing schema is immutable. Technically, it's possible to modify it by either changing the column or bucket size, but that's a costly operation requiring backfilling the dataset.

Bucket size. The Bucket pattern requires setting the bucket size. Unfortunately, finding the right size is challenging if you expect to get more data in the future. If you rely on the current data volume, in the future, you'll create big buckets. On the other hand, if you try to predict the number, there's no guarantee that your prediction will be accurate, and in the meantime, the writers may create more buckets than necessary. Both techniques are acceptable ways to mitigate the problem, but as you can see, they both have some gotchas.

Examples

Amazon Athena is a serverless query service implementing the Bucket pattern at the logical level. Put differently, it doesn't write any data. Instead, it only applies the existing bucketing logic to the tables already stored on S3. For that reason, if you issue an INSERT INTO query into a bucketed table, you will get an error.

To configure a table as a bucketed table, you have to define the bucket columns in the CLUSTERED BY statement, plus set the bucketing format. In Example 8-9, the visits table is bucketed by the user_id column in the Apache Spark format.

Example 8-9. Bucketing configuration in AWS Athena

```
CREATE EXTERNAL TABLE visits (...) ...
CLUSTERED BY (`user_id`) INTO 50 BUCKETS
TBLPROPERTIES ('bucketing_format' = 'spark')
```

Apache Spark creates a bucketed table by calling the bucketBy function, which applies the modulo-based algorithm mentioned in the implementation section to the bucket columns (see Example 8-10).

Example 8-10. Bucketing in Apache Spark

```
input_dataset.write.bucketBy(50, 'user_id').saveAsTable(table_name)
```

Pattern: Sorter

Colocating groups of records in buckets is not the only storage optimization technique. Another technique that helps eliminate data blocks that are irrelevant to queries relies on data storage order.

Problem

You decided to store data in weekly tables to leverage the Fast Metadata Cleaner pattern. Although it made your daily maintenance task less painful, it didn't improve the query execution time. You don't want to change this idempotency strategy, but at the same time, you would like to reduce data access latency. For that reason, you're looking for a solution that could speed up query execution. The good news is that you know the types of users' queries. Most of them will filter or sort by the event time column.

Solution

Knowing which column or columns are commonly used in sorting or filtering is a good way to implement the Sorter pattern to optimize data access.

You start the implementation by identifying the sorting column or columns. Next, you have to declare the sorting column(s) in the table's creation query. Thereafter, the database will take care of organizing the written rows according to the defined order.

Thanks to the sorted storage, any query targeting the sorting column(s) will be able to skip irrelevant data blocks, very often thanks to the metadata information associated with each of them. Figure 8-4 illustrates this optimization, and if you need more details, you'll find them in "Pattern: Metadata Enhancer" on page 251.

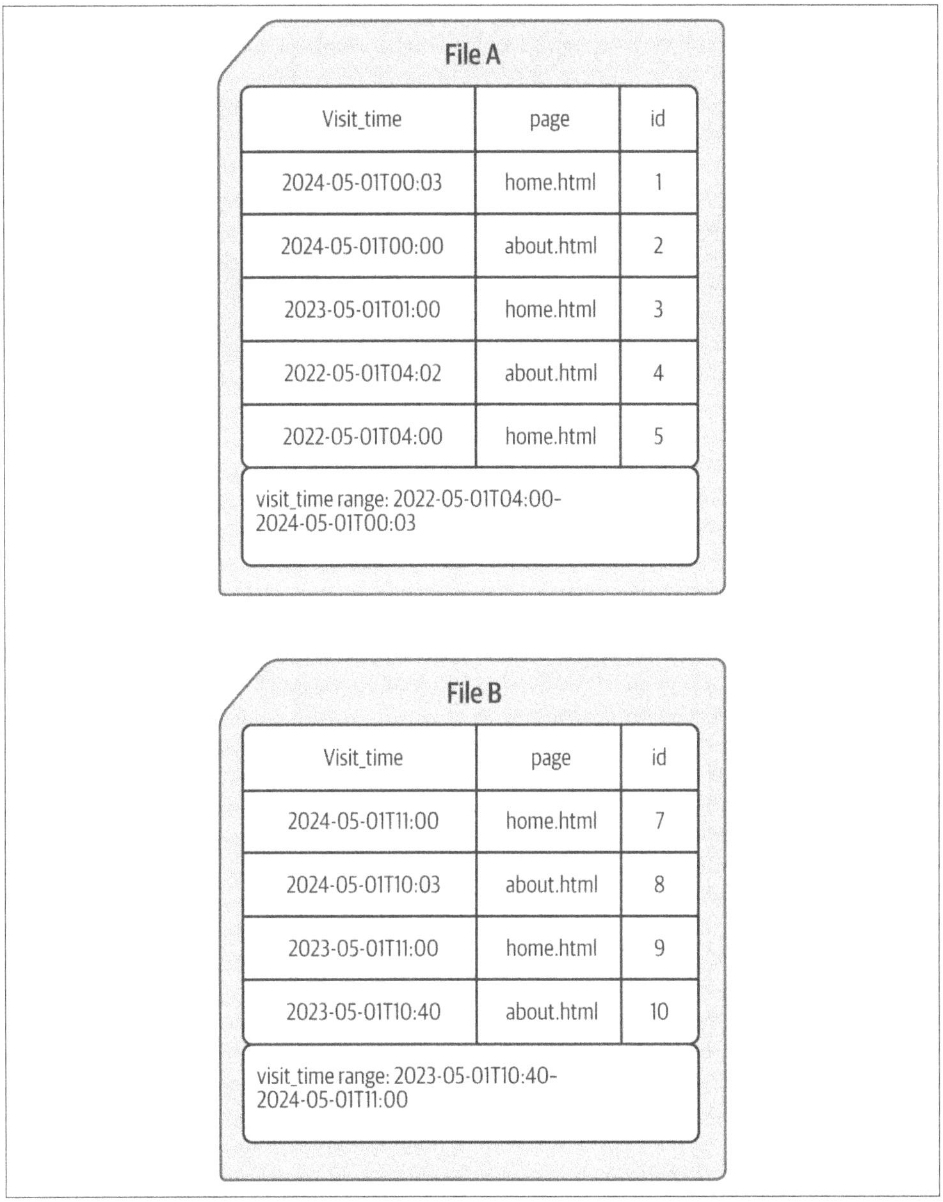

Figure 8-4. Metadata information for data skipping (note that if a query targets `visit_time` *within one of the ranges, the query engine can avoid processing one of the files)*

Curved sorts is a variant of the classical top-to-bottom sorting algorithm, where the results are sorted vertically. A popular example of this, especially thanks to recent advances in the table file formats space, is Z-order. Instead of lexicographical order, this method colocates rows from x-dimensional space.

Explaining the Z-order algorithm in detail is out of scope of this book,[1] but fortunately for you, table file formats like Apache Iceberg and Delta Lake implement it natively. However, it's important to understand why Z-order works better than lexicographical order for multiple columns. To help you grasp this, let's analyze how both methods store a dataset sorted by columns x and y, as shown in Figure 8-5. As you will notice, Z-order reduces the number of data blocks to read thanks to a different, curved data organization layout.

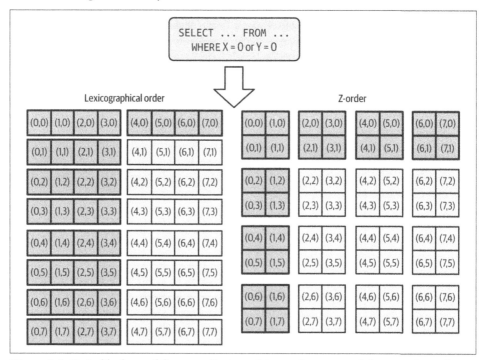

Figure 8-5. Data blocks read for a predicate and two-column sorted datasets (note that lexicographical order reads nine data blocks, while Z-order only reads seven)

---

1 You can find more information about it in two O'Reilly books: *Delta Lake: The Definitive Guide* by Denny Lee, Tristen Wentling, Scott Haines, and Prashanth Babu (2024) and *Apache Iceberg: The Definitive Guide* by Tomer Shiran, Jason Hughes, and Alex Merced (2024).

Z-order became famous with Delta Lake and Apache Iceberg, but it has been around for longer. Among other data stores, Amazon Redshift provides a Z-order-like sort implementation based on Z-curves with the *interleaved sort keys* feature. Classical sorting is present in data warehouses such as GCP BigQuery and Snowflake via clustered tables.

Sorting Versus Clustering

Z-order is also referenced in the context of clustering due to colocating related records in the same files. However, it does this by effectively sorting data on disk, like a lexicographical sort would do. For that reason, Z-order is classified here as an example of the Sorter pattern.

Consequences

A presorted dataset has a positive impact on the reader's performance. However, it negatively impacts the writer.

Unsorted segments. Sorting may not always be an instantaneous activity. This means that whenever you write new records, there will be some unsorted blocks that will not benefit from the Sorter pattern's optimizations. To mitigate the issue, you may need to schedule the sorting actions in the data writing job or outside of it. Keep in mind that integrating the sorting action with the data writing process will impact the execution time.

Composite sort keys. When you use composite sort keys in the lexicographical order method, keep in mind that the queries should always reference the sorting columns preceding the one(s) you're targeting. Otherwise, despite sort declaration, the query engine will still need to iterate over most of the data blocks. Let's illustrate that with a simple case of a sort key composed of a visit time and a page ID column. Figure 8-6 points out the rows involved when the query targets both columns, and the rows impacted by the read when the query filters only on the page ID.

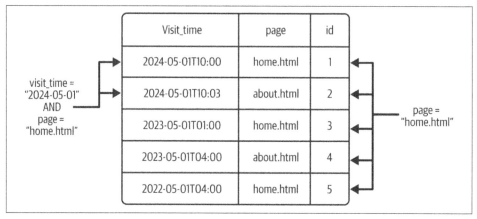

Figure 8-6. A table sorted by `visit_time` *and page, and rows impacted by querying both columns (left side) or only one of the columns (right side)*

Mutability.   Although it's often possible to change the sorting keys after creating them, you must be aware that the operation may need to sort the entire table. Depending on the table's size, this can be costly.

Examples

Let's start this section with a cloud example. GCP BigQuery implements the Sorter pattern via clustered tables. A clustered table requires the declaration of the sorting columns as part of the CLUSTER BY statement (see Example 8-11).

Example 8-11. Clustered table for `visit_id` *and page columns in BigQuery*

```
CREATE TABLE `dedp.visits.raw_visits`
PARTITION BY DATE(event_time)
CLUSTER BY visit_id, page
```

Although the clustered table will improve performance when it comes to targeting the visit_id and page columns, it will not help that much if you only need to filter on the page column. Curved sorts solve this issue. Let's see how by using a Delta Lake Z-order compaction. Creating a Z-order-compacted table requires calling the optimized API with the columns that should be used to create this curved distribution. Example 8-12 shows this initialization step.

Example 8-12. Z-order compaction with Delta Lake for the `visit_id` *and page columns*

```
DeltaTable.forPath(spark, output_dir)
  .optimize().executeZOrderBy(['visit_id', 'page'])
```

As a result, Delta Lake will compact data files to better organize the records inside the rewritten files.

Read Performance Optimization

The patterns from this section extend the data organization techniques presented so far to optimize data access.

Pattern: Metadata Enhancer

The first technique you can leverage to optimize reading performance uses metadata. This is one of the reasons why columnar file formats such as Apache Parquet have been viewed as disruptive changes in the data engineering field for many years.

Problem

You partitioned your JSON dataset horizontally by event time, hoping to reduce the execution time of batch jobs. And it worked! However, your company then hired new data analysts who are also working on the same partitioned dataset but are targeting only a small subset of rows from one partition.

Since the partitions are big, data analysts complain about the query execution latency and increased cloud bills as they're relying on a pay-as-you-go querying service. After the first analysis, you find out that the data analysts' queries always load the full dataset and only later apply the filtering logic. You would like to reverse these two operations and apply the filtering logic before loading the dataset into the query engine.

Solution

An easy way to optimize the query execution time and cost is to skip all irrelevant data files before loading them for processing. That's where the Metadata Enhancer pattern comes into play.

The implementation consists of collecting and persisting statistics about the stored records in a file or database. Since we mentioned the files in the problem statement, let's discover this integration first.

The Metadata Enhancer implementation for files applies to columnar file formats such as Apache Parquet, in which each data file contains a footer with additional metadata. As per its name, the columnar file format stores a column in each file. The statistics are local to the file (i.e., they describe only the values from the file). Figure 8-7 shows a simplified version for an age column with attached statistics.

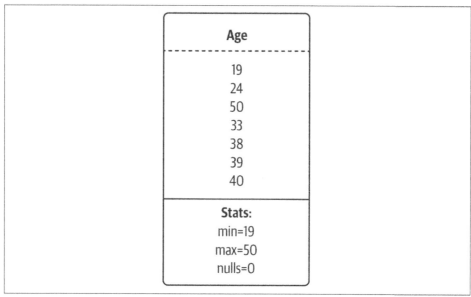

Figure 8-7. A simplified example of the metadata footer with a data summary for the stored records in an Apache Parquet file

As you've likely noticed, the footer includes a range of possible values that are automatically computed while a file is created by the data producer. Now, when a user queries the age column as part of the predicate (for example, SELECT ... FROM table WHERE age > 50), the query execution engine can simply verify in the metadata footer whether the requested age is included in the file. Since the footer is smaller than the data block, the filtering operation relies on a reduced dataset and consequently is much faster than opening a larger portion of the data to analyze each entry separately. That said, there is still the overhead of reading all the footers to know where the relevant records are, but the overhead is incomparably smaller than for reading all the data files.

Since Apache Parquet is the storage format used by table file formats, the pattern is automatically available on Delta Lake, Apache Iceberg, and Apache Hudi. But in addition to the Apache Parquet statistics, these formats store additional metadata in the commit log that can optimize readers. Some of this metadata consists of numbers, such as the number of rows created in the commit, the minimum and maximum values per column, and even the number of NULLs in a given column. That way, users can pretty quickly perform queries counting the number of elements or filtering on nonexistent values.

But files are not the only place where the Metadata Enhancer applies. You can find the same kind of statistics for tables in relational databases and data warehouses. The statistics in that context will often be located in a separate table that the query planner will leverage to create the most efficient execution plans.

Consequences

Although it's hard to find drawbacks for the Metadata Enhancer, there is a little one related to the cost of this additional layer.

Overhead. When it comes to columnar file formats, building statistics at writing time is an extra operation the writing job must perform. It can slightly impact the processing time because for each processed column, the job must keep the configured stats.

Additionally, for relational databases and data warehouses, the data store must keep the statistics up-to-date. Otherwise, the execution plan might be far from the most optimal one. To address this issue when statistics are out of date, you can run a command that's responsible for refreshing them.

Out-of-date statistics. Even though statistics are updated automatically for relational databases and data warehouses, the update process may not be immediate. Often, its execution is controlled by certain thresholds, such as the number of rows that have been modified since the last update. Consequently, if your table undergoes small changes from time to time that don't reach the thresholds, the statistics can become out of date over time.

To mitigate this issue, you can refresh the statistics manually with commands like `ANALYZE TABLE`. But keep in mind that this might add temporary read overhead on the database to process the table and generate updated statistics.

Examples

To start this section, let's look at the most basic example with Apache Parquet. The writing step in Apache Spark requires using an appropriate data writer (see Example 8-13).

Example 8-13. Writing an Apache Parquet file

```
input_dataset.write.mode('overwrite').parquet(path=get_parquet_dir())
```

Statistics are created for you under the hood. You can see their content by running a Docker command like the one in Example 8-14.

Example 8-14. Apache Parquet metadata analyzer command

```
docker run --rm -v "./output-parquet:/tmp/parquet"
  hangxie/parquet-tools:v1.20.7  meta
  /tmp/parquet/part-00001-3c52ae6f-aeea-4364-aac3-7fc69d63e898-c000.snappy.parquet
```

The output should print statistics for each column. Example 8-15 shows this for the ID column.

Example 8-15. Apache Parquet statistics for the login column

```
"NumRowGroups": 1, {"PathInSchema": ["Id"], "Type": "BYTE_ARRAY",
 "Encodings": ["PLAIN", "RLE", "BIT_PACKED"],"CompressedSize": 180463,
 "UncompressedSize": 200035,"NumValues": 5000,
 "NullCount": 0, "MaxValue": "fffbe4f8-8d88-43d2-a9a5-54bf536de75b",
 "MinValue": "0018e1dc-1b80-4410-92f6-5261d2dadf35",
 "CompressionCodec": "SNAPPY"}
```

Delta Lake adds an extra layer on top of the Apache Parquet metadata. This layer is present in the commit logs and also contains metadata to accelerate data processing operations. As for Parquet, you don't need to generate those values explicitly. That's done by the data processing framework under the hood. As a result, you should receive entries like those in Example 8-16.

Example 8-16. Statistics in the Delta Lake commit log

```
{"commitInfo":{"timestamp":1716954694590,"operation":"WRITE",
"operationMetrics":{"numFiles":"1",
"numOutputRows":"6100",
"numOutputBytes":"50437"}," ...}
{"add":{"path":"part-....-c000.snappy.parquet, "size":50437,
"stats":"{
 \"numRecords\":6100,
 \"minValues\":
   {\"type\":\"galaxy\",\"full_name\":\"APPLE iPhone 11 (White, 64 GB)\",
    \"version\":\"Android 10\"},
 \"maxValues\":
   {\"type\":\"mac\",\"full_name\":\"Yoga 7i (14\\\" Intel) 2 in 1 Lapto◆\",
    \"version\":\"v17169535721658688\"},
 \"nullCount\":{\"type\":0,\"full_name\":0,\"version\":0}}"}}
```

Pattern: Dataset Materializer

Costly operations pose another challenge to improving data access. If you need to write a query that involves some shuffle and CPU-intensive transformations, and if you need to run the same query over and over again, performance may suffer. Surprisingly, you could benefit from data duplication to improve data reading performance.

Problem

You wanted to simplify the process of querying multiple partitioned tables of the same dataset to get the past three weeks of data. You created a view, but consumers weren't fully satisfied. They complained about latency, and because the view runs the underlying query each time, you can see their point. However, you want to solve this issue and provide them with a better-performing single point of data access.

Solution

When the computation of results is slow, the simplest solution is to avoid the problem by materializing the data. That's what the Dataset Materializer pattern does.

The implementation starts by identifying the datasets that should be materialized. After the identification step, you need to implement the materialization. Typically, this will involve querying the data with the appropriate SELECT statements and maybe combining multiple datasets with a UNION or JOIN operation. Then, the created query is later used to materialize the dataset as a materialized view or a table in your database.

Which of the materialized view and table techniques should you chose? The biggest difference between them is related to refreshes. Manual refreshes of materialized views are possible, but modern data warehousing solutions support automatic refreshes under some criteria as well. For example, Amazon Redshift supports this feature via an AUTO REFRESH YES option defined in the CREATE MATERIALIZED VIEW statement. However, the refresh isn't meant to be run immediately after you change the underlying tables. Its execution depends on the current workload on the database or the size of the data to refresh. Therefore, the logic, albeit automated, is less predictable. Besides Redshift, materialized views are available in other data warehousing solutions, including GCP BigQuery, Databricks, and Snowflake.

On the other hand, when you use a table as the storage for the materialized dataset, you'll be responsible for refreshes, without the possibility of leveraging any automatic refresh feature. In exchange for this extra work, you get extra flexibility as the table may benefit from other storage optimization techniques—including partitions, buckets, and sorting—which may not be available for a materialized view. All this gives you more work to do but also provides more operational flexibility and optimization techniques.

Consequences

While you may be thinking that refreshing is not an issue, I have bad news. It may be.

Refresh cost. As you can imagine, whenever you need to refresh the view, you need to rerun the creation query. If this setup query is costly, perhaps because of the data volume or the type of operations, it'll impact the resources of your database, including the ones available for regular users interacting with other tables.

To overcome this issue, you can use an incremental refresh (i.e., integrate only the most recent changes into the view). This fits perfectly into insert-only workloads where historical data doesn't change and the refresh only appends the new records.

Modern data warehousing solutions support incremental refreshes out of the box. That's the case with Databricks and GCP BigQuery. However, their incremental refreshes don't support all SQL operations, and sometimes, they will still refresh the whole dataset.

Data access. Because the materialized dataset combines multiple tables, it may be challenging to apply consistent data management, including retention or access configuration. Typically, if a user doesn't have access to one of the building tables, you should continue to deny access to the view, or you should implement one of the options in the Fine-Grained Accessor pattern, if possible.

Data storage overhead. Materialization does indeed optimize access, but it trades optimization for storage. If storage is a concern for you, you may opt for a mixed implementation of the Dataset Materializer pattern, in which only some of the view's datasets get materialized and the others live as regular, recomputable parts.

Examples

GCP BigQuery is a cloud-managed data warehouse that not only supports materialized views but also let you configure an automatic refresh of them. Example 8-17 shows a materialized view that's refreshed every 15 minutes.

Example 8-17. Query creating an automatically refreshed materialized view in BigQuery

```
CREATE MATERIALIZED VIEW dedp.visits.visits_enriched
OPTIONS (enable_refresh = true, refresh_interval_minutes = 15)
AS SELECT...
```

There's one thing to notice, though: automatic refreshes are rarely guaranteed to run just after you modify the base table. This is also true for BigQuery, which should run the refresh within five minutes of the change. But if there is not enough capacity, the refresh will be delayed.

That's why as an alternative, you can use a manually refreshed materialized view. PostgreSQL provides a REFRESH MATERIALIZED VIEW command that integrates new data into the view, as shown in Example 8-18.

Example 8-18. Refreshing a materialized view with PostgreSQL

```
REFRESH MATERIALIZED VIEW dedp.windowed_visits WITH DATA;
```

As for the incremental version of the Dataset Materializer pattern, let's analyze how to integrate new visit counts. First, the input table has an `insertion_time` column that corresponds to the writing time of each row. The idea is to use this column to query only the rows added after the previous execution and combine the result with the existing dataset. As you can see already, the solution combines the Incremental Loader pattern with the Merger pattern.

Example 8-19 shows the SQL query executed at each run to update the number of overall visits per user by combining existing counts with new records.

Example 8-19. Incremental version of the Dataset Materializer pattern

```
MERGE INTO dedp.visits_counter AS target
USING (
  -- 2024-11-09T03:27:32 is the time after the previous insertion_time
  SELECT user_id, COUNT(*) AS visits FROM dedp.visits
  WHERE insertion_time > '2024-11-09T03:27:32' GROUP BY user_id
) AS input
ON target.user_id = input.user_id
WHEN MATCHED THEN UPDATE SET count = count + input.visits
WHEN NOT MATCHED THEN INSERT (user_id, count) VALUES (input.user_id, input.visits)
```

Pattern: Manifest

The last read access performance challenge concerns data listing, which can be slow, especially for object stores with many files because this will result in many API calls. Even though you can try to mitigate this issue by parallelizing the listing operation, there is a better way.

Problem

You have created an Apache Parquet dataset in your object store. Your batch jobs are now performing very well, and their decreased execution time has also reduced your cloud bill. As a result, your company has asked you to create a data warehouse layer. One of the requirements is the exposition of this Apache Parquet dataset to the data analysts team. Unfortunately, when you did your first tests, the execution time was not as good as for the batch job producer. You found out that the slowest operation lists the files to load from your object store, and you would like to avoid this costly step.

Solution

To overcome a repeated listing operation problem, it's better to list files only once or not at all if the data producer can record filenames beforehand. That's the premise of the Manifest pattern.

Table file formats such as Delta Lake, Apache Iceberg, and Apache Hudi are the first implementations of the pattern. They write the list of files created within the given transaction to the commit log stored in the metadata location. That way, when a reader needs to access the data files, it can simply get them from the commit files, without performing any listing of the underlying storage. In the context of the Manifest pattern, these commit logfiles act as manifest files, meaning files providing all necessary and important information about the data.

The alternatives to automatically managed manifests are manually created manifests that may require a prior listing operation. They can be particularly useful if many different readers operate on the same dataset, for example, as part of the Fan-Out patterns in Chapter 6.

In addition to their utility in data reading, manifests can play a crucial role in writing. Amazon Redshift uses a manifest file in the COPY command that loads new data into a table. For each loading operation, you can define a different manifest file with a dedicated list of files to upload. This materialization can be incredibly helpful in implementing idempotent pipelines, like the ones in Chapter 4. A similar implementation exists for the Storage Transfer Service on GCP. This offering relies on manifest listings to copy files from other cloud stores to GCS.

Consequences

As you can see, the pattern offers efficiency and optimization, but there are trade-offs with complexity and overall size.

Complexity. If you need to add the manifest creation step, you'll add some extra complexity to the execution flow. However, manifest creation is a rather simple operation consisting of listing recently written files. Having this extra complexity in the pipeline should be easier to accept than running a slow and unpredictable listing action many times.

Size. Manifests can grow really big. That's particularly apparent if the input location has many small files or if the data producer is a continuous streaming job. In that case, it's common to see manifests of several gigabytes in size. Some of the implementations may have a maximum size limit for a manifest file or a retention configuration for the entries present in the file.

The size issue was present in the early days of Apache Spark Structured Streaming. When you were using the framework to write files, in addition to creating new files in the output location, the job was adding their names to a manifest file. Over time, the manifests were continuously growing, and sometimes the jobs couldn't even restart because the manifests were too big to restore. Since then, the issue has been fixed (see SPARK-27188 (*https://oreil.ly/Cewc7*)).

Examples

Let's see how the Manifest pattern can enable two different technologies to work together. The goal of the first example is to create a so-called external table for a Delta Lake dataset in BigQuery. To start, you have to generate the manifest file from Delta Lake. The operation is just a matter of calling a `generate` function (see Example 8-20).

Example 8-20. Generating a manifest file in Delta Lake

```
devices_table = DeltaTable.forPath(spark_session, DemoConfiguration.DEVICES_TABLE)
devices_table.generate('symlink_format_manifest')
```

The generated manifest contains all files used by the most recent version of the Delta Lake table (aka snapshot). The next thing to do is to reference this file as part of the external table creation statement (see Example 8-21).

Example 8-21. External table creation with a Delta Lake manifest file

```
CREATE EXTERNAL TABLE IF NOT EXISTS `dedp.visits.devices`
...
OPTIONS (
    hive_partition_uri_prefix = "gc://devices",
    uris = ['gc://devices/_symlink_format_manifest/*/manifest'],
    file_set_spec_type = 'NEW_LINE_DELIMITED_MANIFEST',
    format="PARQUET");
```

Another use case of the Manifest pattern occurs in Redshift, which can enforce the idempotency of the `COPY` command with the list of files to load to the table. If before loading the files, you create the manifest and associate it with the job's execution, you'll be able to use the same manifest file for any replayed job's runs. Example 8-22 shows an example of the operation using a manifest file composed of two required data files.

Example 8-22. Manifest for data loading in Amazon Redshift

```
COPY customer
FROM 's3://devices/manifest_20250601_1031'
...
MANIFEST;
# manifest_20250601_1031
{"entries": [
 {"url":"s3://devices/dataset_1","mandatory":true},
 {"url":"s3://devices/dataset_2","mandatory":true}]}
```

Data Representation

Data storage is not only about organizing storage or optimizing read performance. Both are crucial steps to make a dataset useful, but they're missing one piece: data representation, which answers the crucial question of what attributes will be stored together and thus what tables you're going to create.

Pattern: Normalizer

The first data representation pattern favors decoupling, which is great for keeping a dataset consistent by not duplicating the information.

Problem

You defined a data model for the visit events from Figure 1-1. A colleague pointed out some data duplication. In fact, your visits table stores event-driven attributes, such as visit time and visited page, but also immutable attributes, such as device name, operating system name, and version. The immutable attributes are repeated for each visit row, leading to increased storage and slow update operations whenever these attributes are modified.

You were asked to review your design and propose a model that addresses the issues of data repetition and slow updates.

Solution

In the context of our problem, the separation can be understood as normalization since we try to reduce repetition by representing each piece of information only once. From there comes the name of the next pattern, the Normalizer pattern.

The Normalizer has two possible implementations called normal forms (NF) and the snowflake schema. Despite their different names and technical details, the two share the same high-level design process that follows these steps:

1. Defining the business entities. First, you establish a list of terms involved in your data model. For the sake of our website visits example, the terms could include *visits*, *devices*, *browsers*, and *link referrals*.

2. Describing the business entities. Then you define the attributes of each entity. For example, if the entity you are describing is a browser, its attributes could include the browser name and version.

3. Defining the relationships among the business entities. Finally, you define the dependencies between the business entities. For example, a visit would depend on the availability of a browser, while a browser would depend on the availability of an operating system.

As for the specific implementations, let's start with the NF-based approach. It's widely used in transactional workloads that mainly involve writing operations occurring at a fast pace. The NF design helps eliminate data quality–related issues by reducing duplicates and, consequently, the volume of data to write. The model respects the following forms:

The first NF
> After you apply this form, the columns of your table should have nonrepeating atomic values, and each row should be uniquely identifiable by a primary key.

The second NF
> Here, each column must depend only on the primary key. In other words, a non-primary key attribute must be described by all primary key attributes.

The third NF
> This form guarantees that there are no transitive dependencies between nonprimary attributes. In other words, all nonprimary columns should depend only on the primary key.

More Normal Forms

Even though there are more NFs, the three we just explained are the most commonly used. Knowing them should be enough to implement the Normalizer pattern.

To help you understand these NFs better, let's take a look at three examples, each of which shows a broken version of one of the forms:

1. The first NF. Table 8-1 contains repeating attributes in the comments column. To normalize this table, you should extract each comment to a dedicated games_ comments table.

Table 8-1. The first NF, broken

Name (primary key)	Comments
Puzzle Tour	["…", "…"]
Runner	["…"]

2. The second NF. Here, you have a table with a composite primary key. As you can see in Table 8-2, our games table has a primary key (PK) composed of the name and platform. According to the second NF, all other columns should fully depend on both key columns. However, that's not the case for the platform language, as it only depends on the game platform. To normalize this table, we should create a new table in which we store the platform and the platform language.

Table 8-2. The second NF, broken

Name (PK)	Platform (PK)	Release year	Platform language
Puzzle Tour	iOS	2023	Swift
Puzzle Tour	Android	2024	Kotlin
Runner	Android	2024	Kotlin

3. The third NF. To help you understand the last form, let's stay with our gaming example. Table 8-3 shows the schema breaking the third NF because of a transitive dependency. This dependency comes from the studio country column as its value doesn't depend on the game's name but on the studio's name. To fix that, we should create a new studios table and put all related information inside it.

Table 8-3. The third NF, broken

Name (PK)	Studio	Studio country
Puzzle Tour	Studio A	Italy
Runner	Studio B	Portugal

The NF model was the first implementation of the Normalizer pattern. Even though this model is often used in transactional workloads of relational databases, it also has a dimensional model variant that's present in analytical workloads. In a nutshell, a *dimensional model* is a design composed of one fact table and multiple dimension tables. A *fact table* represents an observation, such as an ecommerce order or a website visit, while a *dimension table* describes the observation by providing extra context, such as product information for the order or the browser configuration for the visit. Those are the shortest definitions possible, but if you need to know more about fact tables and dimension tables, there is plenty of great reference material.[2]

One of the dimensional models, and (by the way) another implementation of the Normalizer pattern, is the *snowflake model*. In this model, the fact table is described by multiple dimension tables that in turn can be described by other dimension tables. Figure 8-8 shows a central fact table decorated with dimensions.

---

2 Ralph Kimball and Margy Ross, *The Data Warehouse Toolkit: The Definitive Guide to Dimensional Modeling*, 3rd ed. (Wiley, 2013).

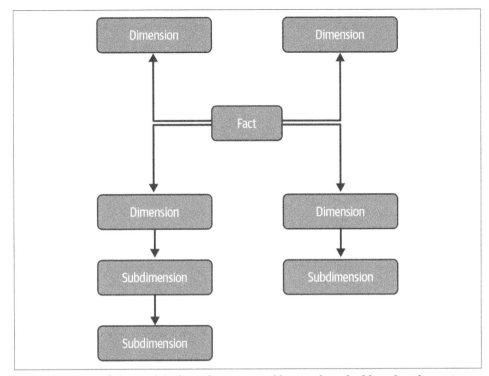

Figure 8-8. Snowflake model where dimension tables are described by other dimensions

As you can see, one dimension like the date can be normalized into subdimensions, such as quarters or months. The snowflake model tends to move attributes repeated multiple times to a dedicated subdimension table.

From both NFs and the snowflake model, you can see that the most important goal of the Normalizer pattern is to prioritize data consistency over any eventual performance optimizations. This means easier updates since any given update will be immediately reflected in all related tables.

Consequences

Complexity is one of the biggest drawbacks here, but that's the price you have to pay if you need to keep the data consistent.

Query cost.   The Normalizer pattern favors data split into multiple places. That translates into relying often on JOIN operations for querying data. Unfortunately, joins can be costly in a distributed environment as they involve exchanging data across the network.

Even though that's the price you have to pay for better data consistency, there are technical solutions that can reduce network traffic, such as colocating smaller dimension or entity tables with bigger ones, so that the joining remains local to the node.

Another mitigation technique consists of using the *broadcast* mode (i.e., sending these smaller tables to all compute nodes to avoid other, usually more expensive data distribution methods).

Broadcasting Big Tables

The easiest approach to broadcasting a big table is to reduce its size by applying filters. If that's not possible, you can eventually try to configure your data processing layer to broadcast tables of larger size. In Apache Spark, you can control that part with the `spark.sql.autoBroadcastJoinThreshold` property.

Archival.   The next challenge comes from archival needs. A dimension or entity table can be time sensitive. For example, our product table may have different prices over the years, and from your query layer, you may want to find out what the price was on a specific date.

You can easily mitigate this issue with the SCD techniques we introduced while exploring the Static Joiner pattern in Chapter 5.

Examples

First, you're going to see the NF. Figure 8-9 demonstrates how to create tables for a visit event from our use case dataset. As you can see, there are many tables you can create.

There are some important things to notice here. First, browsers and devices attributes are on dedicated tables. They can't be part of the `visits_context` table since the browser or device doesn't depend on the visit. They're different entities that can be shared across different visits. Second, the records on the `visits_contexts` table are not on the visits table because putting them there would involve repeating groups and thus break the first NF.

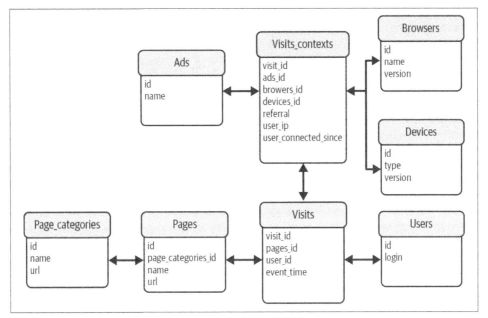

Figure 8-9. Visits in normalized form. The `visit_id`, `pages_id`, `user_id`, *and* `event_time` *columns compose the primary key of a visit.*

As you can see from the diagram, if you want to get a full picture of a visit, your query will be verbose. Example 8-23 shows this overhead for Apache Spark and Delta Lake.

Example 8-23. Joining normalized datasets

```
context = (visits_context
 .join(ads, visits_context.ads_id == ads.id, 'left_outer').drop('id')
 .join(browser, visits_context.browsers_id == browser.id, 'left_outer').drop('id')
 .join(device, visits_context.devices_id == device.id, 'left_outer').drop('id'))

page_with_category = (pages.withColumnRenamed('id', 'page_id')
  .join(categories, pages.page_categories_id == categories.id, 'left_outer')
  .drop('id').withColumnRenamed('page_id', 'id'))

full_visit = (visits
 .join(context, visits.visit_id_event == context.visit_id, 'left_outer')
 .drop('visit_id_event')
 .join(users, visits.users_id == users.id, 'left_outer').drop('id')
 .join(page_with_category, visits.pages_id == page_with_category.id, 'left_outer')
 .drop('id').withColumnRenamed('visit_id', 'id')
)
```

From that, you can deduce that the fully normalized datasets are not easily queryable and may not perform well on big datasets due to the number of joins. You'll encounter the same problem while designing a snowflake model for our visits use case. Overall, to get the full picture of a visit, the model still requires a lot of joins, like the ones in Example 8-24 for combining dates and pages.

Example 8-24. Querying overhead for a simplified snowflake schema for visits

```
page_w_category = dim_page.join(dim_page_category,
 dim_page.dim_page_category_id == dim_page_category.page_category_id,
 'left_outer')
date_with_month_and_quarter = (dim_date
 .join(dim_date_month, dim_date.dim_month_id == dim_date_month.month_id,
 'left_outer')
 .join(dim_date_quarter, dim_date.dim_quarter_id == dim_date_quarter.quarter_id,
 'left_outer'))

full_visit = (fact_visit
 .join(page_w_category, fact_visit.dim_page_id == page_w_category.page_id,
 'left_outer')
 .join(date_with_month_and_quarter
 fact_visit.dim_date_id == date_with_month_and_quarter.date_id,
 'left_outer')
)
```

Pattern: Denormalizer

Knowing that joins can be costly, a simple optimization technique is to reduce or avoid them. Unfortunately, that causes side effects that you'll learn more about in a few minutes, after discovering the next pattern.

Problem

You were called to help a company that implemented a relational model on top of their data warehouse storage for analytics. They didn't notice any issues in the first few months, as the data volume was low. But then their product became incredibly successful, and their data analytics department started to complain about the query execution time.

You performed your preliminary analysis and learned that the most expensive solution involves joining all eight of the tables involved in 80% of queries. Thanks to your previous experience, you have an idea how to create a better solution for the issue.

Solution

The stated problem is a typical scenario where the Denormalizer pattern can help. Unlike the Normalizer, it tends to reduce and even eliminate all joins from the query.

The elimination approach consists of flattening values from all joined tables into a single row so that there is no need to exchange data across the network. How? There are two different ways to do it:

Just as regular columns
> Here, each column from the joined tables is copied as is. A user can access them directly as top-level columns from a SELECT statement.

As nested structures
> In this approach, all rows from the joined tables can be put into one column in the target table. Typically, you will rely on the STRUCT type that's available in modern data stores to represent complex types. As a result, the user will need to access the attributes of this column instead of accessing the column directly.

An example of the first implementation could be storing the visits from our use case alongside referential datasets, such as users and devices, in the same table. This design approach is also known as One Big Table, and you can see it in Table 8-4.

Table 8-4. Denormalized visits table

visit_id	user_id	user_name	device_id	device_full_name	visit_time	visited_page
1	409	user ABC	10000	local computer	2024-07-01T09:00:00Z	home.html

In the second approach, the Denormalizer pattern reduces the number of joins by flattening related tables. This is typically the usage in dimensional models with the *star schema*. Although the star schema also uses the fact and dimension tables, unlike the snowflake schema, it doesn't accept nested dimensions. Put differently, dimensions describing other dimensions are now present in the highest-level dimension table (Figure 8-10).

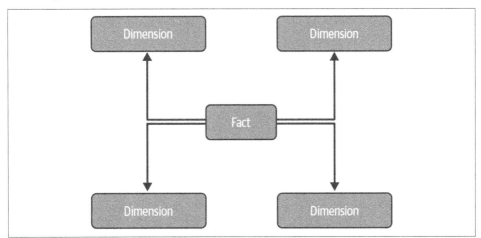

Figure 8-10. Star model with only one dimension table level

With the Denormalizer pattern, the query cost is significantly lower, thanks to the reduced network traffic needs.

The Normalizer and Denormalizer patterns are not exclusive, though. If you still care about consistency, you can apply one of the Normalizer's models first and create the denormalized version on top of it for querying. To keep them in sync, you can leverage one of the sequence design patterns covered in Chapter 6.

Figure 8-11 shows an example of a workflow in which we first create a normalized snowflake schema and later use it to build a corresponding One Big Table optimized for reading. Both datasets are accessible to users, but you can also decide to hide the snowflake schema and treat it like a private reference model for the tables you expose.

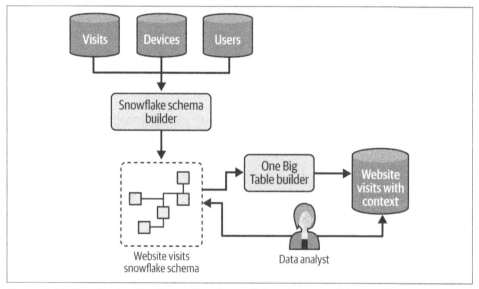

Figure 8-11. Combining the Normalizer (snowflake schema builder) and Denormalizer (One Big Table builder) design patterns, both available to the data analyst

Consequences

Even though the Denormalizer optimizes data access, it sacrifices data consistency.

Costly updates.   Since all attributes are now duplicates, updating one will potentially require changing multiple rows instead of one in cases of normalized storage. This is technically feasible but will be more expensive than the normalized approach.

There is no magic solution to mitigate the issue. The only viable mitigation strategy relies on what you consider the denormalized table to be. If you consider it to be a snapshot (i.e., what your data looked like at a specific point in time), you will not need any updates. Otherwise, you may simply need to accept the fact that you need to perform a more expensive update operation to have quicker response times.

Storage. Storage is another concern. You will probably repeat the same information from the joined tables multiple times, which may end up taking up some space in your database. Fortunately, there are various encoding techniques that can reduce the storage footprint.

A popular and easy space-optimizing encoding strategy involves using a dictionary. The dictionary builds a mapping between the real values and their more compact representation, and it uses the compact values in the columns. An example of such a mapping would be transforming long string columns into integers, such as {1: "long name...", 2: "long name, next...", ...}. In addition to saving space, these techniques can improve performance. For example, the query engine may decide to check for the existence of a value by verifying the dictionary instead of reading the dataset.

One big antipattern. The One Big Table solution, despite its good intentions of flattening records and reducing query time, can end up as an antipattern if it doesn't follow any domain-oriented logic. Let's take a look at an example of the One Big Table group's attributes, such as a user's details, a list of their past orders, columns for their current visit to our website, and finally, their favorite color.

If the user's favorite color and past orders have nothing to do with the visit, One Big Table ends up as a trash bag that you put things into, but from outside, you don't really know what's inside.

How can you know when to stop while choosing attributes to combine? Your intuition about the domain knowledge should help here. If you don't know it that well, a good exercise is to try to give a name to the table. If you end up using a lot of conjunctions such as *and* or *with*, it may be a sign that you've put too many unrelated attributes together.

Examples

The first example of the Denormalizer pattern is One Big Table that combines all related elements and stores them in the same table. Creating this table can be costly, but the good news is that you pay the cost only once per update operation. All subsequent readers will take advantage of it and experience much faster operations. Example 8-25 shows the costly writing and cheap reading of a table combining visits with pages and categories.

Example 8-25. Writing and reading One Big Table

```
# writing
page_w_category = dim_page.join(dim_page_category,
 dim_page.dim_page_category_id == dim_page_category.page_category_id,
   'left_outer')
date_w_month_quarter = (dim_date
 .join(dim_date_month, dim_date.dim_month_id == dim_date_month.month_id,
   'left_outer')
 .join(dim_date_quarter, dim_date.dim_quarter_id == dim_date_quarter.quarter_id,
   'left_outer'))

full_visit = (fact_visit
 .join(page_w_category, fact_visit.dim_page_id == page_w_category.page_id,
   'left_outer')
 .join(date_w_month_quarter, fact_visit.dim_date_id == date_w_month_quarter.date_id,
   'left_outer')
)

full_visit.write.mode('overwrite').format('delta').save(get_one_big_table_dir())

# reading
visits_table = spark_session.read.format('delta').load(get_one_big_table_dir())
```

When it comes to a slightly normalized denormalization storage, the star schema, the writing step creates more tables, which also has an impact on the reading step that requires joins. That was not the case previously as all combined data was flattened. Example 8-26 shows this impact.

Example 8-26. Writing and reading for a star schema

```
# writing
page_with_category = dim_page.join(dim_page_category,
   dim_page.dim_page_category_id == dim_page_category.page_category_id,
   'left_outer').dropDuplicates()
page_with_category.write.mode('overwrite').format('delta').save(output_page)

date_with_month_and_quarter = (dim_date
 .join(dim_date_month, dim_date.dim_month_id == dim_date_month.month_id,
 'left_outer')
 .join(dim_date_quarter, dim_date.dim_quarter_id == dim_date_quarter.quarter_id,
 'left_outer')).dropDuplicates()
(date_with_month_and_quarter.write.mode('overwrite').format('delta')
  .save(output_date_dir))

visits_dataset = (spark_session.read
  .schema('visit_id STRING, event_time TIMESTAMP,  page STRING')
  .format('json').load(input_visits_dir))
fact_visit = (visits_dataset.selectExpr(
 'visit_id', 'HASH(page) AS dim_page_id',
  'HASH(TO_DATE(event_time)) AS dim_date_id',
```

```
  'DATE_FORMAT(event_time, "HH:mm:ss") AS event_time'
))
fact_visit.write.mode('overwrite').format('delta').save(output_visits_dir)

# reading
fact_visit = spark_session.read.format('delta').load(output_visits_dir)
dim_date = spark_session.read.format('delta').load(output_date_dir)
dim_page = spark_session.read.format('delta').load(output_page_dir)

full_visit = (fact_visit
  .join(dim_date, fact_visit.dim_date_id == dim_date.date_id, 'left_outer')
  .join(dim_page, [fact_visit.dim_page_id == dim_page.page_id], 'left_outer'))
```

Summary

In this chapter, you learned about data storage design patterns. The first section was dedicated to partitioning strategies. You saw two approaches, horizontal and vertical. The horizontal approach operates on whole rows and is a good candidate for low-cardinality values, such as event time values. Vertical partitioning works at the attributes level, so it splits one row into multiple parts stored in different places.

Although partitioning is a great data storage optimization strategy, it won't work well for high-cardinality values, such as last names or cities. Here, a better approach will be the Bucket pattern that groups multiple similar rows into containers called buckets. Additionally, you can leverage a Sorter to enable faster processing on top of sorted data.

The third section covered other access optimization strategies. The first of them is Metadata Enhancer, which tries to reduce the volume of data to process by filtering out irrelevant files or rows from the metadata layer. Next, you saw the Dataset Materializer pattern, which is ideal for materializing complex queries and thus optimizing the reading path by sacrificing storage. Finally, you saw the Manifest pattern, which you can use to mitigate often costly listing operations.

In the last section, you saw two data representation patterns. The first is the Normalizer pattern, which favors data consistency but involves joins. The alternative is the Denormalizer pattern, which introduces a risk of data inconsistency but completely eliminates the need for joining multiple datasets.

And now, unfortunately, I have to disappoint you yet again. Even the best-optimized storage won't be enough to guarantee that other people will use your data. You also need to provide data of the best possible quality, and that's what the next chapter will be about.

## CHAPTER 9

Data Quality Design Patterns

Trust is an important value of a dataset. Exchanging data is like a mutual transaction, in which you either provide or consume a service (dataset). The final goal is to make the producer and consumer happy about this dataset exchange. Unfortunately, you will rarely be excited about working with a dataset that cannot be trusted, as any insights drawn from it could be wrong at any moment.

One of the causes of lost trust is poor dataset quality, which means incompleteness, inaccuracy, and/or inconsistency issues. But the good news is that these issues are not new, and even though data engineers continue to fight against them, there are some design patterns to mitigate data quality issues.

In this chapter, we're going to address data quality issues with the help of design patterns organized into three different categories. In the first category, you will see how to enforce quality and thus avoid exposing data of poor quality to your downstream consumers.

In the next part, you'll see how to address data quality issues at the schema level. Oftentimes, your producers can generate data without any apparent issues, until the day they decide to modify the schema. Depending on the evolution type, this may lead to a fatal failure of your pipeline and thus a loss of trust in your data provider.

In the last part, we're going to see how to guarantee that our enforcement rules today will still be relevant for the data of tomorrow. That's why, in addition to controlling the data and its schema, it's important to observe the dataset and spot any new issues before your consumers do. These observation techniques will help you keep your enforcement rules up to date by providing the freshest overview of the processed datasets.

That's just the context for this chapter. If you are eager to see more concrete examples, I invite you to the first section on quality enforcement.

Quality Enforcement

Ensuring the quality of your dataset means that you will avoid sharing an incomplete, inconsistent, or inaccurate dataset. Quality enforcement is therefore the first category of data quality patterns you'll apply to your pipelines with the goal of sharing trustworthy data.

Pattern: Audit-Write-Audit-Publish

The first way to ensure good dataset quality is to add controls to the data flow. This approach is similar to assertions in unit tests that verify whether your code is performing correctly against an expected input. It's possible to transpose these assertions to data flows and consequently produce the kinds of data quality guards in the pipelines that might stop the whole execution if the dataset doesn't meet expectations.

Problem

Your daily batch ETL job generates statistics for the user visits presented back in Figure 1-1 from Chapter 1. The results have not been good for the past week. In fact, the number of unique visitors dropped by 50%, and the product team considers this to be an issue. As a result, it has started a new marketing campaign to bring visitors to the website.

Today, while you were working on a new feature of this job, you discovered that the unique visitors aggregation is not computed correctly. You informed the product team, which stopped the campaign but asked you to ensure that there will be no similar issue in the future.

Solution

Generated data volume that drops by 50% compared with previous days is a perfect use case where the Audit-Write-Audit-Publish pattern can shine.

Write-Audit-Publish Evolution

The Audit-Write-Audit-Publish (AWAP) pattern is an evolution of the Write-Audit-Publish (WAP) pattern shared by Michelle Ufford at the DataWorks Summit in 2017. The original talk introducing WAP to the world is still available on YouTube at "Whoops, the Numbers Are Wrong! Scaling Data Quality @ Netflix" (*https://oreil.ly/4xACM*). Unlike WAP, AWAP completes the validation logic with the input data verification to perform some usually lightweight validation on the input dataset.

The idea behind AWAP is to add controls (aka *audit steps*) to ensure that both input and output datasets meet defined business and technical requirements, such as completeness and exactness. Figure 9-1 shows a pipeline with these extra audit steps.

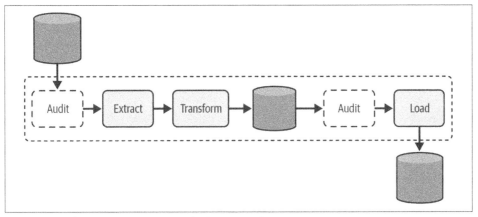

Figure 9-1. The AWAP pattern applied to a pipeline

As you can see in Figure 9-1, the main difference between the two audit tasks is the audited data store:

1. The first audit job is responsible for analyzing the input data source before you start transforming the dataset. Very often, you will limit the validation here to fast operations such as input file format validation, file or table size control, or schema checks. For example, let's imagine you're working on a table that usually has three columns called a, b, and c, and that you want to load a new CSV file to the table. The first audit step could validate whether the CSV file has these three fields present and defined correctly, just by analyzing the first line of the file. Although it's technically possible to validate the full dataset as well, keep in mind that you'll risk reading the dataset twice, once in the first audit step and once in the transformation step.

2. The second audit job validates the transformed data. You can consider it to be an extension of your local unit tests that is going to run on the real dataset. Therefore, the control functions will focus more on the data. For example, if you need to transform columns a, b, and c from the previous point and the transformation should never be NULL, you can add a validation function here.

With these two audit steps, you must be very careful when considering a validation function to be redundant. To help you understand this, let's take a look at an example of the nullability validation from the previous paragraph. If you added this validation on top of the input dataset, you would verify whether the dataset generated by your data provider meets your expectations. On the other hand, if you added the NULL validation to the second audit step, you would ensure that your transformation logic doesn't generate missing values. On the surface, both actions validate NULLs, but as you can see, their intent and scope are different.

A risk with the same validation function is processing the whole dataset many times. If you're concerned about that, maybe because of the data volume you're working on, you should always consider putting the validation action in the most exhaustive place. In the case of our NULL validation, that's the second audit step, where it could detect NULLs coming from both the input dataset and your transformation logic.

Unit Tests and AWAP

Unit tests are important for any system relying on software, including data engineering pipelines. However, with regard to the data, unit tests are static. You create them at some point in time that may reflect current reality but may not represent what will happen in the future. For that reason, I mentioned that the audit steps from the AWAP pattern extend unit tests on top of the real-world data. But don't get me wrong, unit tests (which are local) should always be the first line of defense against any data quality issues caused by incorrect business logic implementation.

Validation in audit steps can operate at the records level and thus validate attributes of particular records, or it can operate at the dataset level to verify overall properties, such as data volume, distinctiveness of particular columns, or even the proportion of NULLs in a column. You may be thinking that the outcome of the audit steps is always a failed pipeline, but it doesn't have to be. Apart from failure, other possible outcomes are as follows:

Data dispatching
> If only part of the audited output dataset is invalid, you can still promote the valid portion to the downstream consumers and keep the invalid records in a separate storage. This sounds like the Dead-Letter pattern, but it's different because there are no unexpected runtime errors. Instead, the dead-lettering logic results from your explicit data control mechanism.

Nonblocking audit
> If your processed dataset has some imperfections, you may want to promote it to the final storage despite the audit errors. In that case, it's good to annotate it as having some issues so that readers can evaluate trust and not process it if the data doesn't meet their expectations. For example, if one of your columns has an unexpected increase of NULL values but the overall dataset looks fine, consumers who don't rely on that column can still use the dataset. Consumers who use the column can also decide to process the dataset, if the proportion of the missing

values is under their acceptable threshold. For the annotation, you can create a data summary entry in a table or in a file, where you would list all possible data quality issues.

The description so far makes it sound like the AWAP pattern works only for batch pipelines. That's not true because stream workloads can also use it with two different approaches depicted in Figure 9-2.

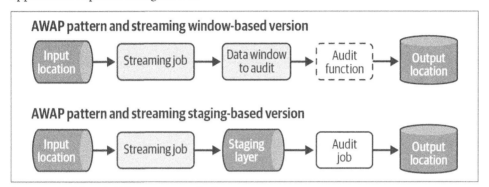

Figure 9-2. *The AWAP pattern applied to streaming*

The first implementation, which is called *window based* in the diagram, creates processing time windows directly in the streaming job. Once the window closes, the job runs data audit steps that can apply one of the strategies (fail/dispatch/ignore) to the buffered records. The second approach, which is called staging based, doesn't modify the data processing logic. Instead, it only changes the output to write transformed records to a staging layer where an audit job can run before eventually promoting the dataset to the final output location.

As you may have noticed, AWAP in a streaming context follows the more classical WAP approach. The first audit step is missing because data is continuously flowing to the system, and in most cases, it should be simpler to validate the records after the transformation step of the streaming job. This is a real-world example of the exhaustiveness rule for validation functions mentioned previously in this section.

Consequences

The AWAP pattern brings extra safety, but it incurs some extra costs.

Compute cost. Depending on the nature of your audit steps, you may have an additional compute cost. Metadata-based operations, such as validating file formats, will be cheap, but operations working on data, such as row-based validations, will be more expensive. But that's the price you have to pay to ensure the quality of generated data.

Rules coverage. Let's stay with the row validation example here. If you need to verify values for each incoming row, you'll define a set of business rules. Unfortunately, as datasets may evolve over time, the rules from today might not fully cover a dataset of tomorrow. For that reason, it's better not to consider the AWAP-controlled pipelines to be 100% reliable. There is still a risk of forgotten or out-of-date validations that, hopefully, you will spot with one of the patterns in "Quality Observation" on page 293.

Streaming latency. AWAP in a streaming context may add some extra latency. For example, if you want to assert a NULL values distribution within a processing window, the data delivery will be delayed by the window accumulation period.

An issue may not be an issue. Keep in mind that an issue spotted by the audit steps may not be a real issue. This may sound surprising, but remember, data is dynamic, and something that appears wrong may turn out to be correct. An example here would be an audit step validating the data volume for our blogging platform introduced in "Case Study Used in This Book" on page 5. If you encounter unexpected success, such as being quoted in social media, normally, you should notice an unexpectedly high number of visits and thus much more data volume to process. Consequently, it doesn't mean something was wrong on the data producer side.

For that reason, you don't need to consider all audit failures to be critical issues. Sometimes, an invalid outcome can only trigger an alert and require further investigation on your part.

Examples

Let's begin this section with an example from Apache Airflow and PostgreSQL, thus SQL-based validation. Example 9-1 shows possible tasks you can create as part of your batch pipeline. First, the pipeline starts by auditing the input dataset with the rules detailed later. If the validation is successful, the pipeline starts the transformation that in turn gets validated before being written to the final data store.

Example 9-1. The AWAP pattern in a batch pipeline

```
audit_file_to_load = PythonOperator(
    task_id='audit_file_to_load',
    python_callable=local_validate_the_file_before_processing
)
transform_file = PythonOperator(
    task_id='transform_file',
    python_callable=flatten_input_visits_to_csv
)
def local_validate_flatten_visits():
 validate_flatten_visits(get_current_context())
```

```
audit_transformed_file = PythonOperator(
    task_id='audit_transformed_file',
    python_callable=local_validate_flatten_visits
)
load_flattened_visits_to_final_table = PostgresOperator(
    task_id='load_flattened_visits_to_final_table',
    sql='/sql/load_file_to_visits_table.sql'
)

(next_partition_sensor >> audit_file_to_load >> transform_file
  >> audit_transformed_file >> load_flattened_visits_to_final_table)
```

The input data audit consists of asserting on JSON lines the correctness and overall file size. Example 9-2 shows a snippet of the validation function; you will find all the code in the GitHub repo (*https://oreil.ly/Rg4wj*).

Example 9-2. Input dataset validation (`local_validate_the_file_before_process ing` function)

```
if f_size < min_size:
  validation_errors.append(
    f'File is to small. Expected at least {min_size} bytes but got {f_size}')
if lines < min_lines:
  validation_errors.append(
    f'File is too short. Expected at least {min_lines} lines but got {lines}')
if invalid_json_line:
  validation_errors.append(
    f'File contains some invalid JSON lines. The first error found was
    {invalid_json_line}, line {invalid_json_line_number}')

if validation_errors:
  raise Exception('Audit failed for the file:\n-'+"\n-".join(validation_errors))
```

As you can see, the final error message includes all the issues the input file can encounter. The same logic works for the processed dataset, in which the audit function relies on the pandas library to look for any NULL values. Remember, our job operates in a constraintless CSV format that requires these extra NULL checks in the audit step. Otherwise, you could rely on the Constraints Enforcer pattern. Example 9-3 shows this extra audit step for NULL values checks.

Example 9-3. Processed data validation example (`validate_flatten_visits` function)

```
required_columns = ['visit_id', 'event_time', 'user_id', 'page', 'ip', 'login',
 'browser', 'browser_version', 'network_type', 'device_type', 'device_version']
cols_w_nulls = []
visits = pandas.read_csv(partition_file(context, 'csv'), sep=';', header=0)
for validated_column in required_columns:
 if visits[validated_column].isnull().any():
```

```
    cols_w_nulls.append(validated_column)

if columns_with_nulls:
  raise Exception('Found nulls in not nullable columns:'+','.join(cols_w_nulls))
```

Let's complete the picture with a streaming example using Apache Spark Structured Streaming. One of the methods for running jobs uses triggers (i.e., time-based expressions defining the execution frequency for the data processing logic). It's a great alternative to processing windows because it's stateless and naturally does not involve state management overhead. First, Example 9-4 shows the code for writing the processed results to a staging table.

Example 9-4. Apache Spark Structured Streaming and a Delta Lake staging table

```
visits = (spark_session.readStream
  .option('kafka.bootstrap.servers', 'localhost:9094').option('subscribe', 'visits')
  .option('startingOffsets', 'EARLIEST').option('maxOffsetsPerTrigger', '50')
  .format('kafka').load()
  .selectExpr('CAST(value AS STRING)')
    .select(F.from_json("value", get_visit_event_schema()).alias("visit"), "value")
  .selectExpr('visit.*')
)
# ...
write_query = (visits.writeStream
  .trigger(processingTime='15 seconds')
  .option('checkpointLocation', checkpoint_dir)
  .foreachBatch(write_dataset_to_staging_table).start())
```

Next, the second job streams the staging table and performs the data quality controls. Depending on the evaluation outcome, it writes the results to the final destination (if there are no issues) or to the errors destination. This logic is omitted in Example 9-5 for the sake of brevity, but you can find it in the GitHub repo (*https://oreil.ly/hBh5R*).

Example 9-5. Audit job on top of a Delta Lake staging table

```
visits = (spark_session.readStream.format('delta')
  .option('maxBytesPerTrigger', 20000000)
  .table(get_staging_visits_table())
  .withColumn('is_valid', row_validation_expression)
)
# ...
write_query = (visits.writeStream
  .trigger(processingTime='30 seconds')
  .option('checkpointLocation', checkpoint_dir)
  .foreachBatch(audit_dataset_and_write_to_output_table)
  .start())
```

Pattern: Constraints Enforcer

The AWAP pattern validates the data directly from your data processing pipeline. Put differently, the implementation effort is on your end. However, there is an easier way to create trustworthy datasets by delegating those quality controls to the database or the storage format, thus relying on a more declarative approach.

Problem

A batch pipeline processes visits from Figure 1-1 (back in Chapter 1) and writes the results back to a table. Even though it has been running without any issues for several months, you're now getting random NULL values for several required fields. The data processing job is already complex, and you want to avoid adding data validation complexity to it. You're looking for an alternative approach that will fail the loading process if there are any data quality errors, such as missing required fields.

Solution

Delegating responsibility for validation to the database is what the Constraints Enforcer pattern is responsible for.

The implementation starts by identifying the attributes that should have the constraint rules assigned to them. It's a very business-specific step, in which the rules can be driven by your product team or legislation. For example, an orders dataset will certainly require some attributes to be defined, such as the order amount and the buyer's billing address. Unfortunately, that's just an ecommerce-specific example, and there is no one-size-fits-all solution.

Once you identify the attributes, it's time for you to assign the constraints. They can be from different categories:

Type constraints
> A type constraint ensures that all values for a given attribute will always be of the same type. It greatly simplifies processing since consumers know what kind of data they're dealing with. Type-based constraints are part of the dataset schema and the backbone of the Schema Consistency pattern.

Nullability constraints
> These define an attribute as never missing or possibly missing. If an attribute is defined as not nullable, a nullability constraint will reject any rows with missing values. On the other hand, if an attribute is configured as nullable, the dataset will accept missing values. This setting also communicates to downstream consumers possible operations to add, such as filtering the column that can have null values to eliminate rows with missing values.

Value constraints

These rely on one value or a set of values or expressions that are allowed for an attribute, plus a comparison operator. A value constraint compares the value from the inserted property with the expected value. If the outcome is negative, the record is rejected with a failure. Examples include x <= NOW() for inserted value (x) to never be in the future, and x BETWEEN 1901 AND 2000 for x to be in the 20th century.

Integrity constraints

These are often part of transactional databases modeled with the Normalizer pattern. In that context, integrity constraints ensure that a value present in a table references a real value present in another table. For example, if a website visit references a page that doesn't exist in the pages table, the integrity constraint will be broken, and consequently, the website visit row won't be added to the visits table.

Although this implementation is commonly present in databases, you can encounter it while working with file formats. For example, Delta Lake includes a CHECK operator that will verify each value against the specified condition. Also, serialization formats such as Apache Avro and Apache Protobuf implement the Constraints Enforcer pattern. They natively cover type constraints, and if you install additional extensions, they may also cover value constraints. You'll see this in the Examples section.

The Constraints Enforcer pattern is informative for consumers, as it defines the dataset's shape and possible values, and interactive for producers, as it prevents them from adding records without passing the expected validation controls.

Consequences

Using the Constraints Enforcer pattern is a definitive way to ensure good data quality. It's simpler than writing data validation logic, but it also has some drawbacks.

All-or-nothing semantics. Most of the time, the constraints defined at the database level follow transactional all-or-nothing semantics. This means that if any of the input rows from the ingested dataset don't respect the validation rules, none of the rows will be accepted.

Also, databases often stop at the first encountered error. If you, as a data producer, generate a dataset with multiple issues, you'll need to go back and forth with the database several times to discover all the problems. To mitigate this problem and compile the full list of issues, you could implement the validation rules on the data producer side—but by doing so, you'd lose the informative and interactive advantages presented earlier in this chapter.

Data producer shift. The Constraints Enforcer pattern is data producer–oriented since it exposes the constraints to the data writer. However, different consumers may have different data expectations. For example, a nullable field in the database may be required for some consumers, and as a result, you, as a consumer, may still need to implement data validation or data filtering logic on top of an already constrained dataset.

Constraints coverage. It's not always possible to cover all validation rules. That's especially apparent with table file formats that, for example, may not cover integrity constraints. The constraints from the AWAP pattern are more flexible as the single limitation is your programming language. Consequently, you may need to complete the database constraints with the ones defined in your data processing job.

Examples

Delta Lake has been referenced in this section in a few places, so let's start with this table file format and see how to apply all three categories of constraints. Example 9-6 creates a table with type constraints and nullability constraints, and then, it defines the value constraint, ensuring that the values in the event_time column are always from the past.

Example 9-6. Delta Lake constraints

```
CREATE TABLE default.visits (
  visit_id STRING NOT NULL,
  event_time TIMESTAMP NOT NULL
) USING delta;

ALTER TABLE default.visits ADD CONSTRAINT
  event_time_not_in_the_future CHECK (event_time < NOW() + INTERVAL "1 SECOND")
```

From now on, if any of the inserted rows violates the specified rules, you will get a DELTA_VIOLATE_CONSTRAINT_WITH_VALUES or DELTA_NOT_NULL_CONSTRAINT_VIOLA TED error. Consequently, none of the records added in the transaction will be written to the table.

Another, perhaps more surprising, place where you can use the Constraints Enforcer pattern is in serialization file formats, like Protobuf. The library implements the type constraint natively, and if you install protovalidate,[1] you can extend the scope with value constraints.

---

1 The protovalidate GitHub repository (*https://oreil.ly/dYoEi*) covers the capacities of protovalidate more extensively.

Example 9-7 shows a visits event annotated with extra validation properties. You can see that we control the minimum length of the visit_id field, the time with the lt_now (aka lower than now) expression, and even specify the page that cannot end with an HTML extension.

Example 9-7. Protobuf and constraints with protovalidate

```
message Visit {
  string visit_id = 1 [(buf.validate.field).string.min_len = 5];
  google.protobuf.Timestamp event_time = 2 [
    (buf.validate.field).timestamp.lt_now = true,
    (buf.validate.field).required = true];
  string user_id = 3 [(buf.validate.field).required = true];
  string page = 4 [(buf.validate.field).cel = {
    message: "Page cannot end with an html extension"
    expression: "this.endsWith('html') == false"
  }, (buf.validate.field).required = true];
}
```

Now, if you call validate(...) on any of the visit class instances and, intentionally or not, break one of the rules, you will get a ValidationError, as in Example 9-8.

Example 9-8. A ValidationError for a broken protovalidate constraint

```
Traceback (most recent call last):
  File "...visits_generator.py", line 39, in <module>
    validate(visit_to_send)
  File "...protovalidate/validator.py", line 61, in validate
    raise ValidationError(msg, violations)
protovalidate.validator.ValidationError: invalid Visit
```

Schema Consistency

The schema constraints you discovered with the Constraints Enforcer pattern solve the data consistency problem. However, schemas have a special place in data engineering that is much more complex than simply defining the field types of a table. In this section, you'll learn about other challenges and how to solve them with two design patterns.

Pattern: Schema Compatibility Enforcer

Datasets are dynamic because their values can change over time, and the Constraints Enforcer pattern validates these evolved entries against a set of predefined rules. But what if I told you that schemas can also have this validation? If that's something new to you, let's take a look at the next pattern.

Problem

You're running a sessionization job that you implemented with the Stateful Sessionizer pattern. It ran great for months, but then the team generating your input data made several changes, and as a result, the job has failed many times in the past month. It turns out, the new team removed the fields used by your application, thinking they were obsolete.

After discussing the issue with your new colleagues, you've asked them to build a solution to avoid any schema-breaking changes.

Solution

To ensure that you as the data producer don't introduce any breaking changes, you can use the Schema Compatibility Enforcer pattern.

Depending on your data store, you'll use one of the three available schema compatibility enforcement modes:

Via an external service or library
> This is the enforcement mode Apache Kafka's Schema Registry uses to expose an API the producers and consumers communicate with. Schema Registry versions each schema and validates schema changes against the configured compatibility rules. Alternatively, instead of a service, you could use a library. For example, Apache Avro has a `SchemaValidator` class that you could use to validate that a schema doesn't have incompatible changes. That said, this library doesn't allow you to set the compatibility rule.

Implicit with inserts
> This is the enforcement mode for table file formats or relational databases. When you create a new table, you define the constraints, such as nullability, type, or accepted range of values. At the same time, you implicitly set the compatibility mode that prevents any record not respecting the constraints from being written. However, there is no way to define an explicit schema compatibility mode as the implementation relies on an external service or library.

Event driven for data definition language (DDL)
> This approach extends the implicit mode. In some relational databases, such as PostgreSQL and SQL Server, you can add event triggers that will run SQL functions before committing any DDL operations such as `DROP COLUMN` or `RENAME COLUMN`. The function logic can include your schema enforcement rules and roll back the operation if a user tries to perform an incompatible change. On the other hand, if you don't need such fine-grained control, you can prevent all schema modifications by not granting the `ALTER TABLE` permission to a user.

All three modes are summarized in Figure 9-3.

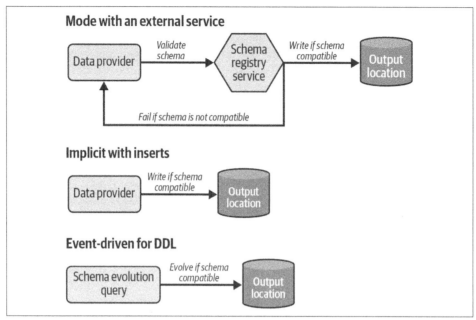

Figure 9-3. Schema compatibility mode workflows

Let's complete this implementation section with an analysis of various compatibility modes you can define for your schemas (if supported by your data store). The schema compatibility mode informs downstream consumers of what evolution they should be ready for. One of the most common compatibility scenarios involves non-transitive rules in which two consecutive schema versions (such as version and version+1 or version and version−1) must remain compatible. The available modes are as follows:[2]

Backward compatibility
> Here, a consumer using a new schema can still read data generated with an old schema. For example, if a new schema has a new optional field, then since the consumer is using the new schema, the added field will simply be missing in the records generated with the old schema.

Forward compatibility
> In this mode, a consumer with an old schema can read data generated with a new schema. For example, if an optional field that was in an old schema has been deleted from a new schema, then the removed optional attribute will be missing from the records produced with the new schema. The consumer will see that the

---

2 The list omits the "None" mode on purpose as it doesn't enforce anything and shouldn't be used as part of the Schema Compatibility Enforcer pattern.

field's value is empty, but the emptiness is already part of the contract as the field was marked as optional and thus possibly empty.

Full compatibility

This mode mixes backward and forward compatibilities, so consumers with a new schema can read data generated with a previous schema, and consumers using an old schema can still access data generated with a new schema.

The compatibilities can also be *transitive*. This means that the compatibility between all past (backward) and future (forward) schemas must be guaranteed. Table 9-1 summarizes these compatibility scenarios.

Table 9-1. Schema compatibility actions summary

Compatibility modes	Allowed actions	Semantics
Backward nontransitive Backward transitive	Delete field Add optional field	Consumers with a newer version can read data produced with an older version.
Forward nontransitive Forward transitive	Add field Delete optional field	Consumers with an older version can read data produced with a newer version.
Full nontransitive Full transitive	Add optional field Delete optional field	Consumers with a newer version can read data produced with an older version. Consumers with an older version can read data produced with a newer version.

As you can see in Table 9-1, the transitive and nontransitive allowed actions are the same. That may be confusing, so let's take a look at an example of backward compatibility to see the transitive mode broken. Our initial schema looks like the one in Example 9-9.

Example 9-9. Initial schema for transitive versus nontransitive allowed actions

```
Schema Order (v0):
  order_id LONG REQUIRED
```

Let's imagine now that we need to add an amount. After all, an order without an amount doesn't make any sense, does it? Since the schema is set to be backward compatible, the amount field must be optional (i.e., it must have a default value, as shown in Example 9-10).

Example 9-10. Backward-compatible version of the Order schema

```
Schema Order (v1):
  order_id LONG REQUIRED
  amount DOUBLE DEFAULT 0.0
```

Turns out, our product team asked us to remove the default as it might lead to erroneous insights on the data analytics side. We can therefore create a new version with the amount field set as required, as shown in Example 9-11.

Example 9-11. Final version of the Order schema

```
Schema Order (v2):
  order_id LONG REQUIRED
  amount DOUBLE REQUIRED
```

For a transitive backward dependency, the last change is not compatible between v0 and v2 since from that standpoint, a consumer using the newest version (v2) can't read the data produced by the very first version (v0). However, the evolution looks fine from the nontransitivity standpoint. Put differently, the consumer using the most recent version (v2) can read a schema produced in the previous version (v1). In that case, even if a data producer omitted the amount field, the schema definition would put a default value in it. As a result, each order would have an amount.

Upon defining the compatibility mode and schema, the data producer interacts with each schema change with this external schema enforcement component. That way, if the produced data contains an evolution not supported by the compatibility mode, it'll be rejected.

Consequences

Even though the benefits outweigh the risks, there are some points to keep in mind.

Interaction overhead.   Schema management, particularly via an external schema registry component, adds extra overhead to data generation. The producer must validate records against the most recent schema version.

Schema evolution.   Schema evolution will be harder with the Schema Compatibility Enforcer pattern. Any schema change must agree with the schema compatibility level defined for the dataset. This may lead to a situation where renaming a field means adding a new field and deprecating the previous one. However, that's the price you pay for having more reliable data. You'll learn more about this aspect in "Pattern: Schema Migrator" on page 290.

Examples

Apache Kafka's Schema Registry is the tool that made schema compatibility enforcement popular among data engineers, so naturally, it's part of the first example. To start, you need to define the schema alongside its compatibility mode. In our case, we're setting the schema from Example 9-12 to be forward compatible.

Example 9-12. Schema to register in the Schema Registry

```
{"type": "record", "namespace": "com.waitingforcode.model","name": "Visit",
"fields": [
  {"name": "visit_id", "type": "string"},
  {"name": "event_time",  "type": "int", "logicalType": "time"}
]}
```

Let's say that a new producer wants to generate a record without the visit_id field. Consequently, since writing a record now involves validating its schema against the Schema Registry, the operation will fail with the exception from Example 9-13.

Example 9-13. Schema compatibility error message

```
confluent_kafka.avro.error.ClientError: Incompatible Avro schema:409 message:
  {'error_code': 409, 'message': 'Schema being registered is incompatible with
  an earlier schema for subject "visits_forward-value",
  details: [{errorType:\'READER_FIELD_MISSING_DEFAULT_VALUE\',
  description:\'The field \'visit_id\' at path \'/fields/0\' in
  the old schema has no default value and is missing in the new schema\',
  ...
```

Regarding implicit enforcement, let's see how Delta Lake solves the issue. The table we're going to work with has been created with the columns present in Example 9-14.

Example 9-14. Initial schema for a Delta Lake schema enforcement example

```
root
|-- visit_id: string (nullable = true)
|-- page: string (nullable = true)
|-- event_time: long (nullable = true)
```

Now, let's imagine a producer who adds an extra column called ad_id. Consequently, since Delta Lake doesn't modify the schema without your permission, it will detect this change as incompatible with the current schema and respond with the exception from Example 9-15.

Example 9-15. Implicit schema enforcement in Delta Lake

```
pyspark.errors.exceptions.captured.AnalysisException: A schema mismatch detected when
writing to the Delta table
...

Table schema:
root
-- visit_id: string (nullable = true)
-- page: string (nullable = true)
```

```
Data schema:
root
-- visit_id: string (nullable = true)
-- page: string (nullable = true)
-- ad_id: string (nullable = true)
```

Pattern: Schema Migrator

Ensuring schema correctness prevents producers from making incompatible changes and prevents consumers from being interrupted if those incompatible modifications are possible. However, one schema-related problem still remains: how to keep consumers safe while giving them the ability to perform breaking schema changes, such as field type evolution and renaming?

Problem

You're looking to improve the structure of the visit events your jobs are generating downstream. From day one, you wanted to be user friendly, and for that reason you have been adding new fields without bothering your consumers. As a result, some of your domain-related fields are dispersed across an entire message that sometimes has up to 60 attributes, which is too many for most uses and makes understanding the domain very challenging.

Many of your consumers are complaining about difficulties related to processing and understanding the complicated domain. Ideally, they would like to have related attributes grouped in the same entity. For example, user-related attributes like login, email address, and age should be part of a single attribute called *user*.

You don't want to radically change the existing schema because that would break its compatibility. However, you do want to improve the organization of the attributes while giving your consumers some time to migrate to the new format.

Solution

You can't solve the problem with the Schema Compatibility Enforcer pattern as it only controls the types of changes that can be made. The solution relies on the Schema Migrator design pattern that enables schema evolution.

Transitive Compatibility

The Schema Migrator requires the schema compatibility to not be transitive. Otherwise, no field removal or renaming would be possible, as the transitive compatibility level guarantees consistency across all versions.

The first step consists of identifying the evolution. Three scenarios are possible here:

Rename

> This will happen whenever you or your consumers find a given attribute name to be wrong or difficult to understand.

Type change

> This is the scenario from our problem statement. Here, we either want to organize a schema better (for example, by simplifying it after multiple changes), or we simply want to optimize it for processing (for example, by adapting a heterogeneous date time text attribute to an epoch timestamp).

Removal

> This is easy if you have a 100% guarantee that there are no downstream consumers processing the attribute you want to remove. If you don't, then you will need to find a substitution for them or even cancel the removal action.

Let's focus first on the most challenging scenarios, the rename and the type change. In both cases, you need to start by creating the new field with the renamed or retyped attribute. Next, you need to agree with your consumers on the transition time. Then, during that period, they will receive the previous and the new attributes at the same time. Only after reaching the deadline can you create a new version of the schema that contains only the modified version of the attribute.

Data Lineage

To detect whether an attribute is used by your consumers or not, you can rely on the Fine-Grained Tracker pattern in Chapter 10.

The removal scenario is slightly different as it requires agreeing with consumers on the field removal period. Again, once the deadline passes, you can create a new schema version, this time without the deleted property.

Consequences

The Schema Migrator pattern relies on a grace period for schema migration. During that time, the old schema is still valid and can be processed by consumers. As you may have deduced, this impacts the data size.

Size impact. This is a natural consequence of the Schema Migrator, which provides some safety mechanisms for performing schema migration but also incurs costs in the form of storage space, network transfer, and I/O as there is more data to save.

For some data formats, having a lot of fields is even officially discouraged. For example, Protobuf, in its "Proto Best Practices" (*https://oreil.ly/I2WTu*), warns against using hundreds of fields because each of them, even the unpopulated ones, takes up at least 65 bytes. The overall size of the Protobuf-generated builders can therefore reach the compilation limits of some languages like Java.

Size also has an impact on the metadata and statistics layer. At the time of this writing, Delta Lake collects statistics on the first 32 columns by default. Although you can change that, it may impact the writing time.

Impossible removal. The Schema Migrator pattern has some implementation limits in the field removal scenario. If a field is used by one of your consumers, removing it will not be possible if you cannot provide an alternative attribute.

Examples

Since the schema migration workflow is the same for various technologies, let's focus here on one data format and understand what happens if the schema migration doesn't follow the Schema Migrator pattern.

The consumer in our example extracts the visits of connected users to a dedicated table with the query from Example 9-16.

Example 9-16. Reading visits of connected users

```
INSERT INTO dedp.connected_users_visits
  SELECT visit_id, event_time, user_id, page, ip, login, from_page FROM dedp.visits
  WHERE is_connected = true AND from_page IS NOT NULL;
```

Now, let's suppose we just realized that the from_page column is poorly named and a better name would be referral. The worst thing we could do, because it would break consumers' workload, would be to run the rename operation directly with ALTER TABLE dedp.visits RENAME COLUMN from_page TO referral. The consumer would not be able to see the new data, as its query will fail first (see Example 9-17).

Example 9-17. Error that might happen without the Schema Migrator pattern

```
ERROR:  column "from_page" does not exist
LINE 2:     SELECT visit_id, event_time, user_id,  ..
```

To avoid this issue, you should migrate the rename by creating a new column first:

Example 9-18. Rename in the sense of Schema Migrator

```
ALTER TABLE dedp.visits ADD COLUMN referral VARCHAR(25) NOT NULL
```

You can remove the previous column only once your consumers adapt their workloads.

Since a similar workflow exists for Protobuf and Delta Lake,[3] I'll omit them from this section, but if you are interested, you can find out about them in the GitHub repo (*https://oreil.ly/aahjn*).

Quality Observation

Remember, datasets are dynamic. They change, and the constraint rules you define today may not be valid tomorrow. That's why it's important to observe what's going on with datasets and be ready to adapt the existing rules or add new constraints.

Pattern: Offline Observer

Observation patterns can be organized according to their place in the data pipeline. The first type of pattern lives as a separate observation component that doesn't interfere with the data processing workflow.

Problem

You started a new data pipeline this month, and you haven't encountered a lot of data quality issues. The dataset is fully structured, and all business rules are correctly enforced by quality enforcement patterns. However, from your previous project, you know this won't last as the upstream dataset will evolve in the coming months. For that reason, you want to monitor the properties of the dataset, such as the distribution of values and the number of nulls per column. Since everything is fine at the moment, this monitoring layer shouldn't block your main pipeline.

Solution

In a scenario when the monitoring shouldn't block the processing workflow, it's best to opt for the Offline Observer pattern.

The implementation consists of creating a data observability job that will analyze the processed records and enhance the existing monitoring layer with extra insight. The insight will depend on the business context, but it can include properties like distribution of values, number of nulls in nullable fields, new but not processed fields in the input dataset, etc. That way, you can store these parameters and spot any data quality issues over time.

The data observability job doesn't impact the data generation process. It runs independently and could even be executed on a completely different schedule. For exam-

---

3 Protobuf's rename operation is safe because the encoded version doesn't store the field's name but only stores its tag. However, changing the type might not be safe, as per the Protobuf official documentation (*https://oreil.ly/H3Eet*).

ple, assuming all your data generators run throughout the day, you may want to schedule all observability jobs to run at night to avoid resource concurrency issues.

Observability Versus Auditing

Observability is not the same as auditing. An audit validates the dataset and is a blocking operation (i.e., whenever it detects some issues, the pipeline will block the pipeline). Observability is a non-blocking approach that monitors the datasets (i.e., it helps detect any issues but will not prevent the pipeline from moving on).

Consequences

Decorrelating data generation from data observation is good as it doesn't impact production resources. Unfortunately, there is another side of the coin.

Time accuracy. Since an offline observation job can run on any schedule, including much later than the data generator, it may not happen on a timely basis. In other words, the insight may come too late since all downstream consumers could already have processed a dataset with new data quality issues.

Compute resources. As the data observation job will be running on the side, you may be tempted to schedule it less frequently than the data generation job. For example, for hourly batch processing, you may execute the data observation job only once every 24 hours. Although this approach is valid, you need to be aware that it may require more compute resources as, instead of dealing with hourly data changes, you'll have to process 24 hours at once.

Eventually, you could consider sampling the observed dataset and therefore using only parts of it. Unfortunately, by extracting a subset to observe, you may miss some interesting observations.

Examples

The first example of the Offline Observer pattern is an Apache Airflow pipeline that runs on a different schedule than the data generation pipeline, asserts the quality of the generated dataset so far, and writes the statistics to a monitoring layer. The overall workflow includes the steps defined in Example 9-19.

Example 9-19. Tasks in an Offline Observer pipeline

```
wait_for_new_data = SqlSensor(...)
record_new_observation_state = PostgresOperator(...)
insert_new_observations = PostgresOperator(...)
wait_for_new_data >> record_new_observation_state >> insert_new_observations
```

Whenever there is new data to process, the observation job records a new observation state that includes the IDs of the first and last processed rows. This operation is required for idempotency to guarantee that in case of any row changes in the observed table, the analysis scope will be the same and thus consistent. Example 9-20 shows the data observation state recording query that's executed as part of the record_new_observation_state task.

Example 9-20. State recording query

```
INSERT INTO dedp.visits_monitoring_state (execution_time, first_row_id, last_row_id)
  SELECT
    '{{ execution_date }}' AS execution_time,
    MIN(id) AS first_row_id, MAX(id) AS last_row_id
  FROM dedp.visits_output
  WHERE id > COALESCE(
    (SELECT last_row_id FROM dedp.visits_monitoring_state WHERE
     execution_time = '{{ prev_execution_date }}'::TIMESTAMP),
    0
  )
```

Later, the Offline Observer pipeline generates the observation by performing aggregations on top of the selected first and last row IDs. The query is present in Example 9-21.

Example 9-21. Data observation query

```
INSERT INTO dedp.visits_monitoring(execution_time, all_rows, invalid_event_time,
 invalid_user_id, invalid_page, invalid_context)
 SELECT
   '{{ execution_date }}' AS execution_time,
   COUNT(*) AS all_rows,
   ...
   SUM(CASE WHEN context IS NULL THEN 1 ELSE 0 END) AS invalid_context
FROM dedp.visits_output
 WHERE id BETWEEN
 (SELECT first_row_id FROM dedp.visits_monitoring_state WHERE
  execution_time = '{{ execution_date }}')
 AND
   (SELECT last_row_id FROM dedp.visits_monitoring_state WHERE
   execution_time = '{{ execution_date }}');
```

Implementing the Offline Observer is also possible for streaming pipelines. As with the batch pipelines, there is a separate job running on top of the processed data and generating observations. In the next example, we're going to analyze the data processing lag of the data producer and some data quality metrics. Example 9-22 shows the metrics for missing rows in an Apache Spark job.

Example 9-22. Offline Observer with Apache Spark Structured Streaming

```
visits_to_observe = (input_data_stream
 .selectExpr('CAST(value AS STRING)')
 .select(functions.from_json(functions.col('value'), visit_schema).alias('visit'))
 .selectExpr('visit.*')
 .select('visit_id', 'event_time', 'user_id', 'page', 'context.referral',...)
 )
query = (visits_to_observe.writeStream.foreachBatch(generate_and_write_observations)
 .option('checkpointLocation', checkpoint_location).start())
```

All of the observation logic is present in the `generate_and_write_observations` function. In the first step, it executes the same data observation query as in the Apache Airflow version presented previously. Then, it performs an extra operation and generates an HTML data profile report with the help of the ydata-profiling library (see Example 9-23).[4]

Example 9-23. Data profiling for the processed dataset

```
def generate_profile_html_report(visits_dataframe: DataFrame, batch_version: int):
 profile = ProfileReport(visits_dataframe, minimal=True)
 profile.to_file(f'{base_dir}/profile_{batch_version}.html')
```

The generated HTML page describes the characteristics of the observed dataset that you can use later to add, modify, or delete existing data quality rules in the enforcement step (see Figure 9-4).

---

4 If you need to set up ydata-profiling, the official documentation provides all necessary information (*https://oreil.ly/xpQaf*).

Figure 9-4. A data profile for the observed dataset

When it comes to lag detection, the function compares the most recently committed offset by the data generation job from the checkpoint location with the most recent offset present in the input topic. Example 9-24 shows this detection logic.

Example 9-24. Lag detection function

```
def get_last_offsets_per_partition(self) -> Dict[str, int]:
 last_processed_offsets = self._read_last_processed_offsets()
 last_available_offsets = self._read_last_available_offsets()

offsets_lag = {}
 for partition, offset in last_available_offsets.items():
  lag = offset - last_processed_offsets[partition]
```

```
offsets_lag[partition] = lag
return offsets_lag
```

For the sake of concision, that was only a code snippet. The whole example is available in the GitHub repo (*https://oreil.ly/G0hyu*).

Pattern: Online Observer

If latency between data processing and data observation via the Offline Observer pattern is an issue, you can opt for a more real-time alternative pattern, which is the Online Observer.

Problem

Last week, your data analytics colleagues complained about an unexpected format in the zip code field. It turns out that there is some data regression in the upstream dataset, and you couldn't prevent it with the data trust rules in place. Your Offline Observer did indeed discover the issue, but since it runs once per week, you couldn't detect the problem before your users did. In the future, you would like to avoid this kind of problem, so you want to be able to keep your consumers from finding out about data quality issues and fix them sooner than after one week.

Solution

The problem we've presented is a perfect example of the Offline Observer's limitations. Thankfully, overcoming it is relatively simple with the opposite pattern, which is called the Online Observer pattern.

The Online Observer still relies on a data observation job to generate all observation metrics. However, the difference between this pattern and the offline approach is the time at which it executes. The Online Observer's job is an intrinsic part of the data generation pipeline, and as a result, the produced insight is available just after the data generation. That approach can help avoid many communication and technical issues with the downstream consumers.

But a question arises: where should we put this observation job? If we reason about our data generator in terms of ETL or ELT steps, the most popular place to put it is after the Transform stage, where you can orchestrate the observation job in the Parallel Split pattern or Local Sequencer pattern (see Figure 9-5).

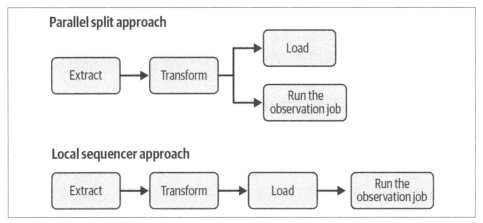

Figure 9-5. Approaches to implementing the Online Observer in a batch pipeline

When it comes to streaming pipelines, you need to integrate the observation logic into the data generation job. Even though this sounds like the batch implementation, there is a significant difference as you will not be able to run the observation step as a separate pipeline. Consequently, any issues with the data observability part, such as unexpected error or memory issues, may impact the whole job. You can try to mitigate this risk by sampling the dataset to perform data observation and then accepting the fact that you'll miss out on some insights during the process. Figure 9-6 shows this dependency between data processing and data observation generation.

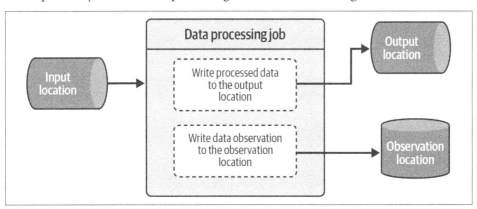

Figure 9-6. Online data observer for a streaming job

Not Only the Data

Even though this section discusses observability related to the processed data, observability covers a wider scope. It also includes technical metadata, such as the CPU, memory, or disk usage of your data engineering tools. Most of the time, they'll be near real-time measurements and therefore available in the Online Observer pattern.

Consequences

Even though the Online Observer pattern addresses the time accuracy issue of the Offline Observer, it has some gotchas.

Extra delays. If you use the Local Sequencer approach to integrate the data observation job, you'll add it as an extra step at the end of the pipeline. Naturally, this will delay the pipeline's completion. It's good to keep in mind that adding this extra monitoring step to the main workflow doesn't come for free.

Parallel splits. The Parallel Split approach adds an extra parallelism to the pipeline by running the observation and data loading steps at the same time. However, it also brings a danger of observing a partially valid dataset. To help you understand what this means, let's look at an example of a dataset with date time attributes loaded into a database. If the date time format is different from the one expected by the database, the database will be missing the date time values. However, the data observation step, since it runs on the loaded dataset directly, will not see this issue.

To mitigate this problem, you should use the Local Sequencer approach that observes the dataset that's exposed to consumers. Eventually, you can decide to apply your data observation scope to the processed and not exposed dataset. In this logic, the observation focuses on the transformation instead of the data loading task. Consequently, even though you might not face any data loading issues at the moment, this strategy may not be relevant throughout the whole lifespan of the pipeline.

Examples

In this section, I'm going to omit the observation code because it's the same as for the Offline Observer pattern and you can find it in the GitHub repo (*https:// oreil.ly/-7S6K*). Instead, let's see how to transform the offline observation code into a more reactive online one. The batch pipeline now integrates the data observation step into the data processing pipeline, and overall, the tasks look like those in Example 9-25.

Example 9-25. Online Observer for an Apache Airflow batch pipeline

```
wait_for_new_data = SqlSensor(...)
record_new_synchronization_state = PostgresOperator(...)
clean_previously_added_visits = PostgresOperator(...)
copy_new_visits = PostgresOperator(...)
record_new_observation_state = PostgresOperator(...)
insert_new_observations = PostgresOperator(...)

wait_for_new_data >> record_new_synchronization_state
  >> clean_previously_added_visits >> copy_new_visits
copy_new_visits >> record_new_observation_state >> insert_new_observations
```

As you'll notice, the observation pipeline from Example 9-19 is now part of the same data generation pipeline. That does indeed involve the potential risk of the pipeline's failure if there are any issues at the data observation level. To overcome this risk, you add a final task that does nothing and that will be triggered independently on the observation job. Consequently, the execution of this task will mark the pipeline as successful even in cases of observation failure. In Apache Airflow, you can achieve this with a trigger rule set to all_done.

What about streaming pipelines? Here, the code is also merged but the operation involves two major changes: lag detection and accumulators. The data reader now includes two extra columns, which are the partition number and the offset position for each retrieved row. Consequently, the lag detector code relies on them to get the most recently processed record in the microbatch. Example 9-26 shows these initial changes with a new class added to store the partition-offset pairs, plus a new accumulator object.

Example 9-26. Online Observer and lag detection adaptation

```
@dataclasses.dataclass
class PartitionWithOffset:
 partition: int
 offset: int


class PartitionToMaxOffsetAccumulatorParam(AccumulatorParam):
 def zero(self, default_max: PartitionWithOffset):
  return []

 def addInPlace(self, partitions_with_offsets: List[PartitionWithOffset],
    new_max_candidate: PartitionWithOffset):
  partitions_with_offsets.append(new_max_candidate)
  return partitions_with_offsets

def write_to_kafka_with_observer(visits: DataFrame, batch_number: int):
 ctx = visits_to_analyze.sparkSession.sparkContext
 max_offsets_tracker = ctx.accumulator([], PartitionToMaxOffsetAccumulatorParam())
```

```
def analyze_generated_records(visits_iterator: Iterator[Row]):
  for visit_record in visits_iterator:
    # ...
    if visit_record.offset > max_local_offset:
      max_local_offset = visit_record.offset
    current_partition = visit_record.partition

    max_offsets_tracker.add(PartitionWithOffset(partition=current_partition,
      offset=max_local_offset))

visits_to_analyze.foreachPartition(analyze_generated_records)
```

Another modification is the use of accumulators to avoid complex SQL queries generating both numbers of invalid rows and max offsets per partition. As a result, the part summarizing invalid rows is also adapted to this new logic (see Example 9-27).

Example 9-27. Online Observer and invalid records summary

```
accumulators = {'event_time': spark_context.accumulator(0),
  'user_id': spark_context.accumulator(0), 'page': spark_context.accumulator(0)}
all_events_accumulator = spark_context.accumulator(0)

def analyze_generated_records(visits_iterator: Iterator[Row]):
 for visit_record in visits_iterator:
  if not visit_record.event_time:
   accumulators['event_time'].add(1)
  if not visit_record.user_id:
   accumulators['user_id'].add(1)
  if not visit_record.page:
   accumulators['page'].add(1)
# ...

observation_dump = {
 '@timestamp': datetime.utcnow().isoformat(),
 'invalid_event_time': accumulators['event_time'].value,
 'invalid_user_id': accumulators['user_id'].value,
 'invalid_page': accumulators['page'].value,
 'all_events': all_events_accumulator.value,
# ...
```

As a side note, *accumulators* are Apache Spark–specific components that run locally on each executor as long as you don't invoke the value method. When the value function is effectively called, the executors send their local accumulators to the main node of the cluster, which performs the results aggregation. In our data observation example, using accumulators is a great way to avoid querying the input dataset twice (once for the lag and once for the invalid columns).

Summary

In this chapter, you learned about three important components you can use to build trustworthy datasets. The first section covered design patterns related to quality enforcement. You saw there how to improve quality in different layers. The first layer was the pipeline, where the AWAP pattern helps you avoid processing and exposing poor-quality data. More protection comes from the databases, where you can define conditions on the inserted fields with the Constraints Enforcer pattern. Finally, you learned about an external component that helps keep the schema consistent within the Schema Compatibility Enforcer pattern.

Although enforcing constraints and controls prevents the publication of poor-quality datasets, it doesn't guarantee that there will be no issues. In fact, it only guarantees that there will be no issues with the rules you defined. But unfortunately, you may miss defining some of them or may simply need to adapt them to the evolved dataset. To overcome the issue of staying up-to-date, you will rely on the patterns from "Quality Observation" on page 293. There, you learned about the Offline Observer and Online Observer patterns, which work on different levels. The former is a detached component that runs independently on the data generation pipeline, while the latter is the opposite. Which approach is right for you depends on your willingness to trade time for accuracy.

With that, we're coming slowly but surely to the end of our data engineering design patterns journey. However, there's one topic left to cover: the data observability that will help you detect issues in your data processing jobs and datasets. That's what the next chapter is all about!

## CHAPTER 10

Data Observability Design Patterns

The data quality design patterns from the previous chapter are crucial to guaranteeing the relevance of your datasets. However, as they focus mainly on the data itself, relying only on data quality solutions won't be enough for you to have end-to-end control of your data engineering stack.

Let's take a look at an example to understand this better. The Audit-Write-Audit-Publish (AWAP) pattern is a great protection mechanism against processing data of poor quality. Unfortunately, even if your AWAP job perfectly detects all issues, you may still be in trouble. An example of this occurs when your AWAP job doesn't run because of an upstream flow interruption and you are not aware of it.

There is good news, though: the data observability design patterns from this chapter fill the gaps left by their data quality counterparts by adding monitoring and alerting capabilities to the system. To address these extra issues, the observability pattern solutions rely on two pillars: detection and tracking.

The detection design patterns spot any problems related to the data or time. They would be great candidates to handle the AWAP's data flow interruption issue mentioned previously. They will also be useful for notifying you whenever your batch job takes too much time to complete.

Tracking design patterns focus on understanding the relationships among datasets, columns, and the data processing layer. They will help you discover the data generation graph that in large organizations often spans across different teams. They are also helpful in understanding the transformation logic for individual columns, especially when it comes to columns created from multiple inputs.

This short introduction should be enough to convince you that observability design patterns, although they might sound like "things the operations team should do," are also important for us data engineers. And to drive this point home even more, let's now turn to the first observability design patterns: data detectors.

Data Detectors

Data engineers process data. Unsurprisingly, the first observability category helps analyze the health of our systems from the data standpoint.

Pattern: Flow Interruption Detector

The first serious data-related issue is dataset unavailability. This issue will have a strong impact on your systems because without any data, your data processing job will not run, leading to data unavailability in its downstream dependencies.

Problem

One of your streaming jobs is synchronizing data to an object store. The synchronized dataset is the data source for many batch jobs managed by different teams. It ran great for seven months until one day, it processed the input records without writing them to the object store.

Because the job didn't fail, you didn't notice the issue. You only realized something was wrong when one of your consumers complained about the lack of new data to process. Instead of relying on consumer feedback, which is not good for your reputation, you want to introduce a new observability mechanism to detect this data unavailability scenario.

Solution

To capture any data unavailability errors, and as a result, increase trust in your data, you can rely on the Flow Interruption Detector pattern.

The implementation of the pattern will vary depending on the technical context and processing mode. Let's start with the stream processing introduced in the problem statement. Basically, you can have two different data ingestion modes here:

Continuous data delivery
> In this mode, you expect to get at least one record every unit of time, like a minute or a second. In that context, the Flow Interruption Detector consists of triggering an alert whenever there are no new data points registered for the specified unit of time, like no data coming in for one minute.

Irregular data delivery
> Here, you expect to see some delivery interruptions that have nothing to do with errors. For example, you might assume that no data will come in for five consecutive minutes. The pattern's implementation in that context consists of analyzing

time windows instead of data points and raising an alert whenever the period without the data is longer than the accepted no-data window duration. Since the data flow is irregular, using the continuous data delivery assumption would result in many false-positive alarms that might lead to alarm fatigue.[1]

Figure 10-1 compares the two approaches. As you'll notice, the only difference between them is the data evaluation period. Continuous data delivery analyzes a specific unit of time (a minute in the example), while for irregular data delivery it monitors multiple consecutive points in time.

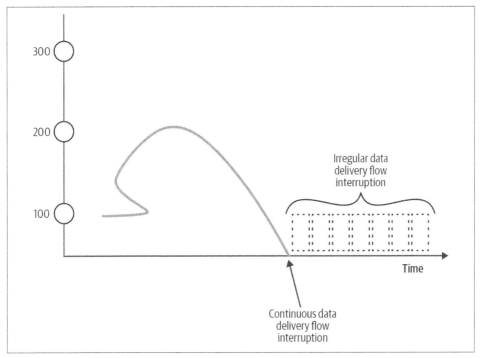

Figure 10-1. Flow interruption detection for continuously arriving and irregularly arriving data

However, data flow interruption can also occur in batch pipelines and data-at-rest databases. Spotting unavailability here consists of analyzing the data freshness of the metadata, data, or storage layer:

---

1 Alarm fatigue (*https://oreil.ly/-H5jH*) is definitely something you want to avoid in order to preserve your resources and remain responsive to issues.

Metadata layer

This layer stores all additional information about the observed table, such as creation time and last modification time. A flow might be interrupted when the modification time hasn't been changed according to the configured threshold. For example, a table with new data ingested hourly could trigger an alert whenever no changes are observed for more than one hour.

Data layer

Generally, interactions with the metadata layer will be less expensive in most scenarios due to more direct access to the information and thus the lack of data processing needs. Unfortunately, your data store may not have the metadata layer available or the update information may be missing. In that situation, you may need to enrich the table with the modification time column to detect a flow interruption if the last update passed the configured threshold. If adding this column is not possible, you can count the number of rows in each evaluation time period and compare the results to see whether there is new data. For example, in our hourly job, if the count doesn't change in two consecutive hours, it'll be a sign of flow interruption. This count-based approach may also require some extra storage to preserve the count statistics for past runs.

Storage layer

The last flow interruption detection strategy is based on the storage layer. Typically, you could use it with any file format, including raw JSON files or more advanced table file formats. The implementation here consists of monitoring the time when the last file was written in a storage space and raising an interruption alert whenever there are no updates within the expected threshold.

Consequences

Flow interruption detection may look simple, but unfortunately, the implementation hides some traps such as the threshold, metadata, and false positives.

Threshold. Finding the perfect threshold for both per-minute and per-window implementations is not easy. Expecting at least one record per minute, as in our previous example, is an easy choice but may not be realistic. If you expect to process hundreds of events or more per minute, you will need to choose a different number.

Relying on the volume observed in the past may be a tempting way to define the threshold. It's often used as the solution to this threshold-finding problem, but it also has a gotcha. From time to time, it can generate false positives, for example, whenever a marketing operation generates more activity than usual.

Metadata. The solution based on the metadata is cheap but may not be perfect. First, this metadata layer with the last modification time or the number of rows may simply

---

not be available for your database. Second, even if the layer is there, the modification can include not only data operations but also metadata changes, such as schema evolution, which obviously doesn't add any new records. You must be careful when evaluating it for the purpose of the Flow Interruption Detector pattern.

False positives for storage. If you rely on the storage layer for flow interruption detection, beware of all housekeeping operations, such as compaction. This operation does indeed create new files, but it doesn't produce new datasets. Instead, compaction simply merges existing data blocks. From the storage's perspective, there is activity, but it will not count as flow continuity since the dataset remains unchanged.

Examples

Let's begin this section with Apache Kafka, Prometheus, and Grafana. To detect the flow interruption, we'll use an expression that evaluates how many records are written every minute (`kafka_server_brokertopicmetrics_messagesin_total`). This is shown in Example 10-1.

Example 10-1. Evaluation of incoming messages per minute for a visits topic

```
sum without(instance)(rate(
kafka_server_brokertopicmetrics_messagesin_total{topic="visits"}[1m]))
```

The next step is to configure the alert to detect an interruption whenever the last values (five in our example) are equal to zero. If this condition is met, Grafana will raise a data interruption alert. Since this operation relies on the user interface and not the code, I'll let you read the screenshot in the GitHub repo (*https://oreil.ly/GZksn*).

The interruption can also be tracked for batch workloads, thanks to the last written message information. PostgreSQL supports this message tracking with a configuration parameter called `track_commit_timestamp`. This attribute enables a `pg_xact_commit_timestamp` function that you can reference in the flow interruption query (see Example 10-2).

Example 10-2. Flow interruption with the last commit time function

```
SELECT
CAST(EXTRACT(EPOCH FROM NOW()) AS INT) AS "time",
CAST(EXTRACT(EPOCH FROM NOW() - MAX(pg_xact_commit_timestamp(xmin))) AS INT) AS value
FROM dedp.visits_flattened
```

The query extracts the last commit timestamp from the current time that you can reference later in your notification layer to trigger an alert whenever the difference is bigger than the accepted flow interruption threshold.

The flow interruption mechanism can also rely on the data producer. Example 10-3 shows a Delta Lake producer that synchronizes data from Apache Kafka with a Delta Lake table. At the end of this action, it also sends a last update time metric to Prometheus. That way, you can use the same time evaluation conditions as shown previously to spot a data ingestion interruption.

Example 10-3. Ingesting the last writing time for a Delta Lake table

```
visits_to_write.write.format('delta').insertInto(get_valid_visits_table())
from prometheus_client import CollectorRegistry, Gauge, push_to_gateway
registry = CollectorRegistry()
metrics_gauge = Gauge('visits_last_update_time',
  'Update time for the visits Delta Lake table', registry=registry)
metrics_gauge.set_to_current_time()
metrics_gauge.set(1)
push_to_gateway('localhost:9091', job='visits_table_ingestor', registry=registry)
```

Pattern: Skew Detector

In addition to data interruption issues, you can face data skew problems that will directly impact your processing layer. An unbalanced and thus skewed dataset can increase processing time or, even worse, trigger a batch pipeline on an incomplete dataset.

Problem

After you put the Flow Interruption Detector in place, some consumers complained yet again. This time, they were unhappy because your batch job processed an incomplete dataset.

You found out that your job worked correctly, but the pipeline processed a half-empty dataset. After talking to your data provider, you learned that there were some data generation issues on its side. You're wondering how to overcome this problem in the future by always processing a complete dataset.

Solution

The situation described in the problem statement is a typical example of *data skew*. Although the term has become popular in data processing to describe a situation in which some tasks have more load than others, *skew* is also a valid word to describe a situation in which a pipeline processes different data volumes in two consecutive executions. Thankfully, the Skew Detector pattern brings you more control over this phenomenon.

This solution consists of three steps. The first step identifies the comparison window. Put differently, you must start by determining which time periods in the pipeline's runs to compare. For example, if you have a daily batch job, you could decide to compare the currently processed dataset with the previous day's dataset.

Once you identify the time periods, you need to set a tolerance threshold. This value determines how different the compared datasets can be. For example, if you set it to 50%, it means that your processing job tolerates working on 50% less or 50% more data than in the previous comparison window. To set up this tolerance threshold, you can analyze the data variations you observed in previous days or directly ask your business users about the expected differences.

The final step consists of implementing the skew calculation. It can be either of the following:

- A window-to-window comparison (as mentioned in the previous paragraph), in which you calculate the percentage difference between two values. It applies to both batch jobs and continuous streaming applications where you might compare data with processing time or event time windows.

- A more complex calculation in which you use the ratio of a standard deviation. Here, you detect how each of the data points deviates from the mean of the dataset. This approach is particularly useful if you need to calculate data skew in a partitioned storage system, such as an Apache Kafka topic or a PostgreSQL table. Thankfully, many of these data stores have a standard deviation function (`stddev`) that you can simply call to get the ratio as part of a formula. For example, in `STDDEV(x)/AVG(x)`, x is the observed metric, such as storage usage by a partition.

The Skew Detector pattern is a good candidate for use in the first Audit stage of the AWAP pattern explained in the previous chapter. It'll then act as a guard preventing the processing of partial datasets.

Consequences

Even though the solution sounds simple, practice reveals some tricky points related to the dataset itself.

Seasonality.   Seasonality is probably the biggest challenge with the Skew Detector pattern. If you assume that each time, the comparison window will get 50% more or 50% less data than the previous window and that that is fine, then you have no issue. But what if that will be true only sometimes or, even worse, never?

The data often relies on your organization's activity. For example, when the marketing department is running ad campaigns, you might get 50% more records than usual. The same variance is valid for a seasonal business where summer may bring more data than the winter season, or the opposite.

Finding a rule under these variable circumstances is not straightforward. To find it, you'll rely on your business knowledge to build the comparison formulas and eventually add some exceptions to ignore or adapt the most variable periods.

Communication.   Even though you're able to define the threshold in the changing environment presented in the previous paragraph, there is still some room left for false positives. An aggressive and successful marketing campaign is one of the examples that can bring much more data than the accepted threshold.

Mitigating the issue requires more communication skills than technical skills as you will need to synchronize with other departments in your organization so that you can adapt the alerts for the chosen time periods and be able to spot false positives.

Fatality loop.   A window-to-window comparison can introduce some fatality loops in cases of skew. Let's get a better understanding of this by looking at an example. You're running a batch job daily, and one day, the skew validation step fails because the dataset is three times smaller than the dataset from the day before. If you don't fix the issue by the next day, the valid dataset from that day will be considered to be skewed since the comparison window is on a day-to-day basis. After all, compared to the failed day, you now have three times as much data.

The best way to fix the issue is to always have a valid and complete dataset for the comparison windows, so you need to ask your data producer to solve the issue. If the fix is not possible before the next pipeline's scheduled run, you can apply the volume comparison not to the day before but to the dataset used by the most recent successful pipeline run, which in our example might be the dataset processed two days ago.

Examples

You already know about the ratio of a standard deviation and how it relates to skew detection. To make this more real, let's see how to write a query to compute the skew in PostgreSQL partitioned tables. The query from Example 10-4 relies on the data catalog's (and hence, the metadata's) `pg_stat_user_tables` to get the number of rows from the partitioned `visits_all_range_` tables and compute the ratio for each evaluation time.

Example 10-4. Computing the ratio of a standard deviation for PostgreSQL partitioned tables

```
SELECT
 NOW() AS "time", (STDDEV(n_live_tup) / AVG(n_live_tup)) * 100 AS value
 FROM pg_catalog.pg_stat_user_tables
WHERE relname != 'visits_all_range' AND relname LIKE 'visits_all_range_%';
```

Later, whenever the standard deviation ratio reaches the configured threshold, you can consider it to be a storage data skew. Again, you will find a full demo in the GitHub repo (*https://oreil.ly/IS1VF*). The STDDEV and AVG functions are pretty common functions in data stores. They're also present in Prometheus, where you can use them to calculate the storage skew for another data store, which is Apache Kafka (see Example 10-5).

Example 10-5. Computing the ratio of a standard deviation for Apache Kafka partitions

```
stddev(sum(kafka_log_size{topic='visits'}) by (partition)) /
  avg(kafka_log_size{topic='visits'}) * 100
```

Now, let's see how to apply the Skew Detector pattern to a data pipeline with the window-to-window comparison mode. To demonstrate this scenario, we're going to use an Apache Airflow pipeline that loads JSON files into a PostgreSQL table. The pipeline's code is shown in Example 10-6. The workflow starts with a sensor (see "Pattern: Readiness Marker" on page 30) that unlocks the pipeline whenever the next partition is created. Later, the compare_volumes function verifies whether the current partition is at most 50% smaller or 50% larger than the previous partition. That's our window-to-window skew validation. If the condition holds, the pipeline moves to the last step, which consists of loading data to a PostgreSQL table.

Example 10-6. Data skew in a data validation task

```
next_partition_sensor = FileSensor(...)

def compare_volumes():
 context = get_current_context()
 previous_dag_run = DagRun.get_previous_dagrun(context['dag_run'])
 if previous_dag_run:
  previous_execution_date = previous_dag_run.execution_date
  current_file_path = get_full_path(context['logical_date'], 'json')
  current_file_size = os.path.getsize(current_file_path)
  previous_file_path = get_full_path(previous_execution_date, 'json')
  previous_file_size = os.path.getsize(previous_file_path)
  size_ratio = current_file_size / previous_file_size
  if size_ratio > 1.5 or size_ratio < 0.5:
   raise Exception(f'Unexpected file size detected for the...')

volume_comparator = PythonOperator(task_id='compare_volumes',
                        python_callable=compare_volumes)
transform_file = PythonOperator(...)
load_flattened_visits_to_final_table = PostgresOperator(...)

(next_partition_sensor >> volume_comparator >> transform_file
>> load_flattened_visits_to_final_table)
```

Time Detectors

In addition to data, time is an important metric for data pipelines. It helps you spot latency issues in your data processing layer.

Pattern: Lag Detector

Speaking of latency, the first pattern from this category defines how far a data consumer can be behind the data producer. This measure is often an indicator for upcoming data quality problems, such as data freshness and data unavailability.

Problem

It has been one week since one of your streaming jobs processed 30% more data than the previous job. Unfortunately, you missed the email announcing this increase, and now, one of your downstream consumers is complaining about slower data delivery. You've promised them that this is the last time. You want to put a scaling strategy in place, but the first required step is to monitor how fast your consumer processes input data.

Solution

A good way to measure how your consumer is doing is to use the Lag Detector pattern.

The first thing to do is to define the lag unit. This choice will depend on the data store. For an Apache Kafka topic, it can be the record position or the record append time. For a Delta Lake table, you can rely on the commit number, while for a time-partitioned data store, you can leverage the partition timestamp.

Upon identifying the unit, you can define the comparison expression that will verify the currently processed unit with the most recent one available in your storage. The difference between them will then represent the lag. Example 10-7 shows a high-level Python algorithm for the lag calculation.

Example 10-7. High-level lag equation; getters will depend on your data store

```
last_available_unit = get_last_available_unit()
last_processed_unit = get_last_processed_unit()

lag = last_available_unit - last_processed_unit
```

In cases of partitioned data stores, like the aforementioned Apache Kafka, you will get a lag measure per partition. That's why the next step will define the strategy for the partitioned results, which can be one of the following:

- If you want to discover the biggest lag, you should call the MAX function on the partitioned results. That way, you will be able to detect the worst-case scenario, even if only one of the partitions lags behind.
- If you want to know how most of the partitions perform, you should use a *percentile* function, such as P90 or P95. That way, you will be sure that 90% or 95% (percentile value) of your partitions are within one lag value. That said, it doesn't mean all of them have the same lag. For example, a lag of 10 seconds for P90 means that 90% of the partitions have a lag of 10 seconds at worst, and some may have less than that.

You can also combine the two approaches to follow an overall latency with a percentile function and the worst-case scenario with the MAX aggregation.

The Average Trap

Averaging is a popular statistical function, but in the context of observability, it hides some traps. Let's suppose that the lag metrics for seven partitions are 10, 5, 30, 2, 3, 5, and 3 seconds. The average lag will be 8 seconds, while the P90 lag will be 18 seconds. Put differently, 90% of the data is processed within 18 seconds, for real! If you just looked at the average of 8 seconds, you could wrongly conclude that the job is performing pretty well. For that reason, percentiles are more relevant for lag detection.

Consequences

Skewed data is a serious consequence for many things in data engineering. The Lag Detector pattern is not an exception here, as you will read next.

Data skew. If you decide to represent the lag as a single unit with the MAX(...) function, beware, because a poor result may not be directly related to your consumer. If, for whatever reason, one partition gets more load than the others, your consumer will naturally process it slower. That doesn't mean the consumer has an issue, though. Instead, you should think of better distributing the data during the writing step so that consumers can work on even partitions.

Examples

Let's see first how to analyze the lag for an Apache Spark Structured Streaming job processing data continuously from an Apache Kafka topic. Apache Spark has a listener's mechanism that you can leverage for lag detection. Our listener will trigger after processing each window of records and compare the offsets of previously processed rows with the most recent ones present in each partition. The snippet from

Example 10-8 shows this step (the full code is available in the GitHub repository (*https://oreil.ly/QLdUz*)).

Example 10-8. Microbatch offsets reader

```
class BatchCompletionSlaListener(StreamingQueryListener):

 def onQueryProgress(self, event: "QueryProgressEvent") -> None:
  latest_offsets_per_partition = self._read_last_available_offsets()
  visits_end_offsets = json.loads(event.progress.sources[0].endOffset)
  visits_offsets_per_partition: Dict[str,int] = visits_end_offsets['visits']
```

After retrieving the offsets, the listener initializes a connection to the Prometheus instance, computes the difference (lag) between the processed and most recent offsets, and sends the results to Prometheus. The second part of the onQueryProgress snippet is in Example 10-9.

Example 10-9. Lag calculation

```
registry = CollectorRegistry()
metrics_gauge = Gauge('visits_reader_lag', '...', registry=registry,
 labelnames=['partition'])
for partition, value in visits_offsets_per_partition.items():
 lag = latest_offsets_per_partition[partition] - value
 metrics_gauge.labels(partition=partition).set(lag)

push_to_gateway('localhost:9091', job='...', registry=registry)
```

Implementing the Lag Detector pattern is also possible for table file formats like Delta Lake. This time, we're going to use a different method of running our Apache Spark Structured Streaming job. Instead of executing continuously, the job will run on schedule, process all data available at a given moment, and stop. That way, you can leverage Apache Spark's checkpoint mechanism and avoid managing the progress manually. For the batch schedule, the job uses the availableNow trigger (see Example 10-10).

Example 10-10. Structured Streaming job with the availableNow *trigger*

```
visits_stream = spark_session.readStream.table('default.visits')

console_printer = (visits_stream.writeStream.trigger(availableNow=True)
 .option('checkpointLocation', checkpoint_dir)
 .option('truncate', False).format('console'))

console_printer.start().awaitTermination()
```

The `query` variable includes the progress information made by the job. That's where you will find the last processed version of the Delta Lake table. You can later read it and send it to the monitoring endpoint (Prometheus Gateway, in our case), as demonstrated in Example 10-11.

Example 10-11. Submitting the last processed version of the visits table

```
last_version = query.lastProgress["sources"][0]["endOffset"]["reservoirVersion"]

registry = CollectorRegistry()
metrics_gauge = Gauge('visits_reader_version',
  'Last read version of the visits table', registry=registry)
metrics_gauge.set(last_version)
push_to_gateway('localhost:9091', job='visits_reader_version', registry=registry)
```

The previous snippet was for the data consumer. But to determine the last written version, the data producer should also emit a metric. Here, the last version can be found directly by running the `DESCRIBE HISTORY` query after generating the data (see Example 10-12).

Example 10-12. Getting the last version of the table

```
# ... data generation step, transaction commit
last_written_version = (spark_session.sql('DESCRIBE HISTORY default.visits')
  .selectExpr('MAX(version) AS last_version').collect()[0].last_version)
```

That way, you can configure your alert as a difference between the last written version and the last read version. If this difference is bigger than the accepted threshold, it can be a sign of increasing consumer lag.

Pattern: SLA Misses Detector

Using the Lag Detector pattern from the previous section is a great way to measure the processing pace of a data consumer. However, it's not a single time-based measure that you can add to your data processing jobs. The lag-based approach can be completed with a solution based on an SLA that directly asserts the execution time of a given workflow.

Problem

Your task is to complete a batch job scheduled at 6:00 a.m. within 40 minutes. Your downstream consumers are critical data pipelines. They must generate various business statistics before 8:00 a.m. You did your best to optimize the job to respect the 40 minute SLA, but you know that unpredictable things happen and the SLA may be broken one day.

For that reason, you want to implement an observability mechanism that will notify you and your downstream consumers whenever the job is taking more than 40 minutes.

Solution

To ensure that your consumers are notified about any latency problems with your batch job, you can use the SLA Misses Detector pattern.

This pattern consists of measuring the processing time and comparing it to the maximum allowed execution time. The implementation depends on the processing mode:

Batch job
> This is the simplest scenario because you will measure the difference between the end time and the start time. If this difference is greater than the defined SLA threshold, then the run will be marked as an SLA miss and an SLA miss notification will be sent.

Streaming job
> If the processing framework works in a microbatch or event time–windowed mode,[2] (i.e., when each stream execution operates on a bunch of data), you can use the same technique as for the batch jobs, to subtract the start time from the end time for each iteration.
>
> On the other hand, if the windowed mode is not supported, the solution consists of measuring the difference between reading and writing each record to the output data store. The gathered metrics can be later aggregated to a MAX or a percentile function to determine, respectively, the longest delay and the overall delay. To gather the metrics, you can use the Online Observer pattern or Offline Observer pattern.

Even though an SLA miss can be related to the lag introduced in the previous pattern, the two detection patterns are complementary but not always interchangeable. A clear example explaining why is a skewed partition in an input data store. If a consumer implements a throughput limitations mechanism to always process the same volume of data, the job will respect the SLA. However, the lag will be continuously increasing as the data on the skewed partition will not be processed as it comes in.

The same dependency is valid in the opposite direction. Let's take a batch job processing data generated daily by an upstream pipeline. At the moment of starting the processing, the batch job won't have any lag due to the daily data processing schedule, but it can still miss the SLA if it takes too much time to complete.

---

2 The processing time window will never be late as it'll always follow the real clock.

Consequences

The SLA Misses Detector pattern is relatively straightforward when it comes to batch pipelines. However, it's more challenging for streaming pipelines, especially due to the data arrival semantics.

Late data and event time. Although processing time is a common unit of measure for calculating SLA misses and the simplest one as well, it's not the only one. You can also use event time and get an idea of the end-to-end time between data generation and processing. It sounds simple, right? In theory, it is, but in practice, whenever you interact with event time, you risk dealing with late data, which from the SLA's standpoint may not be your fault.

Simply speaking, if a producer loses its network connectivity and delivers locally buffered data a few minutes later, your event time–based SLA may not be respected because of the delivery interruption and not because of any data processing issues on your end. But at the same time, late-arriving data may not break your processing time SLA, as it's closely related to how fast the job processes input data, no matter the event time. Put differently, it's based on the current time. The processing time and event time aspects don't cover the same ground, and it's good to separate them when it comes to observing SLA.

Consequently, in this scenario, you will monitor the processing time SLA as the difference between the reading time and the writing time for a record, plus the event time SLA if relevant. The event time SLA will subtract the record generation time from the record writing time. Figure 10-2 depicts this time difference.

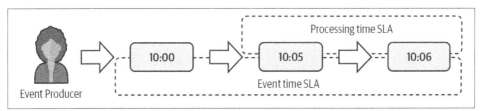

Figure 10-2. Processing time and event time SLAs illustrated

Examples

An easy way to demonstrate SLA monitoring is in Apache Airflow. This data orchestration framework supports an `sla` time parameter that you can define in each workflow's task to be sure it completes in time. Example 10-13 defines an SLA of 10 seconds on `processing_task_2`.

Example 10-13. SLA definition in Apache Airflow

```
@task(sla=datetime.timedelta(seconds=10))
def processing_task_2():
```

Despite this simplicity, the SLA mechanism in the current version of Apache Airflow (2.10.2)[3] exhibits a peculiar behavior. The framework computes the SLA from the execution start time of the pipeline and not the start time of the task. Put differently, for an execution that's scheduled for eight o'clock, if `processing_task_2` starts later than 08:00:10, it will already be considered to be late.

Besides batch systems, SLA monitoring can work for streaming workflows. Our next example uses two Apache Flink jobs. The first of them is a data processing job writing records continuously to another Apache Kafka topic. The output format includes a `start_processing_time_unix_ms` attribute that we're going to use in a second job to calculate the SLA metrics. Example 10-14 shows how this important metric is generated.

Example 10-14. Decorating a record with the processing time attribute

```
def map_json_to_reduced_visit(json_payload: str) -> str:
 # ...
 return json.dumps(ReducedVisitWrapper(
  start_processing_time_unix_ms=time.time_ns() // 1_000_000, ...).to_dict())
```

Now, the second job reads this attribute alongside the writing time to the output topic and computes the difference between the two columns (see Example 10-15).

Example 10-15. Processing execution time calculation for Apache Kafka

```
CREATE TEMPORARY TABLE reduced_visits (
  `start_processing_time_ms` BIGINT,
  `append_time` TIMESTAMP METADATA FROM 'timestamp' VIRTUAL
) WITH ('connector' = 'kafka', ...)""")

sla_query: Table = table_environment.sql_query("""
SELECT
 append_time,
 ((1000 * UNIX_TIMESTAMP(CAST(append_time AS STRING)) +
  EXTRACT(MILLISECOND FROM append_time)) -
  start_processing_time_ms) AS time_difference,
  FLOOR(append_time TO MINUTE) AS visit_time_minute
FROM reduced_visits""")
```

---

3 SLA refactoring is a planned Apache Airflow 3.1 feature detailed in "AIP-57 Refactor SLA Feature" (*https://oreil.ly/hD9Db*), viewed on September 23, 2024.

Next, the SLA monitoring job generates percentiles per one-minute event time windows and emits them to the monitoring stack; from there they can be accessed to create SLA misses alerts. The aggregation step is in Example 10-16.

Example 10-16. Aggregation step of the SLA job

```
sla_query_datastream # ...
 .key_by(extract_grouping_key)
 .window(TumblingEventTimeWindows.of(Time.minutes(1)))
 .aggregate(aggregate_function=PercentilesAggregateFunction(),
   window_function=PercentilesOutputWindowFormatter()
# ...
)
```

The full code and an example for Apache Spark Structured Streaming are both in the GitHub repo (*https://oreil.ly/XUm8o*).

Data Lineage

So far, you have seen solutions for observing the data you're processing. But what happens if the detected issues are not your fault? You saw this in the SLA Misses Detector pattern, where late events can break the event time–based SLA. In this case, you need to know who to ask for help in better understanding the reasons for latency. A great way to get this knowledge is by getting to know the dependencies of your datasets by building a kind of family tree for them.

Pattern: Dataset Tracker

Data lineage patterns operate at the dataset and the data entry levels. Let's start by discovering the dataset tracking that, as the name implies, applies to various data containers, such as tables, folders, topics, and queues. In the end, it creates a dependency tree among these containers to clearly represent data providers and data consumers.

Problem

You're consuming a dataset of poor quality. Your batch job is regularly failing because the schema is not consistent. After investigating, you find out that one of the fields has had different data types over time.

Your upstream data provider is not aware of these changes because it's not the one that generates the dataset. Your data provider is processing data generated by yet another team, so you want to understand the dataset dependency to better detect which team introduces the type inconsistency issue.

Solution

Analyzing dataset composition is a good fit for the Dataset Tracker pattern. The solution creates a family tree of datasets within your organization that you can use to easily discover the dependencies between the datasets and thus also between the teams. Figure 10-3 shows an example for an order dataset combined with two other tables that in their turn are built upon an Apache Kafka topic. Also, each dataset is annotated with the team responsible for maintaining it.

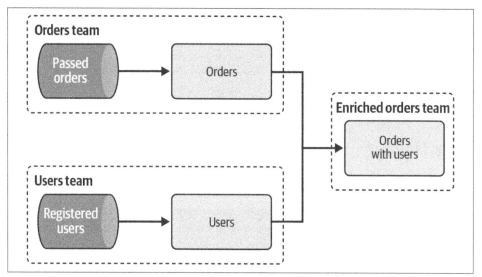

Figure 10-3. An example of datasets tracking in which all three teams are responsible for a dedicated domain and all related data objects (tables, topics, etc.) [4]

When it comes to the implementation, there are two possible solutions. The first uses fully managed cloud services and will be transparent to you, as you will have nothing to do. In this implementation, the dependency tree construction is delegated to a service or framework that analyzes the dependencies among jobs, tables, and dashboards interacting with each dataset. That's how Databricks captures the lineage of its tables registered in Unity Catalog, and it's also the way GCP's Dataplex service automatically records tracking information for other GCP data services, such as BigQuery and Dataproc.

However, the automated version is always limited to specific types of jobs or data stores. For example, even though Dataplex supports lineage from BigQuery data

---

4 This will look familar to a data mesh–driven organization. If you are curious to learn more about this topic, in which dataset tracking is one of the key elements, you can find more information in two O'Reilly books: *Data Mesh* by Zhamak Dehghani (2022) and *Implementing Data Mesh* by Jean-Georges Perrin and Eric Broda (2024).

loading jobs, it doesn't support data loading from BigQuery Data Transfer Service. For that reason, there is a second implementation in which you implement the Dataset lineage on your own. The implementation starts with identifying the inputs and outputs for each query, task, or pipeline. This step can happen at two levels:

The data orchestration layer
Each pipeline that generates a dataset must include the inputs and outputs that will be reported to an external data lineage service. Some of the existing tools, such as Apache Airflow for OpenLineage, can detect dependencies between datasets automatically.[5]

The database layer
Here, your lineage job analyzes the executed queries to identify the dependencies between datasets and saves them in the lineage service. For example, you could build the orders with the users table from Figure 10-3 as `SELECT ... FROM orders o JOIN users u ON u.id = o.user_id`. The database layer identification transforms this query into a tree and extracts all reference tables.

The lineage implementation for the manual version doesn't stop at input/output extraction, though. In addition to this declarative or algorithmic solution, you need a layer that will interpret the identified dependencies and represent them visually. Figure 10-4 shows the full picture of this manual approach. As you can see, this approach brings some flexibility but also requires more implementation effort due to the need to monitor the number of deployed services and interactions among them.

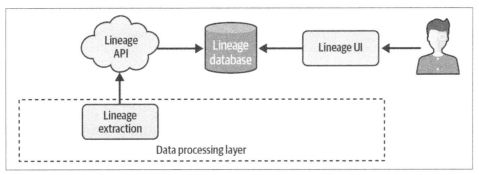

Figure 10-4. The flow for a manual lineage implementation. The fully managed approach follows the same diagram, but the lineage extraction is performed out of the box.

---

5 You can find more details on the integration in the Introduction (*https://oreil.ly/5Wt1s*) and the "Supported operators" section (*https://oreil.ly/RB8xz*) of the Apache Airflow documentation.

Consequences

Even though data lineage is becoming less and less obscure nowadays thanks to the most recent advances in cloud and open source technologies, it also has some gotchas.

Vendor lock. Fully managed solutions like the ones presented with Databricks and GCP often work within the service scope itself. Put differently, if you use them with open source data stores or databases available in other clouds, you may get only a partial view of the lineage.

Custom work. Sometimes, data orchestration frameworks abstract the input/output declaration as they can deduce them from the task configurations. However, that works only if you use the built-in task types. For any custom task type, you may also need to define the input/output resolution logic.

Examples

To demonstrate the Dataset Tracker pattern, let's use the OpenLineage API and Marquez UI.[6] Both are open source solutions that cover existing popular data engineering tools, such as Apache Airflow and Apache Spark.

To connect OpenLineage with Apache Airflow, we need to set the OpenLineage URL (for example, as the environmental variable `OPENLINEAGE_URL=http://localhost:5000`) and install the apache-airflow-providers-openlineage package. Thanks to the native OpenLineage support for various operators like `PostgresOperator`, the lineage setup doesn't require any extra steps on your part. All of the work will be done by OpenLineage extractors, giving you a clear view of how pipelines manipulate your datasets (see Figure 10-5).

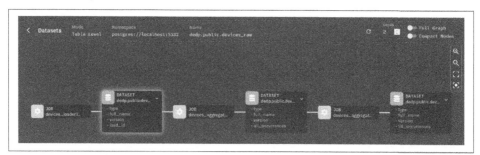

Figure 10-5. Apache Airflow DAG's lineage visualization in the Marquez UI

---

6 The projects are available at the OpenLineage website (*https://openlineage.io*) and the Marquez Project GitHub (*https://github.com/MarquezProject/marquez*).

OpenLineage also works for Apache Spark. All you need to do is include the required OpenLineage dependencies while creating `SparkSession`. Example 10-17 shows how to do this.

Example 10-17. SparkSession with OpenLineage enabled

```
def create_spark_session_with_open_lineage(app_name: str) -> SparkSession:
 return (SparkSession.builder.master('local[*]')
  .appName(app_name)
  .config('spark.extraListeners',
    'io.openlineage.spark.agent.OpenLineageSparkListener')
  .config('spark.openlineage.transport.type', 'http')
  .config('spark.openlineage.transport.url', 'http://localhost:5000')
  .config('spark.openlineage.namespace', 'visits')
  .config('spark.jars.packages', 'io.openlineage:openlineage-spark_2.12:1.21.1')
.getOrCreate())
```

Pattern: Fine-Grained Tracker

Dataset tracking solves the dataset dependency problem, but it automatically brings up another question: how do we track the column(s)? Put differently, how do we determine which input columns compose each output column?

Problem

You implemented the Denormalizer pattern to avoid costly joins in a table. The table has grown to more than 30 columns in three years. Your team's composition changes pretty often, and each time, the new members ask you questions about the table dependencies.

You can answer most of the questions with the Dataset Tracker pattern, but one question remains unresolved. Your new colleagues want to know which columns from the upstream tables use each column from your denormalized table.

Solution

This column-level tracking detail is an ideal scenario for using the Fine-Grained Tracker pattern. It provides low-level details at the column or row level about the data origin.

Let's start with the column level. Some solutions support the Dataset Tracker natively, under constraints. That's still the case with Databricks with the Unity Catalog with the `system.access.column_lineage` tracking table. This feature is also natively present on Azure with the Purview service.

But you can also implement the lineage on your own. In that case, the implementation consists of analyzing the query execution plan and tracking all downstream dependencies for each column. For example, if your query looks like SELECT CON CAT(u.first_name, d.delivery_address) AS user_with_address FROM users u JOIN addresses d ON d.user_id = u.id, the downstream dependencies for user_with_address will be the first_name column from the users table and the delivery_address column from the addresses table.

Figure 10-6 shows how such a column lineage works for the implementations leveraging SQL. As you'll notice, the lineage code analyzes the execution tree to discover all dependencies for the output columns.

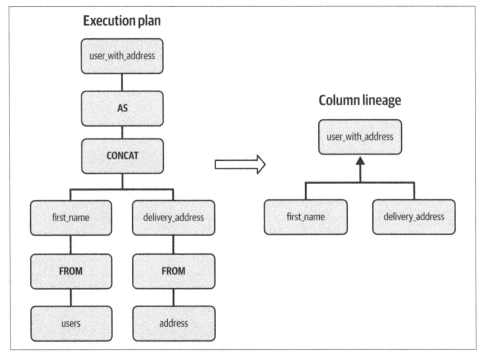

Figure 10-6. Column lineage dependencies for a query concatenating two columns (simplified)

The good news here is that popular data processing solutions like Apache Spark often have native support in data lineage tools, such as the OpenLineage framework.

The low-level tracking might also concern the rows. Here, you would like to know which job produced each row. The implementation consists of adding this information either as an extra attribute or as an additional column, for example, by leveraging the data decoration patterns.

Consequences

The Fine-Grained Tracker provides some extra insight but also has some limits.

Custom code. The column-level lineage analyzes execution plan nodes to detect dependencies. This approach works perfectly well when you use the standard mechanisms of your data processing tool, such as native SQL functions. However, when you transform your data with custom logic, such as programmatic mapping functions, getting the lineage will not be easy. These functions are opaque boxes, where the lineage framework can only see the output but oftentimes doesn't have enough capacity to interpret and understand the coded transformation logic.

Row-level visualization. Dataset and column-level lineage are two common categories in the data lineage world that are widely supported by both the extraction and visualization parts. However, row-level information, although useful, doesn't belong there. It's more of an additional value that can be useful for debugging data quality issues and identifying jobs that write erroneous rows. Unfortunately, the row-level lineage won't integrate with the classical data lineage visualization tools. As a result, you'll need a separate query layer for the row-level lineage.

Evolution management. The transformations that build your column today may change in the future. Consequently, you must ensure that your column lineage solution, either fully managed or customized, supports this evolution tracking. Otherwise, you might get an incorrect view when it comes to defining the origins of a column after the upstream columns have changed.

Examples

Since the Fine-Grained Tracker at the column level for Apache Spark and OpenLineage requires the same `SparkSession` function as in the Dataset Tracker example, let's omit it for brevity's sake. If you are interested, you can find the example in the GitHub repo (*https://oreil.ly/IAxz-*). Instead, let's focus on the row-level lineage, which requires some extra coding effort.

In this example, we're going to use two jobs. The `visits_decorator_job` will write data to a visits-decorated topic, while the `visits_reducer_job` will process this data and write it to a visits-reduced topic. The processing step is irrelevant to our example. That's why we'll focus on the tracking details included in the Kafka record's header.

Example 10-18 shows the row-level lineage for our jobs. As you will notice, both jobs set the same attributes, namely the `job_version`, `job_name`, and `batch_version`. The only difference is the `parent_lineage` attribute present in the `visits_reducer_job`, where you can find the lineage information from the `visits_decorator_job` and thus the data source. Having these upstream attributes makes it easier to understand the workflow and automatically makes any debugging discussions with the data producers easier, as you can provide them with extra debugging details.

Example 10-18. Row-level lineage for Apache Spark Structured Streaming

```
# visits_decorator_job
(visits_to_save.withColumn('headers', F.array(
 F.struct(F.lit('job_version').alias('key'), F.lit(job_version).alias('value')),
 F.struct(F.lit('job_name').alias('key'), F.lit(job_name).alias('value')),
 F.struct(F.lit('batch_version').alias('key'), F.lit(str(batch_number)
  .encode('UTF-8')).alias('value'))
)))

# visits_reducer_job
(visits_to_save.withColumn('headers', F.array(
 # same as for visits_decorator_job, plus the parent's lineage
 F.struct(F.lit('parent_lineage').alias('key'), F.to_json(F.col('headers'))
  .cast('binary').alias('value'))
)))
```

Summary

In this chapter, you learned how to add extra protection to your data workloads by using detectors and trackers. The first section presented two data detector patterns. The Flow Interruption Detector was the first of them. If you have any doubts about the continuity of the data you're processing, the Flow Interruption Detector is an observability solution. Also in this section, you learned about the Skew Detector pattern that you can employ to spot unbalanced datasets and partitions. Using the Skew Detector is a good way to control the completeness of the input dataset, especially for batch workloads working on homogeneous data volumes.

In the next section, you learned about time detectors. They operate in the time space and help spot any latency issues. The first of the described patterns was the Lag Detector. It's particularly interesting to use with streaming pipelines to detect whenever a streaming job falls behind the data producer. Lag detection can be extended with the SLA Misses Detector pattern, which ensures that each data processing task completes within a specified time period.

Finally, in the last section, you learned about the tracking portion of data observability with two data lineage patterns. The first of them focuses on datasets, hence its name, the Dataset Tracker. You will find it useful in big organizations where various teams exchange datasets among themselves and where in the end, you may not know the scope of each team's responsibilities. The Dataset Tracker will provide a global dependency graph among those teams and their datasets. If you need more details, you can leverage the second pattern, the Fine-Grained Tracker. It helps you see not only the big picture but also low-level details of the transformations applied to each column or the jobs producing particular rows.

If you haven't done it already, this chapter should convince you to add the data observability patterns to your system. And by the way, this is the last chapter of this book, but before I let you go—hopefully, to implement some patterns in the real world—I owe you some closing words.

Afterword

The data engineering space has evolved over the last several decades. Before this time, data systems were built on top of proprietary data warehouses, and data engineering was often limited to orchestrating SQL queries from Shell scripts from yet another proprietary data orchestrator.

The world has changed since the Hadoop adoption. The modern data stack of the past—with Hive, Pig, Storm, or MapReduce—expected new coding skills from data engineers. Next came the cloud revolution, which demanded yet another skill set to understand and manage the data infrastructure. Today, we are part of the generative AI revolution that should make the next generation of data platforms more intelligent, enabling simple data access even for nontechnical users.

Despite this continuous evolution, I believe that a well-designed data engineering system is and still will be based on some universal and intrinsic components presented in this book as data engineering design patterns.

Sure, maybe the SQL and Python workloads from today will be replaced by some other query or programming language. Maybe Apache Spark, the table file formats, and the Apache Kafka–compatible brokers used often as examples in this book won't be first-class citizens of the next generation of data platforms. But even though they might not be there anymore, the way you build data systems shouldn't change so drastically. You will always need a way to bring in data either continuously or less regularly. You will always need a way to make your raw and dumb data valuable for the users. And finally, you will always need a way to ensure that all you have implemented and deployed is working correctly.

The data engineering design patterns covered in this book should provide this stability factor in our changing technical world. Thank you for spending time with me, and I hope to see you in the real world to discuss the entrails of data engineering in more detail!

Summary of Patterns

It's unlikely that you'll work with all the patterns at once. You'll face different patterns at different times throughout your data engineering journey, so there's no need to remember all of them by heart. Instead, you should be able to find them easily and adapt them to the problem you're currently facing.

To make this task easier, you can find here a summary of the design patterns presented in the book with quick reminders of their main use cases and gotchas.

Data Ingestion Design Patterns

Pattern name	Use case	Gotchas
Full Loader	Load full dataset	• Increasing data volume for growing datasets • Data consistency during the load process
Incremental Loader	Load chunks of a dataset	• Loading physically deleted rows • Volume of loaded data during a backfilling
Change Data Capture	Load chunks of a dataset as they come	• Setup complexity (database layer) • Changes scope, overall or only after the setup • Data remains at rest
Passthrough Replicator	Replicate a dataset without altering any information	• Serialization side effects, like badly formatted dates • Production resources isolation • PII data • Latency impact if automated via infrastructure • Metadata to replicate if relevant
Transformation Replicator	Replicate a dataset with a custom transformation	• Higher risk of misformatted attributes due to the schema-based transformation • PII data definition up to date
Compactor	Optimize storage of the ingested files	• Compaction frequency impact on resources • Housekeeping job for compacted files

Pattern name	Use case	Gotchas
Readiness Marker	Know when you should start ingesting the data	• Lack of enforcement for the convention-based implementation • Reliability of the readiness definition (e.g., late data)
External Trigger	Efficiently ingest data generated irregularly	• Continuous pulling impact on resources and costs • Lack of execution context • Error management for replayability in case of invocation errors

Error Management Design Patterns

Pattern name	Use case	Gotchas
Dead-Letter	Handle errors without interrupting the main data processing flow	• Snowball backfilling effect • Ordering and consistency • Implementation for error-safe functions • Hidden errors
Windowed Deduplicator	Remove duplicates from the processed dataset	• Space versus time • Not enough for exactly-once delivery
Late Data Detector	Identify late data	• Native support in the API • Lateness strategy
Static and Dynamic Late Data Integrators	Include late data in an already generated dataset	• Snowball backfilling • Storage footprint (small files) • Scheduling complexity • Waste of resources • Limited backfilling for static lookback window • Incremental dataset and backfilling
Filter Interceptor	Identify the condition responsible for filtering out a record	• Runtime impact • Complexity for declarative languages (e.g., SQL) • Streaming for interceptor statistics
Checkpointer	Save the progress of a job	• Balance between delivery guarantee and execution time • Not exactly once!

Idempotency Design Patterns

Pattern name	Use case	Gotchas
Fast Metadata cleaner	Remove dataset at the metadata layer	• Granularity for backfilling • Metadata limits • A more complex data exposition layer
Data Overwrite	Rewrite physical files	• I/O overhead for identifying data blocks to delete • Cleaning operations to reclaim space
Merger	Insert, update, or delete a row	• Unique key requirement • I/O overhead • Incremental dataset and deletes • Incremental dataset and backfilling for data consistency

Pattern name	Use case	Gotchas
Keyed Idempotency	Write a record for a given key only once	• Dependent on the database • Key generation properties, especially for compactable data sources
Transactional Writer	Make the changes visible with an explicit commit action	• Not supported natively everywhere • Commit challenging in distributed environments • Idempotency scope limited to the transaction only (e.g., beware of retries)
Proxy	Expose an immutable dataset from an intermediary layer	• Ease of implementation • Conventional • Extra security required to ensure the dataset is not altered

Data Value Design Patterns

Pattern name	Use case	Gotchas
Static Joiner	Join with a static dataset	• Consistency challenges due to late data • Idempotency may require a specific implementation (slowly changing dimensions)
Dynamic Joiner	Join two dynamic datasets	• Space and exactness trade-offs • Late data integration
Wrapper	Add an envelope to the input record	• Domain split because the attributes of an entity can be present in two places • Payload size
Metadata Decorator	Add extra information in the metadata layer	• Metadata support in the storage layer • Reduce the scope to the metadata only
Distributed Aggregator	Aggregate records in a distributed environment	• Cost of the network exchange • Data skew • Scaling, particularly for reclaiming unused capacity
Local Aggregator	Aggregate records locally, without network exchange	• Frozen scaling • Grouping keys not always shared by all consumers
Incremental Sessionizer	Build sessions on top of an incremental dataset	• Inactivity period impact on resources • Data freshness • Late data and backfilling overhead due to sequential execution
Stateful Sessionizer	Build sessions continuously, with state store support	• At-least-once processing due to checkpointing • Scaling not only for compute but also state • Inactivity period impact on resources
Bin Pack Orderer	Provide an ordering guarantee for partial commits data stores	• Task retries • Extra complexity with the bins creation logic • Bulk size and single requests delivery guarantee
FIFO Orderer	Write records in the order they are input	• I/O overhead and latency for individual requests–based delivery • Not exactly once!

Data Flow Design Patterns

Pattern name	Use case	Gotchas
Local Sequencer	Run tasks in a sequence within the same execution unit	• Boundaries identification • No one-size-fits-all solution
Isolated Sequencer	Run tasks in a sequence across different execution units	• Scheduling, task, or dataset dependency • Communication to avoid desynchronization issues
Aligned Fan-In	Start a task once all parents have succeeded	• Usage of infrastructure resources • Scheduling skew and overhead • Complexity if there are many input branches
Unaligned Fan-In	Start a task independently of the parents' success status	• Visual identification of the unaligned dependency • Partial results annotation for consumers
Parallel Split	Run multiple concurrent branches from a single branch	• Parallelism can still be impacted if task-based dependency is present • The processing layer may require implementation on the orchestration layer (e.g., jobs with different compute needs)
Exclusive Choice	Follow selected execution branches	• Complexity • Hidden logic if the pattern implementer is in the processing layer • Heavy, often data-based conditions
Single Runner	Process data sequentially	• Backfilling performance • Latency
Concurrent Runner	Process data with concurrent runs	• Resource starvation • Shared state

Data Security Design Patterns

Pattern name	Use case	Gotchas
Vertical Partitioner	Easier data removal	• Query performance for reading • Complexity with polyglot storage • Doesn't apply to the raw data
In-Place Overwriter	Remove attributes or rows	• I/O overhead • Cost of interacting with data
Fine-Grained Accessor for Tables	Control access to tables	• Attributes for row-level access policies • Complex structures for column-level policies
Fine-Grained Accessor for Resources	Control access to cloud resources	• Ease of maintenance versus security by the book
Encryptor	Protect data from unauthorized usage	• Encryption overhead • Data loss risk
Anonymizer	Remove protected information from the dataset	• Information loss
Pseudo-Anonymizer	Replace protected information	• Information loss • Possibility of combined identification

Pattern name	Use case	Gotchas
Secrets Pointer	Use credentials without storing them in the code	• Leakage of logs • Refresh for streaming jobs • Setup phase
Secretless Connector	Connect to databases without credentials	• Rotation and maintenance

Data Storage Design Patterns

Pattern name	Use case	Gotchas
Horizontal Partitioner	Store rows together, according to a partitioning column	• Partition granularity • Storage skew • Partition attribute change
Vertical Partitioner	Split a row into multiple partitions with different columns	• Domain split, making the row difficult to seize • Querying overhead as getting the whole row involves joins
Bucket	Colocate high-cardinality records	• Cost to evolve • Direct per-key access, as a bucket involves passing through multiple keys
Sorter	Store data blocks sorted on disk	• Sorting overhead at writing • Composite sort keys
Metadata Enhancer	Leverage metadata layer to optimize processing time	• Metadata creation overhead as an extra step in data writing
Dataset Materializer	Simplify complex data layout by materializing the query as a table or view	• Refresh cost • Data management, such as retention and access policies
Manifest	Avoid listing operation	• Manifest growing too big
Normalizer	Isolate data storage	• Query cost if the query involves multiple tables
Denormalizer	Reduce the number of joins between tables	• Row consistency after updates • Storage footprint

Data Quality Design Patterns

Pattern name	Use case	Gotchas
Audit-Write-Audit-Publish	Ensure the pipeline works on a complete dataset and doesn't expose poor-quality data	• Compute cost for the data-related validation • Not bulletproof and can require adaptations over time • Extra latency
Constraints Enforcer	Ensure data producers don't introduce data quality issues	• All-or-nothing semantics that may cause long back-and-forth loops • Different consumers might expect different constraints
Schema Compatibility Enforcer	Ensure any schema changes will be compatible with consumers	• Additional communication overhead with the schema registry • Schema evolution is more challenging
Schema Migrator	Migrate a schema without breaking your downstream consumers	• Record size can grow significantly • Sometimes, fields simply cannot be removed

Pattern name	Use case	Gotchas
Offline Observer	Implement the observation as a separate pipeline	• Insight can be late • Compute resources might be too big to process the observation dataset
Online Observer	Implement the observation as a part of the observed pipeline	• Extra processing delay • Parallel split is faster, but the observation scope might be different

Data Observability Design Patterns

Pattern name	Use case	Gotchas
Flow Interruption Detector	Detect interrupted data flow	• Rules definition and alarm fatigue: threshold and metadata availability
Skew Detector	Detect storage skew	• Rules definition: seasonality and communication among teams
Lag Detector	Detect consumer latency	• Data skew impact on the consumer
SLA Misses Detector	Detect missed latency expectations	• Late data for event time SLA
Dataset Tracker	Track dataset dependencies	• Vendor locking and support scope for managed solutions • Implementation effort for a custom solution
Fine-Grained Tracker	Track column and row dependencies	• Support for custom processing code • Visualization for row-level tracking • Transformation evolutions

Index

MERGE (UPSERT) command, SQL, 90-91, 93, 99, 202
merge-on-read (MoR) tables, 27
Merger design pattern, 89-94
    blog analytics platform case study, 89-91
    consequences, 91-92
    implementation examples, 93
metadata
    Compactor design pattern, 27
    External Trigger design pattern, 35
    Fast Metadata Cleaner design pattern, 80-86
    Flow Interruption Detector design pattern, 308
    Horizontal Partitioner design pattern, 236
    Metadata Decorator design pattern, 41, 129-132
    Metadata Enhancer design pattern, 251-254
    Online Observer design pattern, 300
    Passthrough Replicator design pattern, 22
    Stateful Merger design pattern, 98
microbatch stream processing model, 236
MIN function, SQL, 51-55
MirrorMaker utility, 23
mode property, Apache Spark, 32
MongoDB, 111
MoR (merge-on-read) tables, 27
mutability/immutability
    Bucket design pattern, 245
    Horizontal Partitioner design pattern, 237
    Keyed Idempotency design pattern, 103
    Proxy design pattern, 110-113
    Sorter design pattern, 250

N

NAMED_STRUCT function, SQL, 129
NF (normal forms), 260-263
nontransient errors, 40
Normalizer design pattern, 260-266
    blog analytics platform case study, 260-263
    consequences, 264-264
    implementation examples, 264-266
NoSQL
    access control, 210
    data decoration, 130
    idempotent key generation, 102
    immutable datasets, 111
NOW() function, SQL, 120
NULL values, 44, 276
nullability constraints, 281

O

Object Lock, 111
observability (see data observability design patterns)
Offline Observer design pattern, 293-298, 318
    blog analytics platform case study, 293
    consequences, 294
    implementation examples, 294-298
OLAP (online analytical processing) cubes, 133
One Big Table, 267-269
Online Observer design pattern, 298-302, 318
    blog analytics platform case study, 298-299
    consequences, 300
    implementation examples, 300-302
on_failure_callback function, Apache Airflow, 180
open-close-open infinite loops, 55
OpenLineage, 174, 323-327
OpenSearch, 111
OPTIMIZE command, 27
optimize keyword, 29
orchestration design patterns, 191-195
    Concurrent Runner, 193-195
    Single Runner, 191-193
ORDER BY clause, SQL, 153
out-of-date statistics, 253
overlapping executions, 61
overwriting design patterns, 80-89
    Data Overwrite, 86-88
    Fast Metadata Cleaner, 80-86

P

Parallel Split design pattern, 182-186, 298, 300
    blog analytics platform case study, 183
    consequences, 183-184
    implementation examples, 184-186
Parquet (see Apache Parquet)
partial commits, 154
partial data, unaligned fan-in and, 180
PARTITION BY expression, SQL, 49
partitionBy method, Apache Spark, 235, 238
partitioning attributes (distribution keys), 235
partitioning design patterns, 234-242
    Horizontal Partitioner, 234-239
    Vertical Partitioner, 240-242
passthrough (extract and load [EL]) jobs, 8
Passthrough Replicator design pattern, 20-23
    blog analytics platform case study, 20
    consequences, 21-22

About the Author

Bartosz Konieczny is a freelance data engineering enthusiast who has been coding since 2010. Throughout his career, he has leveraged major public cloud services and open source technologies—like Apache Spark, Apache Kafka, Apache Airflow, and Delta Lake—to tackle various data engineering problems, including sessionization, data ingestion, data cleansing, ordered data processing, and data migration.

In addition to helping companies bring their data projects to life, Bartosz is deeply engaged with the data engineering community. He provides a comprehensive set of resources to support data engineers in their learning journey, including online and in-person training, data-related blog posts on *https://www.waitingforcode.com*, and conference talks at industry events like the Spark+AI Summit, the Data+AI Summit, and the Big Data Technology Warsaw Summit.

You can reach him at *contact@waitingforcode.com*.

Colophon

The animal on the cover of *Data Engineering Design Patterns* is a queen triggerfish (*Balistes vetula*). It is a large triggerfish native to the coastal Atlantic Ocean and Gulf of Mexico, ranging from Canada and the Azores in the north to southern Brazil and Angola in the south. It is typically greenish or bluish gray on the back and yellow-orange on the belly, with bright blue lines around the mouth. It possesses two dorsal spines that can lock into place to help it remain anchored in crevices, thus protecting it from predators.

Queen triggerfish feed mainly on invertebrates, using their strong jaws and teeth to bite through the shells of mollusks, crabs, and bivalves. They are especially fond of long-spined sea urchins. They will blow water on the urchins with their fins or pick them up by the spines using their teeth and then drop them in an attempt to expose the urchins' more vulnerable undersides.

Due to overfishing, populations of queen triggerfish have declined steeply since the 1980s, and they are classified as near threatened. Many of the animals on O'Reilly covers are endangered; all of them are important to the world.

The cover illustration is by Karen Montgomery, based on an antique line engraving from *English Cyclopedia*. The cover fonts are Gilroy Semibold and Guardian Sans. The text font is Adobe Minion Pro; the heading font is Adobe Myriad Condensed; and the code font is Dalton Maag's Ubuntu Mono.

O'REILLY®

Learn from experts.
Become one yourself.

60,000+ titles | Live events with experts | Role-based courses
Interactive learning | Certification preparation

**Try the O'Reilly learning platform
free for 10 days.**

www.ingramcontent.com/pod-product-compliance
Lightning Source LLC
Jackson TN
JSHW061129120825
89261JS00005B/30